拜啓陳者來ル五月十八日午后五時ヨリ同

六時迄マラカニヤン・パレスニ於テ比島ニ

於ケル大日本帝國陸海軍ノ戰捷ヲ慶祝ス

ル為メ祝賀會相催候間御來駕被下度此段

御案内申上候

　　　　　　　　　　　　敬　具

昭和十七年五月十四日

　　比島行政長官

　　ホルヘ・ビ・バルガス

PHILIPPINE COLLABORATION IN WORLD WAR II

Philippine Collaboration in World War II

by

David Joel Steinberg

Ann Arbor

THE UNIVERSITY OF MICHIGAN PRESS

Grateful acknowledgment is made to the following for permission to quote materials:

The Jose P. Laurel Memorial Foundation
Jose P. Laurel, *War Memoirs*. Copyright © 1962.

McGraw-Hill Book Company
Douglas MacArthur, *Reminiscences*. Copyright © 1964 by Time, Inc.

Meredith Press
Manuel Quezon, *The Good Fight*. Copyright 1946.

Claro M. Recto Memorial Foundation
Claro M. Recto, *Three Years of Enemy Occupation*. Copyright 1946.

Journal of Asian Studies
David Joel Steinberg, "Jose P. Laurel: A 'Collaborator' Misunderstood" (Vol. XXIV, No. 4, August 1965).

To Sally, Jonny
and the Parsonage:
Without whom
This would never exist

Preface

The stark realities of mass warfare and military occupation cast disquieting shadows across modern mankind's belief that primary allegiance must be tendered to the nation-state. The human urge to survive compels the defeated to cooperate with the victors. However, while collaboration abets physical survival, it simultaneously threatens to undermine national allegiance. Not everyone can go into exile or join a guerrilla band, and yet those left in the occupied territory have the greatest need to preserve the sanctity of their national ideals. Allegiance cannot be turned on and off like a spigot, especially during the trauma of occupation; somehow it must be reconciled with the need to survive.

This book is a study of the collaboration crisis which grew out of the Japanese occupation of the Philippines. It is an attempt to delineate how this one society on the verge of gaining its independence struggled to determine its standard of values and its identity. In questioning the use of the pejorative "collaboration" as synonymous with "treason," the book journeys into that critical area of moral history which lies elusively below surface events. Duress compelled the individual and the society to confront values and priorities. Some light may be shed both on the unique aspects of the Philippine situation and on the universal dilemma of the nature of allegiance.

Collaboration remains an explosive issue in the Philippines even a generation afterward. The charges of "treason" and "collaboration" are among the most severe man can bring against man, and the historian has a special obligation to bring sensitivity and compassion to his quest for light. To generate heat by intentionally rekindling the fury of old fires is not history. However, the historian cannot shirk his professional obligation to present all his material frankly. I have tried to combine discretion with honesty and charity with accuracy.

The list of people I wish to thank for their assistance is too long to chronicle here, but I hope that those who have helped will see in the text their deeply appreciated aid. This study began in 1959, when I spent a Fulbright year in Manila. I am grateful to the United States Educational Foundation in Manila, the Woodrow Wilson Foundation in Princeton, and the authorities of the National Defense Education Act in Washington for support. I wish to thank Professor Albert Craig of Harvard for his care while I was his student. I am grateful to the editors of the *Journal of Asian Studies* for granting me permission to use material on Jose P. Laurel which first appeared in their journal. Finally, I wish to express my heartfelt thanks to those numerous Filipino friends who discussed these sensitive issues with me generously and honestly.

Ann Arbor, Michigan

Contents

CHAPTER I

The Web of Filipino Allegiance

Traitors to the high cause of the colored races in the East
—Pio Duran

Man has always craved the security of a well-ordered social environment. Consequently, he has proffered his primary allegiance to those institutions which can give him "order through chaos, direction through space, discipline through freedom, [and] unity through multiplicity."[1] Because this human need is elemental, anyone who violates the standards of his society has been regarded as a pariah. Man has inevitably placed a very high premium on the virtues of allegiance, condemning its violations as treachery and treason. The origin of the word "loyal" is the Latin word *lex*, meaning "law."[2] Treason has always been a fundamental crime, punishable by death. In the nature of allegiance there exists both a voluntary act of commitment by the individual and a coercive demand for obedience by the community. Usually, the individual is fortunate in the coincidence of personal and social aspirations; however, when, periodically, a gap appears between the two, a situation of severe tension inevitably results.

Few problems have plagued modern man more than this dilemma. Allegiance is no longer simply "the tie or obligation of a subject to his sovereign, or government."[3] Western man lacks the luxury of having a clearly identifiable secular or ecclesiastical liege, who demands and receives obedience. Non-Western man lacks the assurance that his nation, his country, and his society can be considered coterminous. The verities of God and country are still influential, but claims on the individual's fealty have proliferated. The dilemma is frequently one of unpleasant choice among conflicting obligations. Each individual must resolve for himself his own set of priorities; each society must struggle collectively to determine for itself its own standard of values.

1

This ubiquitous problem is particularly acute for those who hold authority, since their private dilemma is also often a public one. The twentieth-century leader must somehow evolve a code of behavior which permits him to be loyal not only to his state, his constituted government, and his national ideological credo, but also to his constituents and their standards. The tensions inherent in resolving these often conflicting obligations have produced strain in every modern society—totalitarian or democratic, capitalistic or communistic, colonial or metropolitan. Lurking close to the modern leader is the haunting specter of treason, a specter feared the more because of its multiplicity of meanings. Its usage now embraces domestic demagoguery, as well as ideological apostasy and the sale of secrets. No leader is ever secure today from this accusation. The increasingly complex nature of modern society has obfuscated so greatly the meaning of allegiance that most public officials have come to realize the inapplicability of Polonius' advice:

> This above all: to thine own self be true,
> And it must follow, as the night the day,
> Thou canst not then be false to any man.

The Filipino leadership discovered the enormity of this problem during the Japanese occupation in World War II. As the leaders of a colonial nation about to receive independence from the United States, they were suddenly called upon to respond to Japanese demands. This exigency compelled them to assess both their public posture and their private standard of values. Together with the rest of the nation they relied instinctively on the existing values of the culture for support. This process had the effect of articulating social norms which previously had been inchoate. As a byproduct of the trauma of occupation, each thoughtful Filipino was forced to analyze the values which determined his identity. The war was a great catalyst in this quest, since it required each individual to establish for himself the priorities directing his action. Few Filipinos, especially leaders, were given the luxury of avoiding the acid test of choice.

The war demonstrated visibly the character and strength of Philippine nationalism, establishing the superiority of the national identity over the forces of fragmentation. The war illustrated vividly the previous supposition that a Philippine national identity had emerged from the nearly four hundred years of Spanish-Catholic and American colonial rule. This nationalism provided a basis for common identification among the more than sixteen million Filipinos, in spite of the eleven major language groups, the wide racial and religious differences, and the geographical isolation of the archipelago. The harsh light of military occupation outlined the contours of Philippine allegiance.

In the colonial milieu of the prewar era some doubted the existence of a cohesive nationhood in the Philippines. Claiming that the extant national institutions were the creations of the colonial power, these skeptics defined Filipino identity in terms of the historic accidents of colonialism. Unquestionably, in 1941 Manila was a national capital, from which a highly centralized government ruled effectively. No one, however, was sure of the extent to which people regarded themselves as "Filipinos," saw Manila as the seat of their government, and tendered prime allegiance to the Western concept of the modern nation-state. Was there a dominant culture of the Philippine nation with all its ramifications, or was there only a confederation of Malay peoples, sharing certain common traits and experiences? Was there merely a cultural spectrum embracing the nonintegrated primitive hill peoples, who practiced itinerant "slash and burn" agriculture; the Moslem minority of the south, which retained deep antipathy to lowland Catholics; the rich but feared Chinese minority, who wielded disproportionate economic power; the traditional wet-rice peasant lowlanders; and a small, "Westernized," transitional elite? Or was there a distinctive cultural amalgam, which fused the various external influences—Chinese, Arab, Spanish, and American—with the indigenous Malay culture? In other words, were the Philippines merely a potpourri of noncommunicating, isolated subgroups, or had the components been internalized sufficiently by all the people to form a distinctive Philippine identity? The war demonstrated that there were certain standards and symbols which, by their universality, justified the use of the term "Filipino."

What were these standards and attitudes defining the nation? At the nucleus was a consensus about the role of the individual within his social setting. Unlike the West, which has tended to see human relationships in an I–Thou or an I–It pattern, Filipinos have seen relationships in the social order in a We–They framework of perception.[4] Filipino loyalty has spread out from the center —the immediate family—in ripples. This does not negate the appreciable impact of the pre-Spanish and the Hispanic codes of *amor propio* on modern Filipino behavior. Filipinos have not been immune to the sins of greed, pride, and vanity. The Japanese wartime policy of permitting soldiers to slap Filipinos without just cause rankled the dignity of the individual Filipino and alienated him as much as any single factor. However, in general, the Filipino has been exceedingly sensitive to the old riddle: "If I am not for myself, who will be for me, but being for myself, what am I?" Egocentricity has existed in the Philippines as elsewhere, but the basic social order has focused on the familial "we."

Within this basic structure, Filipinos have traditionally distinguished between the immediate and the distant.[5] The individual ideally should be more loyal to the close family than to the extended family, to close friends than to acquaintances, to the local community than to the distant province, to the personal political leader than to the distant impersonal government agency, to the Philippines than to the metropolitan countries of Spain and the United States, and to Spain and the United States than to the rest of the world. This pattern of concentric circles of allegiance has always placed great emphasis on the personal character of loyalty in relationships. The sense of intimacy in Filipino relationships is expressed in a network of dyads, by definition reciprocal in obligation.[6] Central to Filipino values has been the sense of debt felt by each individual to the network of people who surround and help him. No Filipino dares to ignore this social obligation, called *utang na loob* (an internal debt of gratitude), for fear of being liable to the accusation of *walang hiya* (shamelessness).[7] This code of behavior regulating social contact, which the West has all too often dismissed disparagingly as "concern for face," actually has fulfilled a fundamental human need. Just as Western democracy and liberalism posit the sacred worth of every individual by guaranteeing him his vote and his rights, the Filipino norm acknowledges the reciprocity of all human relations.

The family inevitably has been the primary social unit representing the pluralized self. Kincentric obligations have embraced an enormous number of people, since each Filipino child traced his lineage bilaterally. Because bilateral kinship automatically included the obligation that each spouse accept the obligations due the partner's relatives, whole villages might be interlocked. While distant relatives might not be intimates of each other, the family structure did create an "in-group" which defined the boundaries of a man's loyalties. Like the irrigation system of dikes and paddy fields, the social grouping had to be protected through daily care in order to function at crisis periods.

The concept of familial solidarity was extended to nonfamily via the bridge of ritual kinship, known as *compadrazgo*. This device opened the umbrella of intimate connection to close friends or sought-after acquaintances. "Fictive-kinship," like the marriage alliance, allowed people to formalize their relationships. Based jointly on the pre-Spanish custom of blood compacts and the Roman Catholic concept of ritual godparenthood, *compadrazgo* became a ritual of vital social importance. In 1521 Ferdinand Magellan sealed his new alliance with the Cebu chief, Humabon, by serving as *compadre* (godfather), and the institution developed so strongly thereafter that it transcended its European ritual function.[8] By asking a friend to serve as *compadre* (godfather) or *comadre* (godmother), one could proclaim to the friend and to the world at large the bonds of loyalty linking not only friends but families of friends. Frequently, the system was used to establish life insurance for the child in case anything happened to the parents, and equally frequently it was used as a means of upward social mobility for the child, since the parents tried to get the richest and most powerful friend to accept responsibility. Everything depended on the reciprocal character of the relationship. The child, like Isaac, was the tangible symbol, the living proof of ties of allegiance.[9]

Another communally held bulwark of allegiance among Filipinos has been the intense belief in the omnipresence of the supernatural. Roman Catholicism was adopted passionately but selectively. The grafting of the Spanish faith on to the pre-Spanish Philippines changed both scion and stock. The result has been a Catholicism in which the Filipino has personalized his God, and through this dyadic relationship, he has domesticated his Catholic faith. The connection between man and his maker has been seen in familial terms. God has been revered as "a wise and tolerant father," the Virgin adored as a "kind and loving Mother," and Christ, with whom the average Filipino identifies himself closely, has been pitied as "the beaten, scourged, humiliated, and defeated" son of God.[10] This identification and intimacy with the Holy Family established a cosmic *compadrazgo*. Since Christ had died for each individual Filipino, however humble, the obligations of *utang na loob* dictated that each Filipino remember forever this debt of gratitude, which transcended all repayment. However, the awesome gulf between the lofty majesty of God and the humble station of the Filipino inhibited the Filipino and prompted him to search for celestial intermediaries, just as he utilized human intermediaries in his daily life. He found good advocacy in the apostles, saints, martyrs, and, most importantly, in God's specifically given intermediary for the world, the Rock of Peter, the Holy Catholic Church.

The ecclesiastical power of the Church rather than the temporal power of the Spanish crown was the great Westernizing force in the Philippines. During the centuries of Spanish rule it was the Church which reached into every nook of the country and brought faith and learning to the receptive non-Moslem areas. The periodic visit of the priest was usually the only contact most Filipinos had with Europeans.[11] Catholicism laid the foundation for the modern Philippine nation by creating a common standard of morality throughout the archipelago. Moreover, it was loyalty to the universal and Catholic Church which first gave Filipinos an awareness of a new type of allegiance transcending their immediate, circumscribed world. A sense of *utang na loob* to Jesus for his Crucifixion and the resultant allegiance to Rome taught the Filipinos to live and die with intense loyalty to these distant abstractions. As long as the aims of the Spanish crown and the Catholic clergy were identical, no tension existed, but with the secularization of allegiance in the eighteenth and nineteenth centuries in Spain, a bifurcating wedge began to cleave Filipino allegiance. The Church was figuratively and literally the great structure in each Filipino community. In addition, by its extension throughout the world, the Church transcended the fragmentation of the Catholic world into nation-states, in contrast with Spanish temporal power, which was eventually overwhelmed by nationalism.

It is not surprising that the first expression of Philippine nationalism came through the Filipino desire to gain equal rights as members of the clergy.[12] The Philippine Church had long been torn internally by the struggle between the secular diocesan clergy and the members of the religious orders. The "religious" (also known as regulars, because of the vows they took upon entering their Orders) included Augustinians, Franciscans, Jesuits, and Dominicans. The "religious" represented an enormous percentage of the total clergy in the archipelago, since they dedicated themselves to the hardships of mission stations. Jealous of the autonomy they had possessed initially, they successfully withstood the demands of the secular, diocesan bishops to conduct episcopal visitation. As a consequence of this internal Church struggle, the diocesan authorities resorted to training Filipinos during the eighteenth century in order to have enough secular clergy to meet the pastoral needs of the country even without the "religious," who were always threatening to leave the country rather than lose their autonomy.

In the nineteenth century the rise of nationalism metamorphosed the secular versus regular issue into a racial one. The plethora of Spanish loyalist priests, who had emigrated to the archipelago from the newly independent Latin American nations, the rise of antiliberal sentiment in Spain, and the Catholic revival all combined to heighten the racial distinction between Caucasian and Malay. The loss of most of the empire ended the subtle distinctions which linked the Asian native to the white Spaniard through a myriad of shades of creole and mestizo combinations. Because the racial gradations had suddenly vanished with the loss of the American colonies, a man was more clearly a member of a national racial community. As universality slipped out of the Spanish empire, the confrontation between Filipino and Spanish clerics increased until in 1872 the Spanish temporal authorities executed, because of their clerical nationalism, three Filipino priests during a brief military uprising. The execution of these three—Fathers Burgos, Gomez, and Zamora—who were innocent of the sedition charges trumped up against them, ignited modern Philippine nationalism, and their martyrdom jumped the spark of nationalism from its circumscribed clerical arena to the lay community. In Spanish eyes a native cleric was "an enemy of Spain."[13]

This process of evolving Filipino national identity had to overcome the sense of loyalty most Filipinos have traditionally felt toward their local communities. The sense of affinity for the local over the distant, while consistent with other values, was an inhibiting factor in the formation of modern Filipino allegiance. Although residential affinity was but a further extension of the concept of extended family, it also encouraged communal, dialectal, provincial, and insular isolation. While "geographic ties are not absolute; and propinquity can produce enmity as well as solidarity," most Filipinos have felt a loyalty to their familial area which has increased as they moved further from it.[14] More than nostalgia, such identification has created subcultural allegiances within the society, and it has been only gradually that national identity has begun to achieve primacy over residential affinities.

The strength of this localism has persisted not only because of geographic fragmentation of the archipelago but also because the pre-Spanish community, the *barangay,* has continued to serve as the model for modern political development. Political allegiance has remained reciprocal and personal in large measure because familial polity has retained a dominant position. Despite Spanish and American administrative attempts to redraw *barangay* political organizations to correspond to rational, territorial units, political loyalty has continued to be tendered to the individual rather than to the office.[15] The struggle for local power has been a factional, highly personal competition usually between extended familial organizations. The Western concept of political parties has never dislodged the indigenous fictive-kinship structure dependent on reciprocity. By 1941 this symbiotic relationship, often described in terms of patron and client, created within the imposed framework of American political organization a pyramid of personal patron-client relationships. The mortar of the structure was not allegiance to party or principle but rather loyalty to the individual. A man who supported a rival after accepting the bounty of his own patron was not only thought guilty of *walang hiya* but was also considered to have turned traitor. At the apex of the pyramid were the national leaders, each of whom depended for power on his own personal organization down to the local level. These men were usually strongest politically in the area from which they came, but because they were intermarried and *compadre* to each other, they formed an oligarchy. The power of this elite germinated in the Spanish period and blossomed in the American era.

The claim to political legitimation can be traced back to the pre-Spanish *barangay*, where the local chiefs, the *datus*, exercised political power as patriarchs of familial polities. The Spanish, lacking personnel to rule directly, adopted a policy of indirect rule in which the *datu* was incorporated into the Spanish bureaucracy as the local headman, the *cabeza de barangay*, of the newly structured parish communities.[16] The local *datu* gained not only Spanish and Catholic legitimation but also new opportunities through land acquisition of a magnitude great enough to give him a vested interest in the status quo. At least some of the *datus* evolved into landlords, or caciques, although over the centuries others, through wealth, also attained cacique status.[17] This native elite, also called the *ilustrados*, became a vital bridge between the Spanish, living almost exclusively in Manila and a few other cities, and the mass of the peasantry in the countryside.

One of the salient characteristics of these *ilustrados* was their social mobility. Economic wealth translated into landholding was the necessary prerequisite for membership, but status could and was affected by marriage alliances. These families were rich enough to prove attractive marriage partners for poor Spanish and Latin-American officials. This process, which fed itself, generally permitted a channel for the downward flow of Spanish culture and the upward mobility of Filipinos. Such marriages tended to Filipinize the Spaniard or Latin-American partners and to change the racial status of the children from white to brown. Both phenomena encouraged them to settle permanently on their wife's lands.[18] In this alliance the Filipino family supplied wealth and power to the new husband; he, in turn, supplied status and economic potential through his non-Filipino connections.

While these Spanish-mestizo marriage alliances were undoubtedly the most prominent, of almost equal significance was the emergence of the far larger Chinese-mestizo segment of the elite.[19] The Chinese, who had traded in the Philippines before the Spanish arrived, were the key to the success of the Manila-Acapulco galleon trade, since the galleon depended on Chinese goods almost exclusively.[20] The profits of that trade brought a resident Chinese community to Manila to serve the galleon trade and to supply the demands of the new Spanish sector of the economy. The Spanish came to view the Chinese as vital to the success of the colony and sought to Catholicize and Hispanize them both to guarantee their continued presence and to fulfill the proselytizing mission of the Spanish crown.[21] The Chinese were encouraged to intermarry with Filipinas, and provided they adopted Catholicism, were granted a legal status in the community. "Unlike the *baba* of Malaya or the *peranakan* of Java, the Chinese mestizo in the Philippines was not a special kind of local Chinese. He was a special kind of Filipino."[22] In the mid-nineteenth century there were approximately 240,000 Chinese-mestizos, 20,000 Spanish-mestizos, 10,000 Chinese, and 5000 pure Spanish out of a total population of more than 4,000,-000.[23]

The success of the Chinese-mestizo marriage, in contrast to the more exclusive Spanish-mestizo marriage, depended usually on the brain power and economic acumen of the individual Chinese. Unlike the Spanish-mestizo marriage, which linked the strongest social and political elements in the community, the success of the Chinese-mestizo marriage in social terms had still to be proved by deeds. However, the success of the Chinese within the Philippine economic sphere gave high status and social desirability to such unions. The development of commercial crops—sugar, tobacco, hemp—and the expansion of the economy gave these Chinese-mestizos a vital opportunity for wealth. The Chinese and Chinese-mestizos expanded the Western, commercial sector of the economy into the back regions from the mid-eighteenth century.[24] Ironically, however, it was the growing pressure from the pure Chinese, who began migrating in large numbers to the Philippines during the mid-nineteenth century, as Spain removed the artificial limits on the size of that group, that pushed the Chinese-mestizos into a new nationalist identification as Filipinos. Just as the loss of Mexico sharpened identity through the racial definition of Caucasian and Malay, so too this growing Chinese population forced the Chinese-mestizo either back into a Chinese identity or more usually into a Filipino one.[25] These Chinese-mestizos, who as Catholics, landowners, and entrepreneurs felt threatened by the new immigrants, became another source from which emerged the modern elite. Jose Rizal, for example, the great Filipino patriot, poet, and martyr, was a fifth-generation Chinese-mestizo.[26] Obviously, only a few of these Chinese-mestizos were sufficiently successful to achieve cacique or *ilustrado* status. Many of the new elite also emerged from pure-blooded Filipino families who through hard work, *datu* origins, or good fortune grew rich.

The emergence of these families, whatever their origin, was of paramount importance in the social, economic, and political evolution of the Philippines. Each of these families had open contacts at both the local and Manila levels, serving as the necessary continuum of advisers and bureaucrats to the Spanish officials sent out on tours of duty and as the *principalia,* the local elders, of their home communities. These families became the vanguard of a new self-awareness from which Philippine nationalism has sprung. They were the first to educate their children and to travel abroad. Moreover, their new self-awareness was a key aspect in forging a new Filipino identity. While poorer Filipinos also learned of nationalism and revolution, the wealthy few came to see themselves as the natural leaders of the society and acted accordingly.[27] Power and wealth determined the qualifications of membership rather than the length or purity of the family tree. The community of interest in the emerging social order transcended the distinctions of *indio,* Spanish-mestizo, or Chinese-mestizo. Together they formed the new Filipino oligarchy.[28]

This group must be considered the dominant Philippine social institution of modern times. It was the lubricant for the society. As the arbiter of values it has been the driving force for modernization. It has defined the contours of evolving nationhood and Filipino identity. It first developed a political consciousness and led the periodic fight throughout the nineteenth century for representation in the Spanish parliament, the Cortes. It sent its sons to Europe to be educated and learned from their experiences in the cafes of Europe the vibrant excitement of secular nationalism.

As an embryonic oligarchy, however, it was conservative, expounding an evolutionary nationalism rather than revolution. Even after 1872, when many of this group went into exile because of the reign of terror following the Cavite mutiny and the martyrdom of Burgos, Zamora, and Gomez, it remained nonrevolutionary. The "Propaganda Movement" established by this diaspora argued only for evolutionary meliorism, and the life and writings of its most famous member, Jose Rizal, demonstrated its nonviolent character.[29] As a social reformer, Rizal refused to join the nonoligarchic radical activists, like Andres Bonifacio and Emilio Jacinto, who by the 1890's were advocating, like the Cuban revolutionaries of that period, violence to achieve total independence.[30] Ironically, it was Rizal's martyrdom which finally turned Filipino allegiance away from Spain and ignited the revolution. Significantly, however, even after the revolution began, it was through Pedro Paterno and the traditional elite that the Spanish governor, Primo de Rivera, offered the olive branch to the radical revolutionaries who by then were commanded by General Emilio Aguinaldo. The cease-fire treaty of Biác-na-bató blunted the revolution, and had Admiral Dewey, by a fluke of history, not attacked the Spanish fleet, the conservative elite, led by Paterno and such men as T. H. Pardo de Tavera, might have established a new basis for political collaboration with the Spanish authorities based on Rizal's reforms.

History evolved differently, however, and the United States backed into imperial control of the Philippines. The Americans returned the exiled Aguinaldo and restored initially and inadvertently de facto authority to his radical followers. The United States failed to realize that these revolutionaries had no intention of surrendering their quest for immediate independence merely because America replaced Spain as metropolitan power. The Americans were totally unprepared for the savage war of national liberation waged by the revolutionaries.[31] During these early months of the Insurrection, the Americans discovered good reason to tempt the oligarchy away from Aguinaldo's Malolos government and to collaborate. If they could restore this elite as a counterforce to the Insurrectionist movement by winning over Paterno, Benito Legarda, and others and encourage the elite's own inclination for evolutionary progress, they could use this group as the fulcrum to turn Filipino hostility into friendship. The inducement the Americans offered was a tacit alliance with the United States which would guarantee effectively the destruction of the radical activist threat to the oligarchy's hegemony. Paterno started this process when he broke with Aguinaldo and Mabini over the issue of accepting the Schurman Commission peace offer in 1899. This blow sounded the death knell of the Malolos Republic of the Philippines.

The United States felt compelled to evolve a colonial policy which could reconcile American imperialism with the tenets of American ideology. To achieve this, the Philippines were to be made into a "showcase of democracy" by which the world would be asked to judge the efficacy of the American way. This desire to rework another society in order to make it correspond at least outwardly with the prophetic if secular American credo required as an irreducible minimum the support of the elite. Through the manipulation of the social structure, the native masses were to become America's "little brown brothers." The pragmatic necessity to end the unpopular and embarrassing Insurrection before the next American presidential election in 1904 and the ideological necessity to turn expansionism into altruism by taking up the "white man's burden" drove the Republican policy-makers toward a bargain with the Philippine oligarchy.

American military might succeeded eventually in breaking the Insurrection and, as a result, in discrediting or killing the radical activists who had taken up arms. Simultaneously, the American civil administration weakened the political and economic power of the Spanish Church hierarchy by compelling Rome to replace the Spanish clerics with Americans, by negotiating for the sale of the enormous estates owned by the religious orders, and by imposing on the Philippines the American concept of the separation of Church and state. Into the resultant power vacuum the American administrators, primarily William Howard Taft and Elihu Root, encouraged the elite, the *ilustrados,* to move. They permitted, in the name of private property, the acquisition of the Friar lands by these families. The American goal to establish the trappings of a democratic state drew this elite into political power and also encouraged it to alter the basis on which its Spanish power was constituted. The Philippines needed technocrats, bureaucrats, educators, and professional entrepreneurs to achieve the American plan, and only the landed *ilustrados* had the education and wealth to acquire the requisite skills. The traditional elite utilized its local economic and social power as the basis for modern national control. Bishop Aglipay, the religious revolutionary, who had sought to create an independent Philippine church, and General Aguinaldo, the military-political revolutionary, were soon eclipsed by the American-supported secular oligarchy.

The price the elite paid for this increased power was the taint of collaboration. While the Americans never viewed such cooperation as collaboration, certainly some of the unreconciled revolutionaries such as General Artemio Ricarte and General Miguel Malvar regarded it this way. In a colonial situation, where ultimate power rests with the metropolitan nation, it seems obvious that some form of collaboration is inevitable and that such a term does not take on a pejorative quality until the self-conscious awareness of national identity has taken form. However, it was also true that the Philippine oligarchy had a historic tradition of flexibility toward any metropolitan power which would legitimate its position. Expediency in the face of force rather than idealistic consistency in the face of risk was the historical heritage of the elite during the late Spanish, American, and perhaps Japanese eras.

The pattern which emerged by the time of the first American-sponsored elections in 1907 was, in effect, a continuation of the oligarchic position of the late Spanish period. Although the symbols and techniques altered radically in the American era, the elite continued to espouse an evolutionary nationalism which would lead to independence when the nation was ready. The major spokesmen of this policy became the mestizo oligarchs, Sergio Osmeña and Manuel Quezon. Quezon, who had as a youth served with the Insurrectionists, was won over to the conservative gradualism of collaboration with America, emerging as the most dynamic member of the new leadership. An enormously astute politician and charismatic leader, he eventually gained control from Osmeña of the Nacionalista party, the political vehicle for expressing the policy of gradual nationalism. This party, which Quezon dominated despite periodic revolts by Osmeña and Manuel Roxas, maintained a monopoly of power and permitted Quezon to rule as a semidictator.[32] While responsible ultimately to American authority, Quezon controlled domestic politics almost absolutely, making and breaking men's careers, transferring them from job to job, and sending them on junkets if they dared to oppose him. Only a few, like the opposition leader Juan Sumulong, spoke out against the "feared and detested oligarchy," which kept the "needy classes" from having voice or vote, "even only as minorities."[33]

Sumulong's position was the "road not taken." Clustered around Quezon was a group of politicians and bureaucrats secure in their secondary positions of power, provided that they remained in

Quezon's good graces and that they maintained their own symbiotic patron-client relationships of local power. These leaders were transitional men, who led the drive toward modernization, and by 1941 they controlled the mass media, the bureaucracy, the political structure, and the new Filipino sector of the Westernized economy. They dominated the society so greatly that, except for a few dissenters like Sumulong, most opposition was forced to take extralegal and, therefore, illegal action to try to alter the system.

In effect, the American desire to prove the efficacy of its colonial experiment in the Philippines had as one result this enormous concentration of power. At the price of conceding unbridled influence to the oligarchy America did succeed in winning the allegiance of the elite and, as a direct consequence, the allegiance of the great majority of Filipinos, who followed their leaders faithfully. This was done, however, at the expense of real social and economic reform in the Philippines. The nondemocratic patterns of cacique control were brought into the modern world despite the superficial impositions of democratic institutions. The monolithic Nacionalista party was tolerated in place of an effective two-party system because the Nacionalistas were, for good reason, pro-American. The oligarchy, which had been inhibited by pressure from Spaniards, both temporal and ecclesiastical, was strengthened conversely by pressure from Americans.

This symbiotic relationship between American officials and the Filipino elite, coupled with the genuine effort of Americans to improve the health, education, and welfare of the average Filipino, won Filipino loyalty to the United States. Unlike most colonial experiences around the world, this Filipino loyalty transcended the legal demands for allegiance written into Philippine statute books. Conceding from the outset—albeit somewhat reluctantly—the self-liquidating quality of the American colonial venture, and recognizing that eventual national independence was primarily a question of timing, the American colonial administrations, with the exception of that of General Leonard Wood, yielded power continually. The American policy makers sensed the advantages of appearing as benevolent paternal counselors to the maturing adolescent wards. Implicit in the concept of "little brown brother" was the concession of eventual adulthood. The instinctive familial pattern of the Fil-American relationship triggered within the Filipino the social values of *utang na loob*. In the political realm the debt of gratitude demanded loyalty; the priceless concession of independence demanded of the Filipino acknowledgment of his debt of thanks to the United

States, which, like that of birth itself, could never be fully repaid. The United States, by establishing the image of guardian to the Filipino ward, inadvertently also established the image of *compadre* within the Filipino context. The United States became included in the pluralized "we" of Filipino allegiance. When in 1941 the Japanese attacked, the obligations of allegiance were quite clear.

The new sense of loyalty to the United States could only grow because it encouraged, rather than competed with, Philippine nationalism. The spread of nationalism from European to non-European peoples has probably been the most influential force in the twentieth-century world, and the abnormality of the Fil-American experience can clearly be seen in comparison with that of the Dutch in Indonesia. Because the Dutch strove to inhibit the development of Indonesian nationalism, they generated a residue of hatred which the Americans were able to avoid. Consequently, the response of the Indonesians to the Japanese occupation was in marked contrast to that of the Filipino; Indonesian collaboration with the Japanese was the highest form of patriotism because it advanced Indonesian nationalism. On the other hand, Filipino loyalty to the United States, especially to the self-appointed surrogate of the United States, Douglas MacArthur, reflected the basic, if fortuitous, approach America took toward colonialism. MacArthur, the personification of the best of Americanism to the majority of Filipinos, became the repository of Filipino allegiance because, like the saints and apostles, he was the tangible sign of a complex abstraction. His dramatic flair captivated the imagination of the Filipinos, and his brilliant manipulation of symbols and language permitted him to become a symbol himself.[34]

Within the web of Philippine loyalties there was another fundamental reason for allegiance to the United States. After almost four hundred years of Western colonial control, the Filipino was understandably uncertain whether he was not more occidental than oriental. Despite the color of his skin and his obvious geographic location in Asia, his predominant historical and social experience had been with the West. This Filipino ambivalence has created a natural desire to relate to Western culture, which usually has been dismissed superficially in the West as a desire by the Filipino to be white-skinned. This oversimplification minimizes the real Filipino desire to be accepted as an equal to the white rather than to achieve cosmetic equality. More complex than is indicated in the cliché, "colonial mentality," this drive has evolved out of the pervasive influence Western institutions have had over the centuries. The historic experience has led the Filipino to internalize many Western institutions into his life. Filipinos have felt that they too have a claim on Western culture which must not be denied to them. Through much of Philippine history, however, the Filipinos have been denied the achievement of equality by the West; the sense of sharing at least a partial community of interest and culture with the Americans, therefore, has fulfilled a deep psychic need.

The participation in Western culture has inevitably produced a sharp resultant tension within Philippine society, as, increasingly, the modern nationalist has sought to determine his Filipino identity. The quest for an indigenous, Asian culture predating the arrival of the Europeans has been a constant one since the Filipino became aware consciously of his anomalous situation. This issue, which has been such a major one since the Philippines gained independence in 1946, had also been of concern during the colonial era. Pio Duran, an outspoken propagandist for a Philippines identified primarily with Asia, noted in 1935, for example, that "whether the Filipinos like it or not, nature has thus decreed that their country's life shall be inextricably linked with those of the other countries of the Far East." Duran censured the oligarchy, "the apostates of Orientalism who have aligned themselves with the governing West in an effort to emasculate a portion of the Oriental race," and he asserted that the time was ripe for the Filipinos to join with Japan "in the formulation of a Monroe Doctrine for the Orient." He claimed that "to adopt another course would lay our shores open to attack by our brothers of the Orient, and, what is more, would justify the charge of being traitors to the high cause of the colored races in the East."[35]

The dilemma which Duran posed for the Filipinos became unavoidable when the Japanese occupied the Philippines. Duran, along with others, including the Japanese occupation officials, challenged the direction of Philippine nationalism. The flag, the national anthem, and similar symbols did not determine the ideological structure of the state, since they could be but the external manifestations of the internal social values. The ultimate test of Filipino values was the confrontation of the war, when the web of Philippine allegiance was stretched to the breaking point. The fiber of national values was subjected to intense pressure as each Filipino, and especially the oligarchy, was required to examine the interrelationship of familial, regional, and national obligations. It was ironic that the oligarchs, who had been the key transitional people in forming the new national allegiance, were the ones most troubled in determining their own relative values during the occupation. The critical question must be whether these men, having created and articulated the national consciousness, were guilty of violating, through collaboration with the Japanese, that very code of values. Having shaped the nation during the American era, were they guilty of treason to their own creation during the Japanese occupation?

CHAPTER II

The Heel of Achilles

*The Imperial Japanese Forces have entered on the
wings of victory*

—Tojo Hideki

The initial euphoria felt by Americans when Admiral Dewey defeated the Spanish was soon tempered not only by the Insurrection but also by the reality of the changing balance of power in the Pacific. By 1905 Japan, as a result of victories over China and Russia, emerged as the dominant Asian power. Moreover, the potential Japanese threat of hegemony increased as the fluid diplomatic configuration of late nineteenth-century European power froze in the years preceding World War I. England's anxieties about Europe led to an Anglo-Japanese alliance in 1902. England's recognition of Japanese paramountcy and Europe's increasing self-absorption caused their retreat from the Asian scene. This turn in affairs, together with Japanese power and Chinese weakness, combined to make American policy planners see Japan alone as the future rival to the United states in Asia. In addition, America felt that Japan threatened the stability of peace in Asia. In turn, to Japanese planners America became the only power capable of and interested in checking Japanese imperialism.

Prior to 1941, however, the United States was not willing militarily to oppose Japan's drive for hegemony. While Americans frequently waxed eloquent about the Open Door and the sacredness of Chinese integrity, few felt that East Asia was vital enough to justify the use of force. The traditional isolation of America, its remoteness from Asia, and its primary connections with Europe circumscribed American policy in the Philippines and the Pacific. It became clear to the Korean and Chinese nationalists as well as to the Japanese military that the United States was unwilling to commit troops to fight for anything except the defense of America itself. The discrepancy between American statements and actual intentions created a dangerous inconsistency, since the United States attempted to effect policy goals without paying the price. To avoid an eventual confrontation with Japan the United States had to develop a policy of minimizing liabilities which might ensnare America. Any other policy was bound to create ominous risks.

The possession of the Philippines was one of the most inhibiting elements in the American diplomatic posture in Asia. Strategically, the Philippines were a vulnerable pawn which the Americans were compelled to defend. By 1907 President Theodore Roosevelt saw that the Philippines aggravated the flaws in American diplomacy in Asia. In a letter to William Howard Taft, then secretary of War, he noted that "the Philippine Islands form our heel of Achilles. They are all that makes the present situation with Japan dangerous."[1] Roosevelt argued for Philippine independence as a means of diminishing American military risk, and this theme was repeated with increasing frequency as Japanese imperialism became more blatant through the years. The Japanese action in 1931 in Manchuria encouraged the American Congress to establish a Philippine Commonwealth. Section Eleven of the Tydings-McDuffie Act of 1934, entitled "Neutralization of the Philippine Islands," specifically instructed the American President "to enter into negotiations with foreign powers . . . for the perpetual neutralization of the Phillippine Islands" in order to absolve the United States of any postindependence obligations.[2]

At least until 1946, however, the United States was bound to defend what was, after all, American territory. The American military, charged with this obligation, was aware that the Philippines were a pawn. As early as April 1904, the army chief of staff, Lieutenant General Adna R. Chaffee, proposed a series of war contingency studies between the army and navy. Orange, among the colors of these plans, was designated the code color for a war plan against Japan.[3] The military, aware of the gap between professed aims of political policy and willingness to commit resources to achieve these aims, struggled to evolve a realistic military posture. In effect, the military was told to disguise the "rolled unbrella" as the "big stick." Except for the great base at Pearl Harbor, the government never appropriated sufficient funds to prevent the diplomatic liabilities from becoming military risks. In 1923 General of the Armies John J. Pershing, convinced of the vital military need for Philippine fortification to protect American prestige and to avoid the inevitably arduous task of reconquest in case of loss, urged that a viable defense be established.[4] American policy makers rejected this advice, however, signing instead a pledge of nonfortification as part of the Washington Conference. This fundamental contradiction in American foreign policy in Asia created a gap between military aims and obligations.[5]

The War Plan Orange that evolved posited that in case of an attack by Japan the Philippines were to be held as long as possible so that an American fleet might have time to relieve the siege. This was unrealistic. A determined Japanese bid to take Luzon would have made a long holding action at Manila Bay almost impossible. Indeed, the limitations of congressional appropriations made six months the maximum period an American garrison could survive logistically. War Plan Orange was silent on the political and military consequences of a defeat in the event the fleet did not arrive in time, but at least some people were aware of the risks. Thus, in 1935 the chief of the War Plans Division, General Embick, labeled an inadequately prepared Philippines "a military liability of incalculable magnitude."[6]

During the Insurrection the United States had committed many tens of thousands of troops to suppress Aguinaldo's forces, withdrawing them as quickly as possible after the fighting ceased. The garrison, which in 1913 became known as the Philippine Department, was stabilized at about 10,000 men, one half of whom were Filipino Scouts. There was also a Philippine Constabulary, founded in 1901, which served as a national police.[7] This military situation existed until the establishment of the Commonwealth government in 1935, when, for the first time, Filipino leaders began to evaluate the responsibilities of national security.

American obligations persisted through the Commonwealth period, but, except for the neutralization provision in the Tydings-McDuffie Act, the American government seemed eager to avoid any postindependence involvement. Consequently, while in Washington in 1935, President Quezon approached Douglas MacArthur, who was then completing his fifth year as chief of staff of the United States army. Quezon had known MacArthur when MacArthur had commanded "successively a division and the Philippine Department."[8] He asked MacArthur to come to the Philippines to develop a military plan to make the Islands secure even after the umbrella of American protection was removed. MacArthur, who was completing a military career in the American army for lack of further offices to hold, found the opportunity challenging and accepted with pleasure.[9]

MacArthur was appointed military adviser to the Common-wealth government and was authorized to deal directly with the chief of staff and secretary of War in Washington, but he was basically responsible to Quezon, with whom he developed an increasingly warm and intimate friendship.[10] This relationship was formalized in Philippine fashion when MacArthur invited Quezon to serve as *compadre* to MacArthur's newborn son, Arthur, and Quezon reciprocated by creating for MacArthur the unique rank of field marshal. Quezon personally designed a somewhat theatrical uniform for MacArthur, who, in later years, utilized the hat as a symbol of his and Fil-American resistance.

MacArthur, who rejected the pessimistic opinion of American military planners, was confident that a viable defense strategy could be evolved for the Philippines. He convinced Quezon that his strategy "was a simple one, patterned after the citizen-soldier system of conscription effectively established in Switzerland. The country was divided into ten military areas, each of which was to train 4,000 yearly. There was to be a small professional force which would be charged with their development."[11] MacArthur saw this force both as a means "to build up the health and economic well-being of the trainees" and as a way to deter a foreign aggressor from risking a costly war. Within the limit of $8,000,000 a year, he planned a small "naval arm, the backbone of which would be a fleet of fifty small, high-speed, torpedo-throwing craft and an air force of 250 planes." MacArthur anticipated that by the end of the Commonwealth era the 400,000 Filipino reservists could defend the country, even under a major attack, by retreating into interior positions and becoming a guerrilla movement.

MacArthur's conviction swayed Quezon, who came to propound this theory vigorously. On November 25, 1935, he urged the Philippine National Assembly to accept the plan in order "to serve notice upon the world that the citizens of these Islands are not to be subjugated; that conquest of this nation cannot be accomplished short of its utter destruction, and that destruction would involve such staggering cost to an aggressor, both in blood and gold, that even the boldest and strongest will unerringly mark the folly of such an undertaking."[12] Quezon rejected the provision of the Tydings-McDuffie Act proposing a guaranteed international treaty of neutrality in favor of a self-reliant posture of strength. His advocacy led the Philippine National Assembly to adopt MacArthur's scheme on December 21, 1935.[13]

His optimistic view of postindependence security did little to alleviate the interregnum, during which the archipelago remained vulnerable because of American sovereignty. During the 1930's, however, few Americans and even fewer Filipinos were aware of the degree of vulnerability. The image of American strength, the serene picture of the Stars and Stripes waving gently under tropical skies, disguised the precarious situation. This false sense of security, coupled with a chronic problem of tropical inertia, kept the Philippines from maintaining the annual schedule proposed by MacArthur. Consequently, when Major Dwight Eisenhower left MacArthur's staff in 1940, there were only 100,000 reservists of dubious training, instead of the projected 140,000 men, and there were less than 100 pilots trained to fly only forty of the proposed 250 planes.[14] In other words, despite the blueprint, the real burden of defense still rested with the American military and its operational War Plan Orange. However, that plan, despite its revision in 1938, was made increasingly obsolete by growing Japanese air and naval power. It was also severely crippled by the failure of the democratic powers to enlarge their armaments to match the rapid expansion of those of Japan, Germany, and Russia. Few weapons trickled to the Philippine garrisons, and these were inadequate technologically.

Anxiety about Japanese aggression grew even though the arsenals did not. After the Marco Polo Bridge incident in North China, Filipinos and Americans belatedly awakened to the growing risk. Japanese immigration and economic investment in the Philippines appeared increasingly as a devious plot. Growing Fil-American anxiety transformed the legitimate desire of Japanese business for trade into the specter of yen diplomacy.[15] Vested Fil-American interests cloaked their desire for exclusive monopoly in the guise of new patriotism, but the transfer of hostility from the Japanese imperial threat to the overseas community was very widely made. The Japanese businessman's claim for good-neighborly friendship was heard by Filipinos as "Asiatic Monroeism," which they thought would mean "economic pauperism" and "political extinction."[16]

Increasing anti-Japanese sentiment during the 1930's alarmed the local Japanese officials, who were legitimately anxious to protect Japanese nationals and investment in the Philippines. They attempted improvement of the Japanese image by sympathetic propaganda and by official protest to the United States high commissioner and to President Quezon. The Japanese consul general in Manila, Uchiyama Kiyoshi, intending to clarify policy, introduced to Tokyo a plan he had devised for the improvement of relations. He urged the Japanese to "publish a pro-Japanese newspaper, manipulate the representatives, join hands with the opposite faction, stir up anti-American sentiment, arouse public opinion in Japan, and . . . adopt other behind-the-scene measures."[17] Uchiyama further urged that the key theme for Japanese propaganda should be the then accurate statement that in the Philippines Japan desired trade without territory. Japan did not decide upon a military invasion of the Philippines until the fundamental decisions of global strategy were taken during the period between the German invasion of Poland and Pearl Harbor. Certainly, the local Japanese population and officialdom had reason to feel that Filipino hostility was unfair persecution.

To counterbalance anti-Japanese sentiment, local Japanese officials and businessmen were willing to spend large sums of money. Vice-consul Kihara became a famed entertainer and lavish gift giver.[18] Japanese funds were also used for lobbying and for creating "dummy corporations" in which famous Filipinos were won over to serve as figurehead officers in Japanese-controlled companies. Jose Laurel, Pedro Sabido, and many other ranking officials were retained at one point or another during this period to lobby and to serve Japanese interests. The Japanese government paid handsomely to avoid restrictive legislation, and the Japanese-owned B.B.B. brewery in Manila supplied more than one free beer for the "sake" of goodwill.

A few, like Pio Duran, argued for the Japanese cause, stating that "no other sound recourse is open to the Filipinos than to side with their Japanese brothers of the North and help them preserve Asia for the Asiatics."[19] Unabashedly Japanophile, Duran claimed that Japan's bad image in the Philippines was due to the malicious propaganda of the Americans, who, he said, took "advantage of every opportunity to malign the good name of the Japanese and to picture that country as a warlike nation awaiting the first opportunity to seize the Philippine Islands."[20] Men like Duran were uncritical in their admiration of Japan, highly esteeming the totality of Japanese power and culture. As a group they represented only a minute percentage of the national leadership.

A much more important group of the oligarchy was attracted to certain Japanese institutions, despite its anxiety about the increasing threat of Japanese militarism. These men envied the way the Japanese elite had seemed to succeed in modernizing Japan without diminishing their own power. Sharing with their Japanese counterparts a fear of a radical peasantry, they identified with Japanese authoritarian control. Oligarchs of this persuasion similarly favored movements like the Falange in Spain. The rigid control of

Japanese class structure and the seemingly universal acceptance of social status naturally appealed to men already at the top in their own society. Japan, unlike the Philippines, seemed graft free; it seemed to have mastered Western science while retaining Eastern morals. Together with their technological success, the Japanese seemed to have found an ideological framework unifying the nation. Japanese trains actually ran on time. There was, therefore, a legitimate feeling that the Philippines, like the rest of Asia, could profit from the Japanese experience. Few among the Filipino prewar elite remained uninterested in at least some Japanese institutions and solutions.

Ironically, another group attracted to Japanese institutions was made up of radicals, who were greatly feared by the oligarchy. As in Japan itself, the distinction between radical left and right was blurred. Prewar Philippine radicalism turned right and emulated Japanese ultrarightist organizations, whereas in the postwar era this same basic movement assumed a leftist, communist guise as the Hukbalahap. The most active prewar radical manifestation was the Sakdal movement. Organized in 1930 among discontented tenant farmers and patterned vaguely after radical Japanese agrarian models, it advocated the overthrow of the Commonwealth government. Promising a redistribution of land, including Church holdings, a reduction in taxes, and totalitarian government, the Sakdalistas had some ties with late nineteenth-century radicalism as well as with Japanese secret societies. As with the later Hukbalahap, the movement was primarily indigenous, adopting from the outside useful symbols and connections. The Sakdal party was led by an able politician and poet named Benigno Ramos. In 1934 he succeeded in winning three seats for the party in the congressional election. In 1935, at the height of the depression, he led the movement into an openly revolutionary phase. In that year Quezon fired Ramos from his civil service position in the Philippine Senate.[21] Ramos appealed for aid to the Japanese secret societies, the military, and the Japanese government, but with little success, and the resultant agrarian revolt, though bloody, was soon suppressed. At its peak the Sakdals claimed 68,000 members. After the revolt the movement declined but never died, surviving in modified form as the Ganap party. Ramos fled to Tokyo, but under pressure from the Americans, the Japanese government permitted his extradition. The Japanese could not afford to befriend this radical and his party too openly without risking the total alienation of the conservative Filipino elite. Ramos was jailed without Japanese protest.

As Japanese imperialism became more menacing throughout the later 1930's, Japan became increasingly the enemy, despite sympathetic interest at both ends of the Philippine political and economic spectrum. Commitment to Philippine nationalism was an overriding passion, and Japan appeared as a threat to the success of a postindependence Republic of the Philippines. Consequently, most patriotic Filipinos rallied to the evolved obligations of national identity, which dictated a communal recognition of this rising threat. The new Filipino left—the intellectuals, the embryonic labor movement, and the socialist and communist groups—joined, as elsewhere in the world, a united front with the conservative right in order to protect the new nationalism from external threat. The primacy of this new allegiance linked otherwise hostile groups within the society to rally behind the national leadership of Quezon and the Nacionalista party.

The fall of France in the spring of 1940 was followed in September by a German-Italian-Japanese axis alliance, which acknowledged "the leadership of Japan in establishing a New Order in East Asia." When, during the next spring, Foreign Minister Matsuoka negotiated a pact of neutrality with the Russians, Filipinos and Americans began to fear a Japanese effort to gain empire while the rest of the world was diverted by the European war. On April 1, 1941, President Quezon created the Civilian Emergency Administration (CEA) to prepare civil defense plans for the country. Later in the month, an alien registration law was passed, primarily to check on the overseas Japanese. In early June the Philippine National Assembly passed Commonwealth Act No. 620, which yielded emergency powers to the president, including near dictatorial police and confiscatory authority. During this period Quezon frequently reiterated that the Philippines would fight with the United States against Japan: "Our stakes are our own future independence and assurance that that independence may endure."[22]

On July 22, 1941, Japan moved into Indo-China. This calculated Japanese decision was the step which President Roosevelt felt America could not let Japan take. Four days later, Roosevelt froze all Japanese assets in the United States, impelling both sides toward a confrontation.[23] In early August, Japan finally decided firmly to avoid a war with Russia in Manchuria and Siberia and to turn southward. The Japanese navy, unhappy over its failure to obtain what it considered sufficient oil concessions during the Kobayashi and Yoshizawa trade missions to the Dutch East Indies, argued that Japan could not wait past early 1942 to decide on policy. It was assumed that military balance of power would shift against Japan so decidedly that there would be little chance for success. At the Imperial Conference of September 6, 1941, Admiral Nagano Osami urged that Japan strike south to guarantee the vital oil flow for Japan. If not, he warned, Japanese reserves would be used up, and Japan would become so dependent on American oil as to inhibit Japanese maneuverability.

The Indo-Chinese confrontation finally galvanized the American government into a crash military program to catch up with the totalitarian powers. Supplies began to flow to the Philippine garrison, but it was impossible to reinforce every American garrison around the world at once. The forty-year gap between American policy and power could not be logistically redressed in a few months. A feverish effort was exerted nonetheless. The day after Roosevelt froze Japanese assets, General George Marshall, the chief of staff, cabled General MacArthur that he was being recalled into the American army "as Commanding General, United States Army Forces in the Far East [USAFFE]"[24] This new command included "the Philippine Department, forces of the Commonwealth of the Philippines called into service of the armed forces of the United States for the period of the existing emergency and such other forces as may be designated to it." MacArthur's command included 22,532 men in the Philippine Department of whom 11,972 were Philippine Scouts, in addition to MacArthur's partly trained Filipino army.[25]

It was dangerously late and United States global priorities placed the Philippines fairly low on the list. Supplies were slow in coming and insufficient. By late November 1941, the United States military build-up had barely begun. There were only thirty-five B-17 bombers and 107 P-40 fighter planes, though more were on order.[26] In the months after MacArthur was recalled the size of the American garrison had increased by only 6083 men.[27] In order to help combat this situation Quezon on August 19, 1941, broadcast a speech to the United States. He said that "the stand of the Filipino people is clear and unmistakable. We owe loyalty to America and we are bound to her by bonds of everlasting gratitude. Should the United States enter the war, the Philippines would follow her and fight by her side."[28] Quezon's emotional declaration that the Filipinos "stand with the United States in life and in death" implied, especially in Filipino terms, a United States obligation of reciprocity that Americans, because of insensitivity and global strategy, did not meet.

MacArthur believed that the Japanese attack would not come before April 1942. Indeed, the day after the Japanese fleet had secretly sailed to attack Pearl Harbor, he met with United States High Commissioner Francis B. Sayre and Admiral Thomas Hart to explain why the attack would come in the spring.[29] Admiral Hart and the military planners in Washington thought differently. Some three days earlier, on November 24, Washington had notified all Pacific commanders that war was probable and that a "surprise aggressive movement in any direction, including [an] attack on the Philippines or Guam was a possibility."[30] MacArthur's meeting with Sayre and Hart had been held because a second "final alert" had just been received which indicated that "hostile action [was] possible at any moment."[31] Despite these warnings based on the Japanese code breaker, MAGIC, MacArthur, along with the Hawaiian commanders, appears to have discounted the risk.[32] The Japanese attack on the Philippines did not come until some hours after the Pearl Harbor bombing. The news, cabled to MacArthur between three and four in the morning, awakened the sleeping commander of a sleeping garrison.[33]

President Quezon was so unprepared for the Japanese attack that the outbreak of hostilities caught him at the summer capital of Baguio. Just after dawn on December 8, Quezon was called by his secretary, Jorge Vargas, who reported that "both the United and Associated Press" had telephoned him the news of war; MacArthur's staff apparently never relayed the information to the Philippine executive.[34] By seven that morning Quezon had committed the full prestige of his office and his person to the Allied cause. "The zero hour has arrived," he said, "I expect every Filipino—man and woman—to do his duty. We have pledged our honor to stand to the last by the United States and we shall not fail her, happen what may."[35] At breakfast Quezon watched a formation of Japanese bombers fly over Baguio to bomb Camp John Hay. By the end of lunch another group of bombers had flown over Clark Field, the airbase at Fort Stotsenberg, and had destroyed the bulk of the American bomber fleet, which was caught lined up in rows on the ground. Despite the period of grace for American commanders in the Philippines, "as at Pearl Harbor, the Japanese achieved complete tactical surprise."[36] The "significance of these events" was clear; "the Japanese had removed at one stroke the greatest single obstacle to their advance southward."[37]

Many Americans and Filipinos explained initial Japanese success in terms of a well-organized fifth column of former Sakdalistas and overseas Japanese. Fil-American military failures were attributed to prior intelligence obtained through spies. This assumption, although it was erroneous, helped cushion the shock of defeat. Most Japanese were interned within a few hours and no network of spies was utilized by the Japanese military. The truth, which became increasingly plain with time, was that the Japanese just did not need such assistance.[38]

Fil-American forces soon made the frightening discovery that much of their equipment was old and defective. In some cases only one out of six shells fired actually exploded. Initially, despite American weakness in men and materiel, the Americans could not believe that the Japanese could win. They doubted, irrationally, that Japan had the sufficient power, organization, and logistical skill to mount a major invasion against the Philippines. In the early days of the war it was believed by some, for example, that Japanese planes were being piloted by Caucasians, since racial arrogance made it almost impossible for some Americans to comprehend that the Japanese were skillful enough for pinpoint bombing. This erroneous judgment not only produced an underestimation of Japanese ability but also heightened despair among the Filipino troops at American defeat. When Filipinos realized that the Americans had grossly minimized Japanese military prowess, they tended to overcompensate by exaggerating Japanese power. As a result of the smashing and rapid-fire Japanese victories throughout Southeast Asia, many Filipinos incorrectly decided that the war would last for a very long time and adjusted their behavior to that estimate.

This estimate gradually came into direct conflict with the emotional response made by the Filipinos to the American side. A few days before the war broke out Quezon summarized this emotional attitude while addressing the students of the University of the Philippines. Speaking on Philippine Heroes Day, he outlined the grim basis of Filipino allegiance for the next years. After praying to God that the nation be spared war, Quezon suggested two reasons why it would be a "good thing for us" if God willed it otherwise. Stressing the obligations of *utang na loob*, he said "it will give us an opportunity, before we finally sever the ties that bind us with the United States in 1946, to show the American people that our gratitude to the American flag for all the manifest blessings it has brought us is so deep-seated we are willing and ready to lay down our fortunes and our lives in its defense." Quezon's second reason reflected not the traditional Filipino values but a new concept acquired during the American era. In Puritan-ethic terms, he saw the war as a good experience "because it will teach our youth—that, reared in the ease and comfort of an American-protected market, has whiled away its time in luxury and frivolity—how to suffer and how to die. For no nation is worth anything unless it has learned how to suffer and how to die."[39]

Quezon spoke for his nation. In the early days of the war, before the Filipinos knew of the enormous extent of the American defeats and felt the despair of occupation, they entered the war with the totality of a unified, aroused nation. The Philippine nation committed itself to the Allied cause and mobilized all its resources at Quezon's command. Immediately after hostilities began, Quezon rushed back to the capital, where he met with the Council of State to ratify this decision.[40] On December 10, the day the British capital ships "Prince of Wales" and "Repulse" were sunk by Japanese airpower off the coast of Malaya, and the American naval base at Cavite was similarly destroyed by Japanese bombers, Quezon and the Council ratified the war decision. The following day Quezon sent a special message to the Phillippine Congress requesting emergency legislation and congressional concurrence with his repeated assurances to Roosevelt of Filipino loyalty and "determination to place at her [America's] disposal all the man power and resources of our nation."[41]

The requested concurrence was given immediately in Resolution No. 115, which pledged "the full support and cooperation of the Filipino people to the government of the United States" and authorized "the President of the Philippines to place all resources of the country at the disposal of the government of the United States for the prosecution of the war to its successful conclusion."[42] Since the Philippines lacked the ultimate sovereignty to declare war independently, this Resolution was tantamount to such a declaration. The Congress also certified the results of the November 1941 presidential and congressional elections. A few days later it granted Quezon further emergency powers to do whatever he might deem necessary during the war, including the legislative authority to alter the debt, levy taxes, raise money, promulgate or extend laws that usually required legislative approval, change the structure of government, make appointments, and act in any way necessary to preserve the state.

Quezon devoted prime attention to civil defense and war relief. He worked closely with Teofilo Sison, director of the Civilian Emergency Administration (CEA), for the protection and evacuation of the Manila area. He also met with General Guillermo Francisco of the Philippine Constabulary in order to achieve a proper mobilization of its 6000 members. With Vice-President Osmeña he toured the countryside and the city of Manila. Wherever he went, Quezon remembered receiving a triple manifestation of allegiance as the crowds shouted, "Mabuhay [Welcome]—long live America, the Philippines, and President Quezon!"[43]

Battles are not won by sentiment, however, and the military situation was critical. The destruction of the American fleet at Pearl Harbor and the British capital ships off Malaya gave Japan mastery of the sea. The triumph of Japanese air power permitted comparable mastery in the air. An invasion could be made with impunity. The Japanese victories of the first seventy-two hours successfully aborted any real hope of the arrival of an American relief convoy in the Philippines in time to raise a siege, but MacArthur knew that his orders were still to persist against the Japanese as long as possible. By December 12, only four days after hostilities began, MacArthur summoned Quezon to a conference to inform him of the probable necessity of evacuation to Corregidor, the fortified redoubt at the entrance to Manila Bay. Quezon was shocked that MacArthur was already planning such a drastic retreat. He later recalled that "it had never crossed my mind . . . that there would ever come a time when *I had* to go to Corregidor. I was no *American* Governor-General, but the *Filipino* President of the Commonwealth. . . . I was, therefore, wholly unprepared for the startling message from General Mac-Arthur."[44]

This conference shocked Quezon into an awareness of the gap between the fulfillment of his obligations to America and to the Philippine people. Suddenly aware of the tension he demurred, "But General, why would I have to go to Corregidor in that case? The military defense of the Philippines is primarily America's responsibility and not mine. I have already placed every Filipino soldier under your command." Noting that his first duty was toward the civilian population, he went on to say, "Were I to go to Corregidor, my people would think I had abandoned them to seek safety under your protection. This I shall never do. I shall stay among my people and suffer the same fate that may befall them."[45] MacArthur countered by arguing that "it was his duty to prevent" Quezon from "falling into the enemy's hands." He noted that as long as Quezon was "free, the occupation of Manila, or even of the Philippines, by the Japanese Army would not have the same significance under international law as if the Government had been captured or had surrendered."[46]

This was the beginning of the collaboration dilemma for Filipino leaders. Did Quezon, confronted with the reality of a Japanese military victory, have a higher obligation to continue in office in order to attempt to alleviate the suffering of his people, or did he have a higher obligation to avoid collaboration in order somehow to preserve the integrity of Philippine values and institutions? Quezon wrestled with this problem after his meeting with MacArthur, finally resolving it with the help of his wife, Doña Aurora, who urged him to see his duty in the broader context. "But this is war," she said to him, "total war. . . . The winning of the war is the only question before us. Nothing else matters."[47] Quezon, the first to have to make this decision, was more fortunate than his aides, since he was able to make it free from the physical shadow of Japanese bayonets.

Quezon did not have very much time to brood about the correctness of his choice. Ten days after meeting with MacArthur, on December 22, Japanese bayonets and samurai swords were glittering on the Luzon beaches of Lingayan Gulf to the north of Manila. The Fourteenth (Watari) Japanese Army, with a total strength of 43,110 men, landed from eighty-five transports.[48] Two days later approximately 7000 additional troops landed to the south of Manila at Lamon Bay.[49] The master plan of Japanese military strategy posited a giant pincer operation around Manila, to be completed in fifty days; this would permit a large percentage of these Japanese troops to be sent as vital reinforcements in the drive toward Australia by the end of March 1942.

The Japanese military apparently had been convinced that the decisive battle for Luzon would be fought around Manila rather than in the Bataan Peninsula, where War Plan Orange determined that the last stand be made. Although War Plan Orange must have been known to Japanese military intelligence, it was not considered still to be operational. When, in October, the Fourteenth Army staff met under Commander-in-Chief Homma Masaharu, this possibility of American action was quickly discounted, even though Chief of Staff Lieutenant General Maeda Masami raised it as a tactical consideration.[50] It is impossible to understand how the Japanese could have been so confident that MacArthur's defensive plans would include a fight for Manila rather than a retreat to Bataan, but Homma's misplaced confidence cost him dearly. War Plan Orange III, in its revised 1938 form, was followed closely by MacArthur, who withdrew his troops into the Bataan Peninsula, which was to be defended to the "last extremity."[51] Tragically for the Fil-American forces, the fleet which was supposed to relieve the Bataan garrison was a rusting, twisted group of hulks at Pearl Harbor.[52]

To execute War Plan Orange III MacArthur had to manage a difficult withdrawal in order to avoid the pincer attack of the Japanese troops. With great bravery by the Fil-American troops the retreat was successful; General Jonathan Wainwright's troops managed to hold the critical bridge at Calumpit until the Allied troops had passed. Once he had ordered the withdrawal into Bataan, MacArthur also declared Manila an "open city." Since the city had no strategic value, he shifted all the supplies he could to the war zone and moved his and High Commissioner Sayre's headquarters to Corregidor. He notified Quezon that he too would have to move and informed him that he could take only a skeleton staff.

Quezon selected Vice-President Osmeña, Chief Justice Jose Abad Santos, General Basilio Valdes, and a few others to accompany him. The other members of the cabinet, the Council of State, and the government were informed that they would remain behind, awaiting the Japanese occupation. At the final full cabinet meeting on Christmas eve, the basic question of conduct under occupation came up again. Quezon urged his aides to protect the civil population by "performing neutral functions pertaining to municipal administration and the administration of justice. . . ."[53] However, Jose Laurel asked Quezon what they should do if the Japanese required them "to do many things which are inimical" to the Philippine or American governments. Laurel was afraid Quezon might disapprove of what these men did and might accuse them of disloyalty when he came back. After the war Laurel recalled that Quezon said he would check with MacArthur to get instructions. Laurel further remembered that Quezon relayed MacArthur's reply: "What can you do under the circumstances? You have to do what they ask you to do except one thing—the taking of an oath of allegiance to Japan."[54]

These alleged instructions, which, it must be noted, gave the elite very wide latitude, became a cornerstone in the postwar defense of the oligarchy. They have been accepted unanimously as valid and accurate. While there have been many versions of the story with altered details, the actual quotation rarely varied from account to account.[55] Quezon in his autobiography is, unfortunately, silent. He urged his aides to minimize the suffering of the people, and his final instructions as he recalled them were only to "keep your faith in America, no matter what happens. She will never let you down."[56] He commented that he was consoled by the fact that he was leaving behind key men on whom he could depend to do their duty by their country, regardless of the risk to their lives and fortunes. He was silent on whether he transmitted specific instructions attempting to define the acceptable from the treasonable. While Quezon's parting with Jorge Vargas, his secretary, was particularly tender, it was only an expression of confidence. Quezon recalled later that "no other word was said."[57]

MacArthur, however, denied ever having given the alleged instructions. In a hand-written reply of April 14, 1961, to a letter from the author, he stated: "I gave no instructions to Santos, Roxas, Laurel or any other Filipino leaders on leaving the Philippines to assume command of the Southwest Pacific Area with headquarters in Australia. There was no so-called 'Filipino delegation.' Every Filipino, except those in the armed services, acted according to his own conscience so far as I know. [signed] MacA." The sharp differences, which can never be resolved, further obscure a clouded issue. If MacArthur never gave such instructions, then the prop of higher orders, which absolved the trapped elite of moral responsibility, has been removed. However, even if he had, did the postwar trials at Nuremberg and Jerusalem undermine the defense, that of innocence based on compliance with orders? Whatever Quezon and MacArthur did or did not say before leaving for Corregidor, each ranking Filipino still had the lonely task of determining his own set of priorities. As Quezon's boat slipped across Manila Bay, each of those left behind could only go home, pray, and wait.

With its evacuation and the declaration that it was an "open city," Manila suddenly emerged from its shroud. Between Christmas and New Year's the city and its inhabitants were in limbo. The blackout ended, and the people, not knowing what else to do, came out of their homes. Some Japanese bombing occurred, mostly inadvertently, but far more destruction was caused by the evacuating rear guard of American troops, who ignited anything which might help the Japanese. The oil dumps burned for days, casting a pall of black smoke high over a city afraid that it, like Nanking, would be raped. Tension resulted in looting, as people plunged into the opened warehouses of the American army and then into the unopened warehouses of private business. The city, like the heavy oil smoke, hung in suspension. Far across the shimmering water at the mouth of the Bay, MacArthur frequently looked eastward back to the city. Especially at night, when the outline of his home, the Manila Hotel, was aglow, he would stare out. The Japanese, he stated, "might have the bottle," but he, at least, still "had the cork."[58]

CHAPTER III

Dual Government

*When our actions do not, our fears do make us
traitors.*

—William Shakespeare

On January 2, 1942, the ninth day of Christmas, instead of "ladies dancing," the Japanese army occupied the "open city" of Manila. Instead of the traditional gifts of peace they brought with them the grim specter of famine, destruction, and death. By establishing their occupation in Manila before defeating the Fil-American forces across the Bay on Corregidor, the Japanese also exacerbated the crisis for the nation and for the elite. Two warring metropolitan powers imposed conflicting demands on the colonial Filipinos, and each required support. On Corregidor President Quezon continued to proclaim that the Fil-American forces would beat back the Japanese and that his authority was unimpaired; from this redoubt he demanded unswerving allegiance. In Manila, however, the Japanese immediately began to impose their demands on the civilian population. Insisting that the local and national officials continue in office, the Japanese started to implement their concept of the new order. Two governments, each dependent on force, suddenly faced each other across the Bay. The dilemma of allegiance under occupation had begun.

On January 3, the Japanese commander-in-chief issued a proclamation announcing that "as a result of the Japanese military operations, the sovereignty of the U.S.A. over the Philippines has completely disappeared and the Army hereby proclaims the Military Administration under martial law over the districts occupied by the army." This proclamation, which was the organic act of the Japanese era, indicated that all Commonwealth laws, except those inimical to Japanese interests, would continue in force, and "all public officials shall remain in their present posts and carry on their duties as before." It also conceded freedom of religion and residence to the Filipinos. In turn, it stated that "the purpose of the Japanese expedition is nothing but to emancipate you from the oppressive domination of the United States of America, letting you establish 'The Philippines for the Filipinos' as a member of the Co-Prosperity Sphere. . . ." Filipinos, informed of the Japanese intentions, were warned to refrain from "spreading fabulous wild rumors." They were to reject American propaganda or risk being "severely punished, the gravest offenses being punishable by death, according to martial law."[1]

The following day, January 4, the Japanese brought out the first edition of a newspaper. Appropriating the presses of the Roces family chain of newspapers, they printed limited editions of the *Tribune*, which became their English-language daily, and of its almost identical Spanish and Tagalog counterparts, *La Vangardia*, and the *Taliba*.[2] A few days later they created a liaison office to provide "intercommunication" between the army and the citizenry in order to curb the rash of rumors on which Filipinos were feeding obsessionally and to afford Filipinos a means of redressing abuses suffered at the hands of Japanese troops. Vital services were maintained or begun again under either civilian or military control.

The real Japanese effort, however, was made behind the scenes. Within seventy-two hours of occupying the city, Chief of Staff General Maeda Masami and General Hayashi Yoshide, director-general of Military Administration, began searching for political support among the prewar elite. On January 5 ex-Speaker Jose Yulo responded to this pressure by calling an emergency meeting at his Manila home on Peñafrancia Street. The group, which eventually grew to about thirty men, debated alternative courses of action before deciding on Yulo's plan, which was to stall the Japanese by requesting them to recognize the Commonwealth government.[3] The Japanese political officers rejected this. They expected the Philippine campaign to end within a few weeks; unlike the Filipinos, they knew of the severity of the American defeat at Pearl Harbor. They insisted that the New Order demanded immediate Filipino compliance. On January 8 Vargas was ordered by the Japanese to "organize the Administrative Constitution as soon as possible."[4] In his capacity as mayor of Greater Manila, he was instructed to summon all available prewar officials. He complied by continuing the earlier meetings at Yulo's home. Quintin Paredes recalled that "during the discussions that lasted four or five days, if I am not mistaken, as Secretary Zulueta was leaving the house of Mr. Yulo, he was arrested by the Kempetai [military police]. He was taken somewhere and investigated. The news spread like wild fire and made us all jittery."[5] This was the very effect that the Japanese wanted to produce.

During the fortnight which followed, the Japanese Military Administration increased pressure on these harried Filipinos. Their uncertainty grew even greater as they pondered their decision in isolation, by a tantalizingly few miles of open water, from MacArthur, Quezon, and Osmeña. The crisis was reached when, on January 22, Premier Tojo Hideki said to the 79th Japanese Diet in Tokyo that Philippine independence would be granted "so long as it [the Philippines] cooperates."[6] The reference to a Japanese-sponsored independence was designed to woo the Filipino nationalists and to prod the men meeting at Manila to a decision. Tojo's effort to sweeten the pill of collaboration with nationhood established one of the basic techniques of Japanese policy. It forced an end to the agonizing debate; the time had come to respond. Mayor Jorge Vargas issued a statement to the *Tribune* in which he said that "personally, this confirms my confidence and trust in the true and benevolent intentions of the Japanese Imperial Forces, and I am glad I have been given the opportunity to cooperate and work with them." At the same time, Congressman Benigno Aquino said, "I believe the time has come for every Filipino to stop and ponder on ... why our Supreme Creator ... made us Malays—Orientals and not Europeans or Anglo-Saxons." Aquino concluded his statement by noting that "in essence and spirit, WE ARE ORIENTALS."[7]

The Filipino leaders clearly felt that they should act. These statements represent the first indication that the leadership had decided collectively to cooperate rather than to run any risk to themselves, to their families, and to the population of Manila. On January 23, the so-called "letter of response," which had been debated since the Japanese order of January 8, was finished. Drafted at Yulo's home and addressed to Commander-in-Chief Homma Masaharu, it begged "to inform Your Excellency that, in compliance with your advice, and having in mind the great ideals, the freedom, and the happiness of our country, we are ready to obey to the best of our ability and within the means at our disposal the orders issued by the Imperial Japanese Forces for the maintenance of peace and order and the promotion of the well-being of our people under the Japanese Military Administration." The letter continued: "We have constituted ourselves into a Provisional Philippine Council of State and we are immediately proceeding to draft our Articles of Organization." The document, which listed thirty-four names under it, was signed by only thirty-two men. Both Jose Fabella, who had been in Quezon's cabinet, and Alfonso Mendoza, an anti-Quezon member of the Congress, appear to have decided on principle at the last moment against this collaboration.[8]

General Homma, in his first public appearance, met with the Council of State to accept the letter. He said that he was "extremely satisfied" that such a distinguished group, "having fostered great confidence among the people of the Philippines, have gathered here today to pledge your fidelity to our country and to offer to render your best services . . . for the happiness and prosperity of the Filipino people."[9] Homma indicated that he knew the "historical path" was very difficult, but he concluded that he was convinced that these Filipinos would discharge their obligations satisfactorily. This meeting took place in the former high-commissioner's residence, which looked directly across the Bay toward Corregidor; just over four weeks previously High Commissioner Sayre had evacuated the house.

Immediately after this interchange the Japanese command issued Order Number 1, which directed Vargas to become "head of the central administrative organization—'Chairman of the Executive Commission.'" Vargas was instructed to "proceed to the immediate coordination of the existing central administrative organs in the Philippines, and to the execution of the administration. . . ."[10] The structure of the Commission was modeled on the Commonwealth government, including the secretaries of six departments, who were to form the nucleus of a cabinet. Each appointment made by Vargas required Japanese approval, and each Department was assigned a Japanese technical staff to guarantee that Japanese objectives be fulfilled.[11] Vargas next appointed a committee of Laurel, Paredes, and Marabut to draft "the Articles of Organization of the Philippine Council of State," which formalized the provisional Council into the highest advisory group in the country. This document, issued on January 29, completed the organization of the new Japanese-sponsored government.[12]

Within four weeks the Japanese had succeeded in accomplishing their prime political aim, the active collaboration of the most prestigious Filipinos under Japanese control. This achievement, which occurred while the Fil-American forces were still fighting a few miles away and while President Quezon was still on Philippine soil, must rank as one of the great Japanese successes. A combination of a genuine sense of responsibility toward the civilian population, coupled with a mood of fear, disillusion, and abandonment, produced this cooperation. The Japanese, by threatening and cajoling these men to resume the reins of government for the interim period, managed to keep most of them in active governmental service until the war ended. A few, like the prewar mayor of Manila, Juan Nolasco, went into peaceful retirement after serving during the transitional period. A few more, by resistance or noncooperation, managed to slip from public view. Most, however, discovered that it was easier to start collaborating than it was to stop; the Japanese had managed to vault one of the most difficult initial hurdles of occupation.

Quezon and MacArthur on Corregidor watched this process helplessly. It was particularly traumatic for Quezon, who was, for the first time in his mature life, powerless to influence Philippine politics. Trapped, sick, discouraged, and idle, he was mortified to see his life's work vanish. He had to endure the torture of observing his capital occupied and his leadership overturned. When he realized that Roosevelt's Atlantic First policy made the Philippine operation an expendable pawn in global strategy, he wrote to Roosevelt through MacArthur, who shared his sentiments, and reminded Washington that "this war is not of our making. Those that had dictated the policies of the United States could not have failed to see that this is the weakest point in American territory. . . . Despite all this we never hesitated for a moment in our stand. We decided to fight by your side and we have done the best we could . . . but how long are we going to be left alone?" Quezon asked Roosevelt bluntly "whether any government has the right to demand loyalty from its citizens beyond its willingness or ability to render actual protection." Declaring himself "before the bar of history," and warning Washington that this communication might be "the last time that my voice will be heard before going to my grave," Quezon asked directly if the Philippine garrison had already been written off as lost. "If so," he concluded, "I want to know, because I have my own responsibility to my countrymen whom, as President of the Commonwealth, I have led into a complete war effort. . . . It seems that Washington does not fully realize our situation nor the feelings which the apparent neglect of our safety and welfare have engendered in the hearts of the people here. . . ."[13]

Quezon's veiled threat to transform his despair into some sort of precipitous action worried Washington. Since Quezon's charges had validity, Roosevelt, who was in a very awkward position, cabled back as concessive a message as possible. Playing shrewdly on

Quezon's known admiration for Roosevelt as a leader and as a man, the American President flattered and cajoled Quezon: "I realize the depth and sincerity of your sentiments with respect to your inescapable duties to your own people and I assure you that I would be the last to demand of you and them any sacrifice which I considered hopeless. . . ." Roosevelt followed this disclaimer with just such a request for the sacrifice. Stressing that the "magnificent resistance of the defenders of Bataan is contributing definitely toward assuring the completeness of our final victory in the Far East," Roosevelt expressed his admiration and gratitude "for the complete demonstration of loyalty, courage and readiness to sacrifice that your people, under your inspired leadership, have displayed. They are upholding the most magnificent traditions of a free democracy."[14]

Quezon, encouraged by Roosevelt's attention, broadcast from Corregidor to his people in Manila and elsewhere "to be of good cheer, to have faith in the patriotism of valor of our soldiers in the field, but above all, to trust America. The United States will win this war, America is too great and too powerful to be vanquished in this conflict. I know she will not fail us."[15] However, Roosevelt realized that his influence over Quezon was only to be a short-term palliative, since he already knew that America would fail to hold the Philippines. As early as January 1, Washington had secretly requested that Quezon and Osmeña be evacuated from Corregidor to safer territory. It was felt to be important legally to maintain a Commonwealth government in exile to insure a rallying point against the Japanese and their sponsored Filipino government.

Washington was fully aware of the political strain to which Quezon was subject by being so near and yet so far from power. Long accustomed to authority and honor as the chief of state, Quezon was a man who loved the appurtenances of his office and the thrill of power. It was realized that the emasculation he was enduring on Corregidor tempted him to return to Manila to resume office. The risk that Quezon might be willing to serve in a Japanese-sponsored government in order to retain his paramount political position was one which Washington did not dare to gamble on. Quezon's prestige made him a highly valuable living symbol of the new nationalism, a symbol which could not be lost to the Japanese without incalculable harm to the American war effort.[16] As the weeks of warfare made Corregidor increasingly tormenting to the men living there, Quezon's health deteriorated and further weakened his will to resist.

Quezon, who was constantly feverish because of tuberculosis, became nearly hysterical in early February following a series of Japanese propaganda broadcasts announcing the new government in Manila. He reached the breaking point when he heard an appeal from old General Emilio Aguinaldo, who had joined the new Japanese-supported Council of State. Aguinaldo stated that "my countrymen had to take up arms against the Japanese Army for the simple reason that the Philippines was under the American flag. Now conditions are changed. With most of the country already occupied by the Japanese Army, the fate of the Philippines is definitely decided. To continue fighting against the Japanese Army is not only futile, it will also bring about more useless sacrifices. . . ." Aguinaldo, referring to Tojo's promised independence, continued, "We Filipinos want independence. It is our earnest desire to restore the peace destroyed by this war."[17]

Aguinaldo's February 6 appeal prompted MacArthur to cable General Marshall of the speech and its effect on Quezon. Marshall responded that "the only way to combat statements such as that issued by Aguinaldo is to have our propaganda agencies here contrast against the Aguinaldo attitude the position, example, and statements of President Quezon with the purpose of exciting admiration for the latter and contempt for the former. This effort will be undertaken immediately all over the world and in appropriate languages. . . ." Marshall's effort to publicize "the glorification of Filipino loyalty and heroism"[18] did little, however, to pacify Quezon, who complained bitterly to MacArthur's key aide, Charles Willoughby, that "America writhes in anguish at the fate of a distant cousin, Europe, while a daughter, the Philippines, is being raped in the back room."[19]

In the following days an incensed Quezon devised a method by which the Philippines would be neutralized. The plan, which harked back to the neutralization scheme of the Tydings-McDuffie Act of 1934, was opposed by Quezon's cabinet, including Vice-President Osmeña and Manuel Roxas. Nevertheless, on February 8, having achieved reluctant cabinet support, Quezon cabled Roosevelt that "after nine weeks of fighting not even a small amount of aid has reached us from the United States. Help and assistance have been sent to other belligerent nations . . . , but seemingly no attempt has been made to transport anything here. . . . Consequently, while perfectly safe itself, the United States has practically doomed the Philippines to almost total extinction to secure a breathing space." Quezon asserted "that conditions being what they are we should initiate measures to save the Filipinos and the Philippines from further disaster."[20] He urged immediate independence under a plan which would neutralize the archipelago militarily by a total withdrawal of both Japanese and American armed forces. To Carlos Romulo, Quezon was even more bitter: "We must try to save ourselves and to hell with America."[21]

Secretary of War Henry Louis Stimson, who had known Quezon when he had been governor general in the Philippines, and General Marshall added their voices to those around Quezon who were attempting to dissuade him from this scheme. They reminded Quezon of the longer view and urged him to examine the plight of Korea, Manchukuo, and China under Japanese rule. In a telegram, which they drafted and Roosevelt signed, Quezon was reminded that the sufferings of the Filipino people, cruel as they might be, were infinitely less painful than the sufferings and enslavement which might follow the acceptance of Japanese promises. In instructions to MacArthur (though they were actually designed for Quezon's eyes) Roosevelt gave MacArthur permission to surrender the Filipino troops under his command, but not the American soldiers, "so long as there remains any possibility of resistance." Roosevelt, attempting to manipulate Quezon's attitudes and to shame him, ordered that "so long as the flag of the United States flies in Filipino soil, . . . it will be defended by our men to the death. . . ."[22]

This psychological strategy, coupled with the constant pressure of Romulo, Roxas, Osmeña, and MacArthur, calmed Quezon, who had threatened at one point to resign and had ordered a boat to take him back to Manila.[23] Writing his autobiography several years later in Washington, Quezon related the crisis with a different chronology and emphasis. He claimed that it was MacArthur who convinced him that he would fail to improve the situation by returning to Manila, since the Japanese would utilize his name without permitting him the power to achieve his goals. MacArthur must have played on Quezon's sense of *hiya*, because Quezon related that "my sacrifice would not only have been in vain but might have carried with it my eternal dishonor, for it might not have been possible for anyone but me and my Japanese jailer to have known or to furnish proofs of what I had done or been trying to do."[24]

The Commonwealth government weathered this crisis, but Quezon never forgave Roosevelt for his failure to honor American commitments to the Philippines before European obligations. He felt that when Roosevelt cabled, "I can assure you that every vessel available is bearing . . . the strength that will eventually crush the enemy and liberate your native land," he was fraudulently encouraging the Fil-American garrison.[25] "Now we are in defeat," he said at one point to Romulo. "And why? Because we are not getting protection from those who promised us protection. America is not sending help."[26] The gap between foreign policy and military preparedness which had made the Philippines the heel of Achilles for America took a bitter price of lives, and Quezon, like many after him, held the United States culpable.

This crisis of confidence occurred against the backdrop of steady attrition of the Fil-American forces on Bataan and Corregidor. Japanese pressure forced the American government to consider a strategy for the long road back. Since War Plan Orange had failed to project beyond the siege defense, American military and political strategists had to evolve their plans on an ad hoc basis. MacArthur and Quezon were fundamental to the projected plans of reconquest, and, accordingly, a few days after Quezon was dissuaded from returning to Manila, Washington requested the evacuation of both men. MacArthur, ordered to a new and broader command with headquarters in Australia, sensed the propaganda defeat in his evacuation. "I know the situation here in the Philippines," he cabled Marshall, "and unless the right moment is chosen for this delicate operation, a sudden collapse might occur."[27] Finally prevailed upon to leave Corregidor, MacArthur insisted that his prime obligation was to relieve the Philippines as soon as possible. Evacuated by P. T. boat, he issued a statement which was to become the rallying phrase for Filipinos in the years ahead: "I came through and I shall return."[28]

At roughly the same time Washington moved to protect Quezon and Osmeña, evacuating them first to the southern, unconquered areas of the Philippines, later to MacArthur's new headquarters in Australia, and finally to Washington. Two days before Quezon left Corregidor he appointed his aide, Manuel Roxas, "to act as Secretary to the President. In this capacity you are authorized, when in your judgment the circumstances so require, to act in my name on all matters not involving any change of policy."[29] One of Roxas' duties before his own escape was the secret sinking of the Commonwealth bullion reserves in the waters off Corregidor. A few weeks later, on March 5, 1942, Quezon used his emergency powers to issue Executive Order No. 3, by which he designated Roxas to succeed to the presidency of the Commonwealth in case he and Osmeña did not survive the dangerous escape from the Visayan Islands to Mindanao and on March 26 to Australia. Roxas became the ranking Filipino still free from Japanese control after Quezon's presidential party left.

These evacuations were, of course, closely guarded secrets. The leadership in Manila, which had tried at length and unsuccessfully to communicate with Quezon, was forced to act on its own. A few days after the Japanese had conquered the vaunted fortress of Singapore with great fanfare and Quezon had been evacuated by the Americans with total secrecy, the elite was asked to cable Roosevelt requesting that he end the war in the Philippines. Individually, these men opposed such a telegram, but collectively they acceded to the Japanese request.[30] Jose Laurel recalled that "what the Japanese military authorities wanted had to be done. Consul Kihara received the military orders and instructions for Mr. Vargas. We were made to send cables to President Roosevelt and President Quezon and a manifesto to the fighting Filipinos in Bataan and Corregidor. To save ourselves and avoid retaliatory measures from the Japanese, all these things had to be done."[31]

Only one Philippine government and one colonial power remained in the Philippines by the late spring of 1942. And yet, ironically, dual government never really ended, since two groups of Filipinos continued to speak out seemingly diametrically opposed messages to the nation. Quezon and Osmeña were halfway around the world in Washington, but their appeal to the loyalties of the people remained strong. While the Japanese, with physical control of the Manila elite, had most of the trump cards in their hand, they lacked the ace of trumps. The Commonwealth government which Quezon and Osmeña established in Washington was powerless in the immediate sense, and yet it was also omnipotent. Despite its isolation it remained the government for most Filipinos and continued to command allegiance, even though the Japanese tried to breathe life into their Executive Commission. The failure of the Japanese to bend Filipino allegiance away from the Commonwealth government in exile was a defeat greater in import than the military successes. By the time MacArthur's replacement, General Jonathan Wainwright, surrendered the last Fil-American forces to General Homma in May 1942, the Japanese had already lost the political battle for Filipino allegiance without knowing it. The majority of the nation started counting the days until the return of Quezon and MacArthur to the Philippines would herald liberation.

CHAPTER IV

Japan's New Order:
The Philippine Executive Commission

*In the wake of the sweeping Japanese victories,
the prestige of all Asiatic nations has been vindicated.*

—Jorge B. Vargas

In early 1942 the Japanese confidently expected that military successes would be followed by comparable political victories. All over Southeast Asia the triumph of Japanese arms seemed to be a catalytic force for political cooperation. The short-term outlook was good in Burma, Indonesia, Thailand, and Malaya, and the Japanese appeared to be having equally rapid success in the Philippines. General Wainwright's pathetic surrender order to all Fil-American troops ended any lingering hope that somehow an American relief convoy would arrive in time. The Bataan Death March gave concrete evidence to Filipinos of the totality of the Japanese victory. Having already gained the collaboration of many of the prewar elite, the Japanese had reason to expect that more Filipinos would listen to the Japanese propaganda theme and rally to build a New Order.

The Japanese timetable had been badly delayed by the prolonged resistance of the Fil-American troops. The campaign, which should have ended in March, did not end until May, and Prime Minister Tojo blamed General Homma, who, he felt, had bungled the job.[1] However, with the establishment of peace the Japanese were able to devote themselves to the creation of the Greater East Asia Co-Prosperity Sphere (Dai-Toa Kyoeiken). The critical problem for the Japanese, though, was defining the aims of this sphere. Tensions within Japanese society, primarily between military and civilian elements, frequently generated contradictory goals both at the Tokyo and Philippine levels. The consensus among various Japanese officials was not broad enough to permit the formulation of clear-cut policies. The Japanese administration of the Philippines was often paralyzed by crosscurrents of conflict.

As a result of the political structure created by the Meiji constitution, only the emperor of Japan was in a position to arbitrate among the various agencies of his government. The army and navy each had the right of independent access to the emperor (Iakujoso) and were free to disobey at will the decisions of the prime minister and his cabinet, even when the prime minister was a military man. Since the emperor reigned but did not rule, he rarely interceded; the direct result was that there was no one to control a proliferation of policies. In the Philippine occupation, three separate groups, each deriving its source of power from a different force in Tokyo, were in competition. The most liberal segment reflected the civilian bureaucrats in Tokyo. Embracing prewar diplomats like Consul Kihara Jitaro, this nonmilitary group depended on officials dispatched to Manila in early 1942. The most important man in this category was Murata Shozo, who had been president of the Osaka Shipping Company, the O.S.K., and a minister of communications in one of the prewar Konoe cabinets. Murata's concern to establish a viable sphere was countered most vigorously by the field commanders of the Japanese army, who were responsible through the Philippine commander-in-chief only to the Imperial General Staff in Tokyo and not to the prime minister. These men saw their prime function as the maintenance of combat efficiency to protect the empire; political, economic, and social reforms to win Filipino friendship were inevitably of secondary importance. Between these two groups was the office of the director general of the Japanese Military Administration. The director general was a military major general, but he had as his prime responsibility the political aspects of occupation. While he was responsible directly to the commander-in-chief and the Imperial General Staff, as were the field officers, he was also responsible to the Japanese prime minister through the superintendent general of Military Administration in the Tokyo War Ministry. This office was analogous to the civil affairs-military government section of the United States army, and it wielded the pivotal role in the politics of occupation. The initial director general in Manila, Hayashi Yoshide, was replaced after Corregidor by Wachi Takaji.

These three groups, like their superiors in Tokyo, shared certain goals. Civilian and military officials both agreed on the necessity and wisdom of Japanese hegemony. The civilian agencies were frequently as eager for military expansion as were the military. They agreed that the Japanese need for raw materials justified aggression and that imperialism was a valid expression of political power. Most also believed that Japanese society, which had succeeded in industrializing itself while maintaining a non-Western character, had something both spiritual and practical to offer to every other Asian society. Japanese fanaticism was but one phase of the missionary zeal which governed almost every aspect of prewar Japanese life. Empire satisfied "a psychological craving—the recognition of Japan at her own valuation as the 'light of Asia,'" so that after centuries of feeling inferior and inadequate Japan could "play the part which the Chinese had once played in the great days of the Celestial Empire."[2]

The friction between the civilians and the military stemmed from conflict over the means of achieving these goals. Many of the moderate civilian officials doubted that the Japanese military had the power to sustain the newly conquered empire. They sensed that wish and reality were frequently confused and that the military assumed too readily that any objective could be accomplished by will power. Pride and greed combined to weaken perspectives and to lead to excesses. The insular education of the military leadership in particular led these officers to accept myopically the myths their predecessors had perpetuated to unify Japan. The pragmatism of the Meiji Restoration leadership had vanished by the time of the Showa Restoration of the 1930's. The mystique of Japanese invincibility seemed to be supported by the prewar successes of Japanese expansion. Japanese political mythology was incorporated into government policy formation with eventual disastrous consequences. For example, the Total War Research Institute began a confidential draft of a war plan by stating that "the Emperor is augustly the center of the universe and the origin of morality. The Imperial Country is, therefore, the manifestation of morality and the criterion of the world." Attacking European civilization for penetrating and preying upon the "moralistic East," the document stated that "it is none other than Japan, the Divine Country, that has opposed and rejected that invasion. . . . Now things have come to such a pass that the extortions of America, Britain, and other powers threaten the existence of the Imperial Country. This is intolerable to God and man alike."[3]

The lightning military triumphs at the beginning of the war seemed to substantiate further the divinity of the Japanese mission. But success itself created vast problems and exacerbated existing frictions. Hundreds of millions of people were suddenly under the Japanese flag, and the demand to fashion these disparate areas into a coherent, ideologically justifiable system was strong. The agency developed for this enormous task was the Greater East Asia Ministry, which evolved from the tentative plans drawn up in 1940. On August 1, 1940, Foreign Minister Matsuoka Yosuke first used the phrase, "Greater East Asia Co-Prosperity Sphere."[4] On October 4, 1940, a "very secret" plan entitled, "A Tentative Plan for the Policy toward the Southern Regions" was prepared.[5] As the war drew nearer, the intensity of the planning increased until on March 14, 1941, a "Summarized Plan for the Management of the Southern Areas" was finished.[6] This master plan projected a four-point scheme for the Philippines, stating that the archipelago should become independent as soon as possible, that the Philippines should offer Japan bases and other cooperation, and that there should be close diplomatic and economic ties with Japan. The Greater East Asia Ministry, which Tojo established formally in 1942 to coordinate these plans, was charged with the comprehensive planning of Greater East Asia.[7] A Southern Regions Promotion Training Center was established for the eventual training of some 20,000 Japanese who would expedite the planning.[8]

It was primarily the Japanese military, however, who had to establish an immediate program for transforming Filipino hostility into friendship if the inchoate dream of the Greater East Asia Sphere was to come alive. Despite the conflicts among themselves, the Japanese Military Administration and the civilian advisors as a group realized that if they could not rebuild the economy to provide food and work, and if they could not restore a functioning government to maintain peace and order, they would be doomed to failure. They also realized that if they could not wean Filipinos away from their Western identity and to a sympathetic attitude, all the rest of their reforms would be abortive. Consequently, a prime objective from the outset was a massive propaganda appeal designed to drive a wedge between American and Filipino interests.

The increasingly ideological nature of the war in the twentieth century made it imperative for the Japanese to justify their expansion to the Filipinos in terms other than power politics, economic necessity, and national self-interest. To rule by fiat was not enough; the Japanese wanted to win Filipino support in order to show the world the righteousness of their cause. Like the American attempt forty years earlier, this success would be the external manifestation of the innate worth of the missionary effort.[9] This spiritual dimension of Japanese propaganda had an impact not only in the Philippines but all over Asia, and its long-term effect should not be minimized.

Basing its appeal on an idealized samurai tradition of self-denial and service, the Military Administration emphasized the need for a spiritual rejuvenation by which they thought the Filipinos could realize how obsessively attached they were to Western materialism. Spartan fervor was projected as the secret element in Japan's successful industrialism, and the Philippine nation was urged to adopt frugality in the present to achieve progress in the future. In the first month of the occupation General Homma said that "the people of this country have long been taught by Americans to put too much importance on the material side and physical comfort of life. This tendency must be remedied as Marshal Petain is now urging in France." Homma urged the Philippines "to escape from her former position as a captive of the capitalism and imperialism of the United States, to liquidate the unnatural culture borrowed from a far away country . . . to return to the original features of an oriental people," and to shake off "vanity and the dependent mentality. . . . " [10]

To demonstrate the wisdom of this appeal, the Japanese propagandists tried to depict the Americans as biased, weak, soft, and unworthy of respect. The American prisoners of war were described as "the foul water flowing down from the sewerage of a country that has been formed upon impure foundations and has thus lost its racial pride."[11] The interned American civilian population was labeled "the haughty enemy" who "until yesterday . . . walked through the streets of Manila with their shoulders squared and uplifted noses. They must have been oblivious to the fact that Orientals possessed both talent and power."[12] Many of the atrocities of the Death March and the humiliations of the prison camps were perpetrated to demean Americans before Filipinos.

Japanese propaganda insisted that Filipinos recognize that they were racially and geographically Asian. Homma, for example, in a message on February 11, 1942 (Foundation of the Japanese Empire Day, 2602), commiserated with what he thought was the Filipino yearning "to be free from oppression and the tyranny of the white people. The American influence, which has thoroughly saturated the entire Philippines will now be completely removed, so that you may freely return to the natural life of an Oriental people, thus realizing the ideal of the Philippines for the Filipino."[13] This insistence on an Asian identification exposed one of the basic problems of Philippine social structure, presupposing as it did that the Filipinos craved the eradication of Western influence. In fact, the Filipinos were very ambivalent about their relationship with Western culture and very unsure of their identity. When Homma on another occasion told the Filipinos that "as the leopard cannot change its spots, you cannot alter the fact that you are Orientals," he was appealing for what seemed to him a rational awareness of the Philippine "place in the universal order of things." He asked the Filipinos to probe why they followed "the dictates of Europe and America with an inferiority complex? The time has come," he claimed, "to assert yourselves as an Oriental people."[14]

The Japanese, unable to fathom the degree of tension this propaganda appeal produced in Filipinos, probed candidly but callously into the national psyche. Director General of Military Administration Wachi bluntly reminded the Filipinos that "regardless of whether you like it or not, you are Filipinos and belong to the Oriental race. No matter how hard you try, you cannot become white people."[15] This demand that the Filipinos confront their own racial identity under the compounding stress of war and occupation was as foolish as it was insensitive; it met a frigid response from the Filipinos, who were far too ambivalent to allow conquering generals to tell them how to alter their cultural idiosyncrasies.

The Japanese made up in volume what they may have lacked in astuteness. They flooded the country with a constant flow of mass propaganda, utilizing every technique available. In 1941 the Philippine literacy rate was between 40 and 50 percent, making the archipelago second only to Japan itself in Asia. The Americans and later the Commonwealth government had lavished attention on the schools, creating compulsory elementary education and more importantly, a high social value for education as a means of mobility upward. Almost universally, children could read where the parents could not, and there were few homes, especially in nonremote areas, in which at least one member could not read for the group. Most people who had access to a newspaper could know what it said.

The Japanese published a wide range of periodicals and magazines designed to appeal both to special groups and to the nation at large. They created a giant printing monopoly called the Manila Newspaper Company (Manila Shimbun Sha) and channeled all publications through its controlled presses. This company was placed under the joint control of the Military Administration and a Japanese firm, the Mainichi Newspaper Company (Mainichi Shimbun Sha). In a pattern fairly typical of other industries, experienced civilian personnel came from Tokyo to handle the technical aspects while the Military Administration supplied the copy. Matsuoka Masao, the first president of the Manila Newspaper Company, and his successor, Yamada Junji, were articulate propagandists who not only ran the daily newspapers, the *Manila Tribune*, the *Taliba*, and *La Vangardia*, but also were active public speakers. The top executives of the parent company, the board chairman, Takaishi Shingoro, and the editor-in-chief, Shimoda Masami, were frequent visitors to Manila.[16]

The Japanese appealed through the *Philippine Review*, a literary monthly, to the intellectuals by challenging them "to come out into the open and contribute their mite to the New Philippines" by writing for the journal.[17] At the other end of the propaganda spectrum they produced a series of jingoistic and bloody movies such as "Hawaii Malay Sea Battles," "The Fall of Singapore," and "Conquest of the Southseas." Radio was also used extensively. A major effort was made to impound all short-wave radios capable of monitoring Australia and San Francisco in order to cut off the flow of news from abroad. Listening to such broadcasts became a capital crime, but Filipinos were encouraged to listen to local radio, especially to the broadcasts of the speeches of leading Filipinos, who usually spoke of how the new order would benefit the Philippines. For example, Claro M. Recto, who frequently wrote for the *Philippine Review* and other journals, broadcast that he thought the war was one of "the decisive turning points in the history of the world, for it constitutes the rebirth of the powerful oriental civilization, and the awakening of mighty Asia, under the unselfish leadership of the Japanese Empire, and the Japanese people."[18]

The utilization of famous Filipinos was, from the Japanese point of view, highly advantageous. The Insurrectionary Generals, Artemio Ricarte and Emilio Aguinaldo, spoke extensively from the stump. Ricarte, a dedicated Japanophile, spoke passionately of his personal experiences living in Japan. Aguinaldo, long frustrated by Quezon in his ambition to rule the Philippines, and bitter at the country's failure to render him the homage he thought was his due, spoke with less sincerity but more success than Ricarte. Aguinaldo seems to have hoped that the Japanese would turn to him to head a new government, and, courting their favor, stated that "we should lend our wholehearted cooperation to Japan. . . ."[19]

The most important speakers were, however, the ranking members of the prewar elite serving in the Philippine Executive Commission. Jorge Vargas, as the highest member of this commission, spoke most often, especially when, at state occasions, he said he spoke for the nation. For example, on February 8, 1943, he addressed a mass rally on the Luneta, the parade ground in Manila, to celebrate Premier Tojo's reaffirmation of his pledge to grant the Philippines independence. Vargas, asserting that "Japan has amply proven her high and honorable intentions with acts," spoke of Japan's desire "to liberate the peoples of the Orient from Western imperialism."[20] The Japanese reprinted such speeches and gave them maximum publicity throughout the country.

The Japanese also attempted to eradicate all evidence of the American occupation.[21] Military Ordinance No. 13 established Tagalog and Japanese as the two official languages of the country, banning Spanish completely and permitting English only on a temporary basis.[22] English would have been banned completely except that it was actually the only way in which the Japanese could communicate with the Filipinos. On the first anniversary of the war Vargas issued Executive Order No. 110 to eradicate "all traces of Anglo-Saxon influence" by changing the names of any streets, bridges, towns, or public buildings which had American names. Dewey Boulevard became Heiwa Boulevard, Jones Bridge became Banzai Hashi, and Quezon's name was dropped from the host of streets, places, and towns named after him.[23] Vargas, utilizing this policy to promote the national language, directed that Tagalog be used instead of English in governmental correspondence.[24] Serious thought was given to changing the name of the archipelago to "Mai," an old Chinese name for the Islands, or to "Rizal," "Luviminda," or "Luzon."[25]

Japanese language (Nippongo) became a required subject in all schools. Newspapers ran daily adult education lessons on the back page. A crash program to train language teachers became a central part of the general Japanese effort to reshape the educational system. Textbooks which inculcated a pro-Western sentiment were banned, and others were rigidly censored.[26] The school system, which had been completely closed initially, was allowed to reopen only slowly, as each school was checked out. Higher education all but ceased during the war years; in its place the Japanese established a series of Training Institutes to convert the bureaucracy to a more sympathetic attitude. Japanese culture and ethics were broadcast and publicized, and the Filipinos experienced through a compulsory early morning mass calisthenics radio program, called "radio taiso," a daily reminder of the puritanical Japanese dictum that a healthy mind requires a healthy body.

The Japanese propaganda corps, aware of Filipino history, attempted to woo the Catholic Church. The army had arrived with a large number of Catholic chaplains, who clearly were not required for the few Japanese Catholics. These priests received enormous publicity while celebrating mass, doing good works, and appealing for Christian brotherhood. They frequently referred to Takayama Ukon and other famous Japanese Catholics of the sixteenth century, though they studiously refrained from mentioning the anti-Catholic period of Japanese history, which culminated in the Shimabara Rebellion of 1637 and the total exclusion of foreigners in Japan. A Nippon-Filipino Goodwill Catholic Association was formed in November 1942, and a magazine designed specifically for Filipino Catholics was published. It even ran a special feature entitled "Nippongo in the Altar."[27]

Since many of the ranking clergy in the Philippines, including several bishops, were Americans, the Japanese had the difficult task of circumventing them without alienating the Catholic community. These priests were held in isolation, and diocesan authority was given with the approval of the Papal Nuncio Piani to a Filipino, Bishop Guerrero, and a Japanese, Bishop Taguchi. Theoretically, the Japanese interest in the Church was humanitarian only. The *Manila Tribune* claimed that "the collaboration of all churches is considered a religious enterprise demanded by conscience since it concerns the avoidance of further sufferings, privations, and wanton destruction of lives and properties. . . ."[28]

It was clear that the Japanese hoped to reap considerable advantage from this association, since it linked the most potent institutional source of authority to their side. When independence was promised by Tojo, Bishop Guerrero wrote that "the Filipino Catholic clergy yields to no one in the love of God and Country. We, therefore, greet with sincere joy and profound gratitude the solemn promise made by Premier Hideki Tozyo [Tojo] to grant independence to the Philippines in the shortest possible time."[29] In a circular letter "to all Church Dignitaries and Heads of Religious Organizations" of March 6, 1943, the Vargas Executive Commission through Commissioner of the Interior, Jose Laurel, directly asked that priests and ministers take advantage of every sermon and opportunity to "inculcate in the minds of their faithful or flock loyalty to the constituted authorities and the absolute necessity on the part of all Filipinos" to cooperate "wholeheartedly with the present administration in the establishment of peace and order in every nook and corner of the Philippines." Laurel urged that the sermon each Sunday be used to inform the congregation "of the policies adopted by the government. . . ." This Laurel circular concluded, "far from being political, the collaboration of all Churches is, in the ultimate analysis, a religious enterprise demanded by conscience."[30]

Japanese planners in Tokyo and Manila felt "it would be a good idea to make the controlling or intellectual class travel in Japan and introduce them to the real situation, thus making them discard their idea of relying on Europe and the United States."[31] Conferences and exchanges played an important role; the Association of Greater East Asia Journalists, the Greater East Asia Literary Conference, the Greater East Asia People's Conference, and the Greater East Asia Medical Conference all convened for this purpose. Numerous gratitude missions were also dispatched to Japan.[32] In return, the Japanese sent a constant flow of visitors to the Philippines, including Marquis Tokugawa, president of the Philippine Society of Japan, Uchigasaki Sakusaburo, vice-speaker of the Diet, Dr. Togo Minoru, Tanaka Takeo, Ambassador Nomura Kichisaburo, and others.

A similar effort was made to bring Filipino students to Japan. The International Students Institute (Kokusai Gakuyukai), which had been founded in 1935, was used. In 1942 the Institute moved into the former American School in Meguro in preparation for the first group of students from Southeast Asia.[33] The Filipino students, who were called *pensionados,* were carefully selected, but less on merit than on family connection.[34] They were a first-rate investment for the Japanese, since they linked the two countries together while also providing the Japanese officials in Manila with a potent means of blackmailing the leadership if anything went wrong.

This enormous, multifaceted Japanese propaganda effort failed. It certainly was not aided by the gap between statement and practice, which made most Filipinos discover personally that the claim of Asia for the Asiatics really meant Asia for the Japanese. The Japanese field command, in open disregard for the efforts of the Military Administration, plundered machinery, bullion, and food. While the propagandists extolled the glories of Spartan life over crass American materialism, most Japanese officials and officers commandeered the finest homes and hotel suites, Cadillac and Packard automobiles, and country and yacht clubs. Such exploitation made a mockery of the concept of "co-prosperity." The arrogant behavior of enlisted men, who demanded undue respect from Filipinos in bows and who slapped Filipinos wantonly, further exacerbated the situation.

It would be an oversimplification, nevertheless, to state that if the Japanese had been true to their own ideological commitments they would have won the loyalty of large numbers of Filipinos. Their failure had deeper roots. They never solved the problem of leadership. The nation remained convinced that Quezon was still the leader of the people even though the Japanese accused him of fleeing his people in time of need. From the beginning of the occupation the Japanese realized that their propaganda had to tarnish his image somehow or risk failure, but they never discovered a successful technique. The day Quezon was secretly evacuated from Corregidor, Vargas' daughter, Nena, broadcast to Quezon's wife, Doña Aurora, in an attempt to entice the Quezons back to Manila. Playing on the "suffering" of the Quezons and extending "love, sympathy and affection," Nena Vargas prayed "that the war may soon end and that we shall all be brought together again."[35]

On April 18, 1942, a Japanese military report filed in Tokyo excitedly claimed that Quezon had been assassinated by the American army in order to stop him from returning to Manila to resume his presidency. The report urged that this story receive maximum worldwide coverage.[36] Unfortunately for the Japanese, the story was not true. With Quezon's safe arrival in San Francisco, the Japanese were forced to take public cognizance of his arrival. They unhappily reported, "still unaware of the United States scheme to utilize him as a puppet as well as a source of Anglo-American propaganda, Manuel L. Quezon, former President of the Philippine Commonwealth, arrived in San Francisco. . . ."[37]

The Japanese attempted to establish that he was a prisoner of the Americans, trapped from returning by physical force. In a letter to the *Manila .Tribune* Jorge Vargas wrote that he believed that if Quezon "had had his own way he would have remained and entered into understandings with the Japanese Forces. . . ."[38] A few days later in an inadvertently amusing follow-up editorial entitled, "A Tragedy," the editor noted that Quezon "must suffer the pangs of forced banishment as a virtual prisoner in a place [Washington] which differs from Napoleon's St. Helena only in physical dimension." This editor was "moved by pathos in imagining what he would have much rather done than be dragged away from the country and people he loves." Having bowed respectfully toward Quezon's revered memory, the editorial turned more savage. "Unlike Rizal, who would rather die for his ideal than surrender it, Mr. Quezon lacked the martyr's firmness of character, a character strong enough in ordinary circumstances and equal to minor climaxes, but tragically weakened by the subtle operations of the American way of life which in blinder moments we tried to defend."[39]

A compounding difficulty arose for the Japanese because they were unable to stop the flow of short-wave news from coming into the archipelago, especially from commentator William Winters of San Francisco station KGEI. These transmissions of news, with their encouragement from MacArthur and the Commonwealth government, presented a challenge to the Japanese that required rebuttal. Quezon frequently broadcast to the Philippines, and while in theory no Filipinos were able to listen, the Japanese felt compelled to reply each time. One such editorial rebuttalist admitted candidly that he was "rather reluctant to take issue with the Hon. Manuel L. Quezon, being not a little awed by the august and already somewhat legendary personage who was the supreme leader of the Filipino people until he took French leave of them. . . ."[40] Another in a fit of pique commented that "if Mr. Quezon does not stop planning malicious intrigues and conspiring with the enemy to jeopardize the welfare and happiness of the Filipinos, the Filipino people may eventually be obliged to prosecute him not only for his irresponsibility . . . but also as a scheming malcontent who has plotted high treason. . . ."[41] The Japanese inability to ignore or to tarnish Quezon's paramount position in the Philippines was reflected even in his obituary, in which the *Manila Tribune,* "with a heavy heart," deplored his death, "whatever be his sins and mistakes . . . especially knowing that he died in virtual exile. . . ."[42]

The Japanese were unable to damage Quezon's image. The allegiance he commanded among most Filipinos was a potent force in keeping the Japanese from greater success. Quezon was not, however, the only force frustrating Japanese goals. The Filipinos refused to be ordered by Japanese military power toward an Asian identity. They fervently believed that America would return under General MacArthur's leadership and that real independence would be achieved then. Life under the Americans had major drawbacks (as the Japanese never tired of telling the Filipinos), but the future was predictable and bright under American tutelage. This Filipino response was instinctive rather than rational. From the outbreak of the war the majority of the Filipinos had responded as a nation. This was revealed in their clear-cut decision to fight actively with America as an ally in the struggle against Japan. The bonds of allegiance, alliance, and decision formed then, however irrationally, aborted the Japanese effort before it started. These bonds established the foundations on which the remnants of the Fil-American troops could build a guerrilla movement across the whole archipelago and in every segment of the society.

The resistance to the Japanese effectively continued even after

General Wainwright ordered a surrender of all Fil-American troops. This continuing military effort, waged by pockets of Filipinos in the face of tremendous hazards, was one of the critical factors of the war years. It forced the Japanese to maintain vigilance, casting them in the role of military conquerors just when they were attempting to win Filipino loyalty. Every Japanese decision was directly or indirectly influenced by this fact of continuing belligerency, and the dilemmas posed were enormous. For example, the Japanese could not decide how to handle Filipino prisoners of war. If they were treated as traditional prisoners of war, there was little hope of winning their families and friends to a sympathetic position. If they were sent home without detention, the trained nucleus of an enormous guerrilla movement was being turned free. Since the number of weapons scattered throughout the country was great, the risk created a serious problem. Inevitably, the Japanese were very hostile to these Filipino soldiers at first. Having seen their Japanese comrades killed by Filipino troops during battle, many Japanese troops behaved brutally, forcing Filipino troops to endure hardships of a severity equal to that endured by American troops during the Bataan death march and afterward. The Filipino prisoners were herded into makeshift camps, where terrible atrocities were perpetrated.

During this early period of intense hostility, the Japanese army demanded that Vargas support its treatment of these prisoners. He issued an order which instructed that "no person, including officials of the central Administrative Organization, regardless of their rank, should visit the war prisoners' concentration camps or exert efforts to intercede in behalf of any prisoner."[43] Japanese pressure for this order and Vargas' weakness in issuing it inevitably damaged the prestige his new government had with the people.

As the fighting ended and the Military Administration began arguing for pragmatic charity against the field command's irrational brutality, the policy against the prisoners of war was reversed. The Japanese political officers attempted to capitalize on this benevolence to gain a propaganda victory by arguing that with peace a new era of Fil-Japanese relations had begun. A hastily constructed rehabilitation and indoctrination program was organized for the Filipino troops prior to their discharge. The Military Administration's attempt to salvage something failed. Japanese ambivalence toward Filipino troops resulted in a hybrid policy. The Japanese, having alienated these young Filipinos completely, then proceeded to turn them loose in the society. Within a short period most had joined a guerrilla movement either overtly or covertly.

Armed guerrilla resistance exacerbated an endemic military problem for the Japanese, who were eager to dispatch the maximum number of troops to the combat zone as soon as possible, and it created as well a political alternative to the Japanese-sponsored government in Manila. The Japanese army was unable to pacify the Philippines, with the result that in the political sphere the struggle for the nation's allegiance continued unabated. Since guerrilla groups made clandestine but direct contact with MacArthur's headquarters, they kept the issue of dual government alive implicitly. The fragmentary quality of the initial guerrilla movement evolved into a sophisticated network of guerrilla operations which received coordinated orders from MacArthur's staff. These ubiquitous guerrilla organizations, which managed to broaden the Commonwealth allegiance of the people to include themselves, developed civilian as well as military functions. Each competed directly with the local or provincial governments established by the Japanese and the Executive Commission. Each sapped the authority of these local governments to the extent that Japanese-backed governments existed only where the Japanese garrisons were large enough to force compliance.[44]

The guerrilla movement has become one of the great romantic themes of subsequent Philippine history and lore. The innumerable guerrilla sagas, which are now told and retold, have emerged primarily because the nation felt at the time that this guerrilla resistance was one of the finest hours for the Philippine people. The universality of the movements and the mass participation in them was tangible proof that the initial decision to fight against the Japanese and for the Americans was a commitment of the people. Filipinos continued the fight as staunchly after the formal surrender as before. The nation felt itself part of the front line. This will of the people was virtually an insurmountable obstacle to the Japanese planners. As early as April 29, 1942, Homma touched the problem openly. Expressing his "hearty thanks for the endeavors of many eminent Filipino citizens who with a true understanding of the aims of our new forces have devoted themselves to the task of establishing a new Philippines," he lamented "that there are still others who cannot rid themselves of their pro-American sympathies and who continue to resist in vain without understanding" Japanese intentions. With Draconian severity Homma warned that "they will be annihilated without mercy" and promised that soon "the Philippines will be cleared of these bandits and reconstructed."[45]

When the Japanese discovered that they were unable to destroy guerrilla resistance easily, they sought a political solution. Utilizing the elite cooperation already gained, they requested that the Filipino generals appeal to their former troops. General Guillermo Francisco, who had headed the Philippine Constabulary under Quezon, and who had been the ranking Filipino soldier in Bataan, wrote in a widely distributed "open letter" that "the war in the Philippines has ceased and any further resistance is not only futile but would be classed as outlawry since your status as belligerents has ceased to exist."[46] General Mateo Capinpin also appealed to the guerrillas as did the ranking civilians of the Philippine Executive Commission.[47]

Ranking former command officers were appointed by Chairman Vargas to head the new Philippine Constabulary, which the Executive Commission established as an agency of the Department of the Interior.[48] They were charged with maintaining "peace and order," as coping with the guerrilla problem was frequently described. The Japanese army, which was hesitant to arm the Philippine Constabulary, fearing legitimately that the weaponry would slip into guerrilla hands, assumed the actual military risk of fighting the guerrillas. The Military Administration still tried for as much political and military advantage from the Constabulary as possible. The real problem confronting the Japanese military was not that the guerrillas were militarily strong but rather that they were powerful because they had the tacit approval of the bulk of the population, who also opposed the Japanese. If the Japanese could stop the flow of food, clothing, intelligence, and money from the civilian population to the guerrillas, the bands could be hunted down and destroyed by the Japanese army relatively easily.

To stop this flow, therefore, the Japanese came to realize that they had to rally support to the Japanese-sponsored government in Manila. If they could offer this Filipino government as the carrot, they could wield the stick successfully. To this end they had the Executive Commission establish a Central Pacification Committee under Jose Laurel's direction. The country was divided into seven districts with a key prewar official assuming responsibility for pacification in each.[49] Coupled with this was an increasing demand by the Japanese for a Filipino denunciation of the guerrilla movement. The Japanese, in effect, forced Philippine loyalty to polarize by prodding the national elite to bring its prestige to bear against the guerrillas.

The national leadership rallied to the provincial and municipal politicians, who had been losing out to the guerrillas in what were frequently struggles for local authority. Responding in part because of the patron-client reciprocal relationship of Philippine polity which they had with the local officials, the Manila leadership had to commit its political capital. For example, on April 26, 1943, Vargas addressed the city mayors and provincial governors of the Visayas, the central islands. He urged them "to explain to the people that there is absolutely no reason for any futile and misguided resistance, absolutely no justification for lawlessness and unrest, absolutely no use or purpose in continued disorder." Vargas asked rhetorically if the Filipinos should still fight "for the sake of the sovereignty of the United States and American imperialism? The Tragedy of Bataan," he noted, taught the Filipinos "the bitter lesson that the United States used the lives of the Filipinos to defend purely American interests." Claiming that the flower of Filipino "youth was sacrificed ruthlessly in a senseless prolongation of hostilities, to be afterwards abandoned," he asked "what reason have the Filipinos of the Visayas to make further sacrifices, to shed more blood, to suffer more misery. . . ."[50] In July 1943 he went even further in an address to the Central Constabulary Academy when he claimed that the time had arrived for the Filipinos to relieve Japan of the burden of pacification, "for it is more than enough that she is fighting in the battle fronts of this war for the common interests of all the races of Asia."[51]

A direct confrontation between the Manila elite and the guerrilla movement was the result. After the war Quintin Paredes claimed: "We did not want to establish an army; only a Constabulary for the maintenance of peace and order, and that is the duty of every recognized government."[52] During the war, however, this claim was suspect, because both the Constabulary and the Pacification Committee were concerned less with the normal problems of peace and order than with the particular challenge of the guerrilla alternative. The euphemistic designation, "peace and order," was translated into support of the Japanese war effort by permitting a reduction in the size of the Japanese garrison in the Philippines. Executive Order No. 173 of July 3, 1943, stated explicitly that the Bureau of Information and Public Security of the Executive Commission was created "for the purpose of extending cooperation firmly and effectively to the . . . Imperial Japanese Forces in the Philippines. . . ."[53]

Collaboration produced open conflict between Filipinos. Guerrilla units responded to the increased opposition of the elite by assassinations designed to intimidate the leadership while avoiding savage Japanese reprisals, which always followed any murder of

Japanese. Tee Han Kee, vice-president of the collaborating Chinese Association, Jose de Jesus of the Finance Ministry, and Andong Roces of the *Manila Tribune* and son of Alejandro Roces, were all murdered.[54] The most famous of these assassination efforts was the attempt to kill Jose Laurel while he was playing golf. Violence is endemic in Philippine politics, and at least some of the motivation for these killings or attempted killings might have been personal; however, the basic cause of this violence was the growing polarization of the society, in which the Manila elite seemingly became alienated from the popular will.

This increasing polarization was the result of the Japanese effort to create the new order by allying themselves with the established oligarchy. The Japanese attempted to do what the Americans had succeeded in doing forty years earlier; they tried to create an ideological revolution through the traditional leadership. The Japanese, like the Americans and Spanish before them, struck a tacit agreement with the establishment, in which continuity of power was the price they paid for the desired superficial restructuring of the society. Unlike the Americans of the Taft era, however, the Japanese lacked the time and physical power to crush the opposition. Having cajoled the prewar oligarchy to retain power, they were unable to accomplish the next step of enforcing popular compliance. They ignored potential radical candidates like Generals Aguinaldo and Ricarte, Pio Duran and Benigno Ramos, in their attempt to align the new with the old orders. They could neither ignore nor obliterate the national identity which had grown in the previous forty years and which remained embodied in the Commonwealth government. Had Quezon and Osmeña remained in Manila and cooperated with the Japanese, the situation would at least have been less greatly weighted against them. The shadow presence of the Commonwealth haunted the Japanese, encouraged the guerrillas, and emasculated the impact of that measure of oligarchic support which was achieved.

Every effort had been made to build the new polity with the remaining oligarchs. Vargas was successful in rallying most of the Commonwealth government back to the new Philippine Executive Commission.[55] Moreover, the new government did use the reciprocal local connections of the prewar period to establish channels downward into local communities. In August 1942 Vargas issued Executive Order No. 77, which created the District and Neighborhood Associations (DANAS) "for the purpose of providing means for self-protection under the joint responsibility and thus insuring the stability of the life of the people, through the maintenance of peace and order. . . ."[56] Closely patterned upon the neighborhood associations in Japan (*tonarigumi*), the country was organized into a pyramidal political structure, of which the basic cell was a unit of ten families under a local leader. While patterned on a Japanese rather than on an American or Spanish model, this new system did permit the continuation of the traditional patterns of patron-client polity between the local barrio and the central government. When this system had been fully established, the government claimed that there were 124,000 associations encompassing more than 1,500,000 Filipinos. The DANAS organization was used to control rationing, carry out central governmental orders, conduct indoctrination, and combat guerrilla propaganda.

At the national level the Japanese similarly attempted to alter the structure of the institutions so as to correspond to Japanese models wihout changing the actual political power of the elite. On December 4, 1942, the Japanese abolished all existing political parties, though ostensibly the decision was done voluntarily by the Filipino leadership of each. This action, according to the announcement, ended "all vestiges of American power and authority" as the Philippines returned "to her former Oriental self. . . ." The dissolution of these parties, the dominant Nacionalistas and four splinter groups, was "for the purpose of fostering closer harmony, concordance, and unanimity among all Filipinos. . . ." The announcement continued that such a policy was timely because "the whole world is undergoing complete metamorphosis and social, economic, and political systems of the past are rapidly undergoing drastic changes. . . ."[57]

The Japanese had been unhappy about the existence of prewar parties from the beginning of the occupation. Six months before their dissolution, the *Tribune* reported that the Military Administration had prohibited any form of political activity, but that "notwithstanding this, some government officials and private persons stick to their political bickerings at all times, thus neglecting to perform their real duties for the reconstruction of the new Philippines."[58] Homma, in an address to the Philippine leadership, had specifically urged the elite to "clear the Philippines of sinister influences." After congratulating the leadership for immediately pledging its "loyalty to His Imperial Majesty's Forces," and taking up the task of government, he called on the leaders "to disregard minor differences among yourselves and to unite yourselves on important issues; to avoid partisanship and bring about reforms in all branches of service."[59] The Japanese military, long the opponent of political parties in Japan, branded any sort of party activity anathema.

Retaining the oligarchy as an institution, they urged and effected the creation of a single, nonpartisan, supraparty, modeled on the Imperial Rule Assistance Association founded in Japan in 1940. This new Filipino supraparty was called the Kalibapi (an abbreviation of the Tagalog, Kapisanan Sa Paglilingkod Sa Bagong Pilipinas—Association for Service in the New Philippines). Similar organizations were established by the Japanese elsewhere throughout Asia including the Hsin Min Hui in China and the Concordia Society in Manchukuo. The Kalibapi was proclaimed a few days after the old parties were abolished, when, on December 8, 1942, the anniversary of the war, Vargas issued Executive Order No. 109. The professed aim of the Kalibapi was "to adhere strictly to the policies of the Imperial Japanese Forces in the Philippines in their administration and to render service in the establishment of the Greater East Asia Co-Prosperity Sphere."[60]

The formal launching of the Kalibapi was made on December 30, 1942, the traditional national holiday honoring Jose Rizal, to link this new organ as closely as possible to the mainstream of Philippine nationalism. Vargas became president ex officio, but Benigno Aquino, as vice-president and director general, became the moving force in the organization.[61] On May 18, 1943, Vargas further broadened the Kalibapi by creating a Junior Kalibapi, and by appointing an assistant director general and four directors-at-large.[62]

Because the Japanese placed considerable faith in the future of the Kalibapi, Aquino wielded great power as director general. In this post, perhaps because of ambition, he became an increasingly bold propagandist. He promised that he would "spare no effort to convince and persuade the Filipinos that the only possible salvation of our land and people rests upon the unswerving and unhesitating support of the Co-Prosperity Sphere." Consequently, he urged the Filipinos "to collaborate with the Imperial Forces in these Islands."[63] He noted on another occasion that "a Philippines perpetually dependent on the whims and fancies of the West cannot stand. A Philippines, Oriental in geography, culture, and ancestry, tied to the apron strings, nevertheless, of America is artificial, unnatural, illogical, and untenable."[64]

While some of the prewar elite became increasingly outspoken in their new pro-Japanese positions, others did manage, albeit at some risk, to refuse to serve actively. Men who did only the bare minimum were permitted by the Japanese to slip from view. Indeed, the Japanese were willing to tolerate this situation, perhaps because they managed to retain enough of the prewar officialdom for their purposes. In a "secret" report submitted by Vargas to the Japanese commander-in-chief, Vargas noted that men who had avoided office were able to go into retirement. "In those cases where important provincial, city, and municipal offices were abandoned by the incumbents at the outbreak of the war or where the incumbents refused to reassume or continue in office, the local Japanese military command designated other Filipinos willing to accept the positions vacated. . . ."[65] This significant admission revealed that at least immediate duress was not a direct factor in the decision to collaborate.

The choice of behavior was not always one demanding total abstention or compliance. Jose Yulo, for example, who began the war near the pinnacle of the oligarchy, managed to refuse major involvement during the war, while at the same time he avoided any radical break with the conquering power. When General Homma's replacement, General Tanaka, paid his courtesy call at Malacañan Palace on October 6, 1942, the official list of Filipino hosts who received him placed Vargas first, Yulo second, Aquino third, de las Alas fourth, Laurel fifth, with Alunan, Recto, Paredes, and Sison following. It had been at Yulo's home that the early meetings of the leadership had forged the initial "letter of response," but by February 1943, when the "Manifesto of Independence" was issued, Yulo's name was listed as ninth. And in a series of vignettes continuing throughout 1943 in the Sunday supplement of the *Manila Tribune,* Yulo's biographical sketch was seventeenth.

Such evidence does not prove that Yulo was a hero and that the others were villains; it merely suggests that it was possible for a man to remain aloof and have a good chance of survival. Yulo did not volunteer to do more than the minimum, and his technique succeeded in keeping him out of the limelight. He made few public speeches, and, when he did, he couched everything he said in vague terms. For example, on radio station KZRH he said: "Let us not be carried away by our enthusiasm of the moment, rather let us raise our hearts in thanksgiving to the Almighty who rules the destinies of all peoples, and pray for light and guidance, for strength of will and of spirit."[66]

The Japanese, who clearly preferred Aquino's enthusiasm to Yulo's sobriety, attempted to reshuffle the top leadership to correspond more accurately with the response patterns of the various individuals. Vargas, under instruction, altered the membership of the Council of State by eliminating the unenthusiastic. Yulo, himself, was too important a prewar figure to be dropped, but by Executive Order No. 46 of May 30, 1942, Vargas did drop Jose Fabella and Alfonso Mendoza, the two men who had not signed the "letter of response," as well as Eulogio Rodriguez, Sotero Baluyot, Elpidio Quirino, Jose Zulueta, Dominador Tan, Pedro Sabido, Malicio Arranz, Pedro Hernaez, Jose Osamiz, Ricardo Navarro, Prospero Sanidad, and Eugenio Perez. At the same time, Vargas appointed Pio Duran, Arsenio Bonifacio, Camilo Osias, and Artemio Ricarte to bring the Council up to the newly prescribed limit.[67]

The whole Vargas administration evolved on an ad hoc basis. Since the Executive Commission had been given both legislative and executive functions initially, considerable confusion arose over how the Japanese instruction to maintain existing Commonwealth law was to be carried out. On February 20, 1942, General Homma had issued Order No. 3 to clarify the situation. Four days later his office issued Order No. 5 to clarify Order No. 3. Among the many specific instructions of an administrative and bureaucratic nature, the orders stated as general policy the desire "to rectify the existing tendency of relying upon the United States" and to satisfy the Japanese demands.[68] The orders did not, however, clarify the process of legislative enactment. They did not have to, because in effect the Japanese Military Administration retained the legislative authority and used the Commission as its executive agent.

As chief executive Vargas himself wielded most of the authority which the Japanese were willing to concede to the Commission. He required by Executive Order No. 30, issued on April 9, 1942, that all correspondence go through his office, and he administered a range of executive functions including the Office of the Budget, the government-owned corporations, and the civil service. He referred to his office as the "pivotal position in the compact organization that is the Philippine Executive Commission . . . the nerve center that keeps a steady hand on the pulse of the government."[69] He was most importantly the official spokesman for the government and for the Filipino people.

The only other Filipinos who had comparable power were the director general of the Kalibapi, Benigno Aquino, and the commissioner of the Interior, Jose Laurel. The Kalibapi position was important because the Japanese placed such stock in a mass party and because the director general was able to maintain his Philippine-style political contacts under the cloak of the Japanese-style party. The commissioner of the Interior had authority primarily because the Japanese remodeled this agency to conform closely to the Japanese Home Ministry. The commissioner, by supervising its four divisions—Administration, Law, Public Order, and Games and Amusement Control—and its host of bureaus—Local Government, Constabulary and Police, Religious Affairs, Census and Statistics, and Employment—also retained strong power on the local level. Indirectly, the commissioner controlled marriage and the civil registry and had supervision over local tax appeals, assessments, and provincial, municipal, and city treasurers.

Aquino, who was the first commissioner, and Laurel, who replaced him, also controlled the DANAS organizations through the country and supervised the local governors and provincial authorities, as in Japan. The governor's term was made "subject to the pleasure of the Chairman of the Executive Commission" and under "the new set-up the Provincial Governor is essentially the agent of the Central Administrative Organization in his province. . . ."[70] The provincial official became dependent on the pleasure of the commissioner, with whom he maintained a relationship of *utang na loob* and reciprocity.

Considering the importance of the chairmanship and the hopes the Japanese put in the Executive Commission, it was strange that they retained Vargas in the job for so long and kept Aquino and Laurel in secondary positions. While Vargas had served Quezon long and well as his executive secretary and alter ego, he had never held major elective office, nor had he commanded an independent place in the oligarchic structure. His Commonwealth power merely reflected his proximity to Quezon.[71] The reason that the Japanese kept him in the prime position of power for over eighteen months is enigmatic. Quezon had specifically left him behind as mayor of Greater Manila to maintain the vital services he was so skilled at administering.[72] The Japanese did not have to abide by Quezon's emergency appointment, however, and their retention of Vargas would seem to indicate that they misread the structure of Philippine polity and Vargas' place in it. Vargas lacked the base of independent power which is an essential of Philippine political life and as such he could not inherit Quezon's mantle, although the Japanese tried hard enough to transfer the people's loyalty from the master to his servant.

If the Japanese erred in retaining him in power for such a long time, why did he accept? His initial instructions could well have been read to embrace only the Greater Manila area; his rank was specifically demoted to that of a city mayor, albeit of the great metropolitan complex.[73] Nevertheless, he chose to serve and to cling to power once gained until the Japanese finally had to turn him out of office. Part of his reason lay in his sense of dedication to Quezon, who had instructed him to cooperate. He read Quezon's instructions literally and moved from cautious to active collaboration as a necessary concomitant to this compliance. It was also true, however, that during the period prior to the great global battles of Midway and Guadalcanal, when American military power finally checked Japanese expansion, Vargas shifted from a passive to an active proponent of the new order. Vargas was not alone in his mistaken assessment of the war situation; impressed by Japanese victories he seems to have concluded that Japan would be in the Philippines for years to come. Indeed, since Japanese strategy hoped to negotiate a peace with the West in which America and Britain would accede to at least some Japanese conquest rather than wage a protracted military struggle, Vargas perhaps gambled that the Philippines might be an expendable pawn.

This shift in Vargas' attitude was noted in intelligence reports to the American government. Early in the occupation the first report stated that "Secretary Vargas is loyal to President Quezon's government and to the United States. He considers that it is best that he do what he is doing for the best interests of the Filipino people with a definite idea of preventing suffering. . . ."[74] Six months later the same source was less sure of Vargas' loyalty, reporting that the "subject is suspected by many in the Philippines of being pro-Japanese." Vargas was reported as "living under the fear that the Japanese may suspect that he is insincere in his cooperation with them in which case he feels that he would lose his life." Vargas was still adjudged to be "loyal to President Quezon and to the United States" and not "pro-Japanese," but the absolute certainty of the first report was missing in the second.[75]

This uncertainty was based primarily on the growing sharpness of Vargas' speeches, most of which he wrote himself with the aid of his brilliant young assistant, Leon Ma. Guerrero.[76] Speaking at a parade to celebrate the fall of Bataan and Corregidor, he said on May 18, 1942, that the Filipinos were "grateful for this victory because of the new perspective it has given us . . . [and] because it has vindicated all Asiatic peoples whose rights and genius have been denied due recognition by Occidental civilization." Noting that the fallacy of Western invincibility had been broken, he said, "superiority is not an attribute of a particular color of men, . . . its real source is the spirit, the fountainhead of strength and fortitude. In the wake of the sweeping Japanese victories, the prestige of all Asiatic nations has been vindicated."[77]

The validity of such a nationalist statement was vitiated by its timing, since the victory parade not only celebrated the defeat of the Americans but also of the Filipino troops. Speaking at a rally honoring Rizal on December 30, 1942, Vargas speculated that Rizal would have been scornful "of those who, even in the face of reality, continue to embrace the vanished phantom of Western culture. . . ."[78] Again and again Vargas suggested that "hand in hand, shoulder to shoulder, with all our Oriental brothers, . . . we are ready to build a new Asia for the Asians and a new Philippines for the Filipinos. . . . If we fought on the side of the Americans, . . . we did so only because, at the start of the war, we were subjects of the United States. . . . The Filipino people were never consulted on this war, and they never consented to it."[79] Vargas' argument, which might be impressive in a country like Indonesia, was inaccurate in the Philippines because it attributed to the Filipinos a passiveness they did not evince.

Vargas' increasingly anti-American, anti-white, pro-Japanese sentiments put him at odds with the national decision. Speaking at a rally honoring Premier Tojo on May 6, 1943, he asserted that the Filipinos "were in hopeless bondage to Anglo-American imperialism, and Japan liberated us." After cataloguing how the nation was "deluded," "divided by political dissensions, weakened by limitation and frivolity, [and] oppressed by a sense of inferiority," Vargas lamented that Filipinos "were the orphans of the Orient, the prodigal sons of the Asian race, lost and abandoned in an alien civilization. . . ."[80] Whatever element of truth existed in such statements (and unquestionably Vargas touched on tender issues in the Philippine national character), his effort to bring the light of reason to a nation already emotionally committed in a war was inopportune.

He further flouted this national will by becoming friends with many ranking Japanese officers. To cite one example, he gave a luncheon to honor Lieutenant Colonel Ito Shiro, the commandant of the central Luzon prisoner of war camps. Vargas referred to Ito as a "friend and benefactor of the Filipino people" who by "kindness, courtesy, and considerate treatment" was able to do much "in winning the support and admiration of the Filipino people."[81] Since all the prison camps were notorious, it seemed to many Filipinos to be a gratuitous comment even for a man forced to say things he might not believe.

At a celebration honoring the first anniversary of the establishment of the Executive Commission, the Japanese Commander, General Tanaka, recalled "with great pleasure how Chairman Vargas and the other recognized leaders of the peace-loving Filipino people stood up . . . and courageously stepped forward to collaborate wholeheartedly. . . ." "One year ago," Vargas replied, "the Filipino people, through their chosen leaders, inaugurated a new regime. . . . The inspiring progress we have made constitutes the best justification of the choice we made last year." Pleased to recall that "partisan struggle and disunion" had been left behind, Vargas did not regret the abolition of political parties "which only aroused selfish ambitions and created personal animosities because of the individualistic desire for political power and prestige."[82]

In a speech to a group of Filipino prisoners of war Vargas seemed to imply that he thought their fight at Bataan was folly. "To a group of Filipinos long in public service and to me, who saw beyond the devastation around us, the way to our duty was clear, if difficult. . . . We did not procrastinate; we did not compromise. . . . To this day, we have not regretted having taken that step. . . ." Thanking the Japanese military for the "day by day, acts of charity and mercy," he boldly stated that "it is not resignation to the actuality of a fate that we expect; neither reconciliation to the present state of affairs. The thing most desirable is a full conversion. . . ."[83] Coming only a few months after the Wainwright surrender and the brutal prison camp experience, such enthusiasm jarred Filipino sensibilities.

By mid-1943 Vargas was promising that the Filipinos would stand with Japan "in joy and in suffering, in peace and in war." He committed the totality of national and spiritual resources to Japan and warned that any Filipino who stood in the way of this progress was a "betrayer of the loftiest ideals of our race and nation. No Filipino worthy of the name," he continued, "can desire the return of the American domination without convicting himself of treason and disloyality to the New and Free Philippines."[84] Such assertions transcended reluctant compliance, and an intelligence report to Quezon claimed that "weakness of character has caused him to get further and further involved with the Nips. He is cooperating to a far greater extent than your more loyal friends consider necessary. He apparently is doing this to keep his present leadership stable. He is afraid of being outshone by other aspirants for the job."[85] At no point did Vargas seem willing to risk Japanese ire or to confront the Japanese on any critical issue. To many he appeared as a competent but weak bureaucrat who did exactly what was asked of him both for Quezon before the war and for the Japanese military during it.

Does that explanation account for his behavior completely? Vargas claimed that he had not wanted to accept the chairmanship of the Executive Commission, but that once it was forced upon him he felt that "he might as well do a good job."[86] He maintained that he always tried to aid Philippine nationalism and that he had contributed a new atmosphere of independence for the people by attacking excessive dependence on the Americans. He did not claim any guerrilla connection himself and recognized that each individual had to determine his own priorities. He determined his, and, unlike others, he did not attempt later to explain away his actions.

Was it merely weakness of character, then, which determined his response? Whatever his prewar frustration at always being in Quezon's lee, he was obviously confident of his own capacity. After he formed the Executive Commission, starting from scratch, he seems to have fallen in love with the creation. That it was completely overshadowed by Japanese supervision became less important, perhaps because any government would have been equally overshadowed. He seems to have lost sight of the original purpose for which Quezon gave him responsibility; his defensiveness for his regime was like that of a mother for her child. He must have realized that his government could only survive if the Japanese were successful both in the greater war effort and in the internal dynamics of occupation. Since he seems to have believed that he was already doomed to oblivion or to a firing squad if the Japanese lost, he had little to lose in becoming increasingly pro-Japanese in order to retain power.

The process must have been much more subtle than this, especially since he did not scheme for power initially. It seems likely that he evolved a growing commitment to the Executive Commission as the best technique for coping with the occupation, and then gradually defended his creation (and concomitantly the Japanese) as other Filipinos attacked it. He became hostile to the guerrilla movement because it was contrary to his conception of how to survive an occupation. It is possible that it was the staunchly anti-Japanese (and therefore anti-Vargas) sentiment of the guerrilla movement that pushed him further and further to a pro-Japanese position. In effect, the tragedy for Vargas personally was that almost alone he transferred his loyalty away from the Quezon Commonwealth government to the Vargas Executive Commission. In the conflict between his obligation to Quezon and his faith in himself he apostatized; in Philippine terms he was *walang hiya*.

The pathos of this decision stemmed from the way the Japanese treated him. Increasingly they realized that he lacked charisma and that as a result they were not succeeding in bending Philippine loyalties away from prewar patterns. Vargas was seen as a pliant tool, which they eventually discarded in a frenzied effort to gain Filipino support. The Japanese decided that their only hope of success would be the playing of their last trump card, that of granting independence, before the Americans did, in the most advantageous situation and through the most popular Filipino available. Vargas was shunted to the side, dispatched as window-dressing in the form of ambassador to Tokyo.

CHAPTER V

Independence: The Laurel Republic

*But a small country is a small country, and a weak
people is a weak people. We had no choice and
everything depended on the result of the war.*
—Jose P. Laurel

The trump card of independence was less valuable in the Philippines than elsewhere in the colonial world. Since the Commonwealth was in the final phase of preparation for independence, no one doubted that at the end of the prescribed period an independent Republic of the Philippines would be born. This conviction was a major factor contributing to the initial hostile response of the Filipinos to Japan. Philippine nationalism had ripened to maturity with the blessing of metropolitan America, in sharp contrast to the repressed agonies of the Indonesian, Vietnamese, and Burmese nationalist movements. The fruition of nationalism lowered the worth of the independence issue for the Japanese in the Philippines, whereas, in comparison, it raised to an unassailable position the value of the trump of independence elsewhere. The dream of Japanese-sponsored independence lured Sukarno, Aung San, Ba Maw, and others into collaboration because these men saw no possibility of gaining a similar concession from their own metropolitan power. Many of these nationalist leaders were released from detention by the conquering Japanese armies.

Although the Japanese realized the limited prospects for independence as a means of gaining a pledge of allegiance from the Filipinos, they pursued the policy for whatever it was worth. Tojo had used independence as the initial bait in January 1942, and by the end of that year a tentative draft for independence had been submitted to Tokyo by the Japanese in Manila. This document stressed that independence would "stir up the hope of other Asian countries."[1] Independence was a *sine qua non* from a long-range

Japanese point of view, but the field command in the Philippines was very conservative about advocating immediate Japanese concessions. This general staff, less concerned with winning Filipino friendship, had serious reservations about plunging ahead before it had consolidated its position in the country and had eradicated the guerrilla opposition.

The Japanese political officers in Manila opposed such conservatism strongly. In a "top secret" report to the cabinet, Tojo was urged to make the decision of immediate independence and only then to inform the army command. Tojo was reminded that bureaucratic tensions in Tokyo existed also at the local Philippine level and that the local command in the Philippines wielded enormous power. The prime minister was reminded that his initial promise of independence in January 1942, while the Japanese army was still locked in battle with the Fil-American forces on Bataan, had antagonized the field officers, who considered the timing inappropriate. Since his popularity with the general staff was already low, he was urged to ignore this opposition and to do what the political policy planners thought vital. The report urged that Philippine nationalism be encouraged, except where it hindered specific Japanese objectives. The Philippine national flag and anthem, which the commander-in-chief had banned during the hostilities, had to be restored; the propaganda stress on Japanese institutions had to be deemphasized in favor of Filipino institutions. Finally, Tojo was urged to define clearly the relationship between the field command and the political officers by prohibiting military interference in nonmilitary matters. This was urged "in order to make clear the spheres of administration. . . . Let the personnel of the gunsei [Imperial General Staff] recognize that it is the gunsei which is to be the consultant organization for the gyosei [Murata Shozo and the Military Administration]."[2] Unfortunately for Filipinos and political officers alike, the Tokyo cabinet lacked the muscle to impose its will upon the Imperial General Staff in Japan or in the field.

Tojo still pressed for rapid independence despite military opposition. In early May 1943 he visited Manila to encourage the Japanese garrison and to dramatize independence. His visit was publicized widely, and his presence lent prestige to the Executive Commission. The news media repeated constantly that no American President had ever bothered to come to the archipelago, but that Tojo, in the middle of a total war, felt the Philippines important enough to visit. Huge crowds were mustered to see him, and he dined with ranking Filipinos. Briefed by Murata Shozo and General

Wachi, he used social functions to evaluate the Filipinos he met. A few days after his visit, Greater East Asia Minister Aoki arrived to conduct a more detailed analysis than Tojo personally had time to make.

At the opening of the eighty-second Diet in Tokyo a month later, Tojo promised "independence in 1943" for the archipelago. By a happy coincidence his speech came on the eve of the eighty-second anniversary of Rizal's birth, and maximum coverage was again given to the independence pledge. The *Manila Tribune* editorialized that "henceforth, every Filipino who refuses to collaborate in the supreme task of preparing the Philippines for independence in 'the course of the current year' is a traitor."[3]

Beneath the glitter of publicity, however, the Japanese were still desperately searching for some leader capable of winning Filipino loyalty away from the Quezon government in Washington. The Japanese knew that Generals Aguinaldo and Ricarte, Benigno Ramos, and others would take the job willingly, but none of these men had the necessary stature within the Philippine social and political structure to accomplish Japanese aims. They looked to the prewar oligarchy and initially to former Chief Justice Ramon Avanceña and to Manuel Roxas as their best candidates. Vargas and Aquino had been rejected because, while they seemed interested in the job, they had not given the Executive Commission the necessary charismatic leadership.[4] Ramon Avanceña was subsequently eliminated because he was already over seventy.[5] Despite his distinguished position as chief justice for twenty-five years, he was too old and clearly unwilling to cooperate or to assume an active role in government.

Consequently, Japanese attention focused on Manuel Roxas, Quezon's heir presumptive. Roxas, who had been born in 1894, was politically the most powerful of the younger generation. He had served as liaison between Quezon and MacArthur on Corregidor and was intimate with both these men. Quezon had left him with extraordinary powers as secretary to the president. He had escaped from Corregidor to Mindanao before Wainwright surrendered the fortress, but eventually he was captured by the Japanese. The local commander did not realize his identity at first. When he was discovered, the field command ordered his execution. He was saved by the defiance of Colonel Jimbo Nobuhiko, who as chief of staff in Davao had the responsibility for the execution. He defied the execution order by appealing it to the Military Administration, who remonstrated vehemently with the commander-in-chief to save this poten-

tially valuable Filipino. The Military Administration argued successfully that to execute this influential leader would be to guarantee
the failure of the Japanese political program. The Military Administration was well aware that the field commanders had already done
perhaps irreparable harm when they had executed Chief Justice Jose
Abad Santos. Such brazen intimidation was self-defeating.

Colonel Jimbo wrote after the war that "the order for a secret
execution of this heroic man was obviously against the International
Public Law and also against the principle of the Japanese morality. I
vowed to myself, 'He [Roxas] must not die.' "[6] As a result of this
intercession, Roxas was permitted to return to his Manila home,
where he remained in awkward retirement. The General Staff was
unhappy that this high-ranking officer on MacArthur's staff was free,
but the Military Administration convinced them that Roxas was the
ideal leader of an independent Philippines as pledged by Tojo.

The pressure on Roxas mounted as the Japanese attempted to
lure him into active participation. He claimed that a coronary condition prohibited his positive response, but the Japanese refused to
relieve the pressure on him. Intelligence to Quezon indicated that
"Manoling [Roxas] will be the first President in name—whether
he wants it or not—provision being made for Aquino to perform the
functions of the office. . . ."[7] As a result of such reports, MacArthur
and Quezon decided to attempt an evacuation, despite the incalculable risks to Roxas, to the Fil-American intelligence network, and to
the rest of Quezon's former aides. A submarine rescue was planned
and indirectly Roxas was secretly informed "that the Chief wants
him [Roxas] to follow his own judgment as to evacuation. If he
feels he can serve better away from enemy pressure, arrangements
can be made for his early evacuation." Roxas was notified that he
could bring his family but was warned to "be careful as the Chief
does not want him to run any risks."[8] The plan, which went awry
before Roxas was ever implicated, was reluctantly abandoned by
MacArthur's staff as too dangerous.

The Japanese pressure on Roxas reached a crescendo in the late
spring of 1943, when the Military Administration finally decided
that he would not cooperate sufficiently. The Japanese abandoned
their efforts, and switched their attention to Jose Laurel, who also
attracted them.[9] They noted that Laurel had obtained a doctorate
of jurisprudence in Japan in 1938, that he had been a prewar lobby-
ist for Japanese business interests, that he had sent one of his sons to
Japan for military training before the war, and that he had spoken
very favorably about some Japanese institutions. Most importantly,

they read enormous significance into the June 6, 1943, guerrilla assassination attempt against him. They wondered why the guerrillas attacked Laurel but not Aquino, Vargas, or any of the others, and concluded that he must have been more pro-Japanese than even they had realized. Having read events in this way, the Japanese must have seen the assassination as some divine omen which suddenly resolved their leadership dilemma. Unfortunately for them, however, this construct was not valid and they misjudged the significance of the shooting and Laurel's motivation for accepting their offer.

In the immediate postwar era, Laurel claimed that he had been forced into accepting the presidency. He maintained that his cooperation was *ex necessitate re* and that "forced collaboration is not collaboration. Voluntary collaboration as a means of national survival and to tide over our people to better times is not punishable."[10] In Laurel's postwar defense he projected himself as a devoted patriot whose one and only aim was to serve his nation selflessly. He claimed that he acted merely on MacArthur's original instructions and was free of any more complex motivation.

The evidence may support a more complicated explanation. He seems to have accepted the presidency because he wanted to use the power of that office, albeit circumscribed by the Japanese occupation authorities, to effect reforms which he felt were essential to the fabric and growth of Philippine society. Laurel was far more than the weak puppet, as was claimed of him by his postwar enemies, and he was far less than the self-sacrificing martyr, as was claimed of him by his friends. He thought that he could achieve certain goals despite the occupation, or perhaps even because of it, and he gambled on that assumption. It happened that both the Japanese and Laurel agreed on the value of a strong executive, but they differed sharply on the reasons for wanting one in 1943. Laurel's intention of wielding authority firmly was antithetical in many ways to the Japanese desire for a pliant but charismatic Filipino.

The attempt on Laurel's life left him critically wounded, and he was confined to a hospital bed for seven weeks. He survived because of the intensive efforts Filipino and Japanese specialists were ordered to give him by the Military Administration. Doctors were flown from Tokyo especially to care for him. If he had wanted to avoid further involvement in any Japanese-supported government, his wounds afforded him a perfect excuse to go into semiretirement, at least. If Roxas managed to avoid Japanese pressure with a slightly irregular electrocardiagram tape, Laurel, near death from his wounds, could have opted to avoid their offer if he had wanted to. Nevertheless, exactly twelve weeks after he was released from the hospital, he was inaugurated as the first and only president of the Japanese-sponsored republic.

After the war Laurel openly admitted that on his accession to power, "I boldly announced my *national policy,* my *political ideology,* and my *moral philosophy* in my speeches, interviews, and conferences."[11] In 1943 Laurel wrote a short book, subsequently published under the title *Forces That Make a Nation Great,* in which he avowedly codified his aims. He admitted that his "suggested reform is comprehensive and far-reaching and implies a complete renovation of the individual and collective life of the Filipinos, the overhauling of institutions and laws, the adaptation of our system of jurisprudence to what is genuinely autochthonous, and the revision and reorientation of educational policies, particularly in reference to ethical and civic instruction in our schools"; Laurel concluded by urging the formulation of a system of government which would be responsive to the new exigencies.[12]

Laurel chafed at those many aspects of Philippine life which he viewed as wasteful and deleterious. His own values were not in harmony with the main elements of his culture, which he thought lacked discipline, control, and purpose. He was lured by much in the Japanese social fabric which he believed would have a beneficial effect on Philippine life, if it could be transplanted. "The integrity and compactness of the Japanese family," were to Laurel, "not only a source of communal strength because of the ever-pervading authority and responsibility of the heads of families, . . . but with the political concept happily conceived regarding the divinity of the Emperor as the supreme patriarch of the nation, they make for a strong and cohesive people ever united to move and to act, to fight and to die at the behest of their August Ruler." He felt that "Japan has succeeded in cementing the lasting foundations of her national existence through the family system," which, he implied, was unlike its Filipino counterpart in being "one of the secrets of her almost incredible spiritual strength and power."[13]

Japanese society seemed to Laurel to be graft-free; it reinvested its profits in preference to siphoning them off for fleeting luxury consumption. He admired the apparent domestic tranquillity, in which all classes appeared to accept their respective places willingly, and he envied the way the Japanese educational system focused on self-sacrificing service to the state. He noted that in Japan "the regimentation implied by the compulsory education of the masses may give a Filipino observer the impression that the system is un-democratic." Rejecting this estimate, he continued that "in education what is needed is not democracy, . . . but regimentation, not liberty but discipline, not liberalism but correct orientation, not flexibility but rigidity in the formation of the desired mould of citizenship."[14] Such views indicated that Laurel was dubious about the influence of American materialism, educational theory, and individualism, all of which had permeated Philippine culture prior to the war.

Instead, Laurel was concerned with the importance of "racial pride in shaping the destiny of a nation."[15] This pride, he felt, was the critical ingredient in Japanese nationalism which had led to such striking results. Frugality, hard work, and sacrifice were virtues he felt his own society sorely lacked, in contrast to Japan, where "no sacrifice was too great if it was made, in the words of the Imperial Rescript on Japanese Education, to 'advance public good and pro-mote common interests.' " He reminded his countrymen of the Japa-nese saying, "Life is nothing, duty everything," noting that "out of that fine moral concept has stemmed the might and solidarity of the great Nippon Empire."[16] Laurel puritanically demanded of himself rigid standards both physically and mentally. He thrived on the early morning "radio taiso" calisthenics. Born into what he must have viewed as a lax and corrupt, if lovable, society, he marveled, often mistakenly, at efficiency elsewhere. This puritanical disposition is reflected in some of the chapter titles of *Forces That Make a Nation Great:* "Honor," "Frugality and Cleanliness," "Self-Reliance and Perseverance," "Man Perfects himself by Working," "The Value of Ethical Principles," and "Truth, the Mother of All Virtues."

The role of the emperor as a symbol for the nation fascinated him. He was aware of the impact of this symbol in creating cohe-siveness; he thought Philippine nationalism needed something of "similar compelling force and dynamic reality."[17] In the Philippine context, the presidency could fulfill this function, and at the same time it could provide a mechanism for reform from the top. Laurel had watched Quezon manipulate the office without taking maximum advantage of the full range of power available. Since Quezon thrived on dissent, factionalism, and the combat of politics, he did not seem to Laurel to develop presidential power coherently or systematically. Months before Pearl Harbor, Laurel is quoted as supporting emergency powers for Quezon because he felt that "con-stitutional dictatorship" was in keeping with a worldwide trend in which "totalitarianism [was] gradually supplanting democ-racy."[18] Laurel felt that "in the interrelationship of powers of government a center of political gravity must, in the nature of things, be provided. Such a center must necessarily be the Executive. . . ."[19]

Japan's phenomenal development "within half a century from primitivism to modernism, from obscurity to primacy as a world power has been due, in the main," Laurel deduced, "to its system of government which is characterized by massive powers rigidly centralized, but exercised with wise benevolence. . . ."[20] He seems to have hoped that Japan's experience could be duplicated in the Philippines through a strong, centralized, authoritarian president. He posited that a president aware both of the symbolic possibilities of the office and of the opportunities of power within the office could alter the society profoundly.

Laurel was a devout nationalist who hated colonialism. He frequently spoke out against the American colonial legacy. "We are weary," he said during the war, "with the pretentions of the 'White man's burden' which more often than not has only served to cloak the exploitation of weaker peoples."[21] He reasoned that "if the Americans are no longer here and we are earnest in our desire for independence, we should not want them to come back."[22] After the war, he maintained that the Japanese "offer of independence could not have been rejected for historical reasons and as a matter of national dignity." After noting that generations of Filipinos had fought and worked for independence, he suggested that his generation "could not afford to appear in the history" of the Philippines as the one which "offered to become free, rejected the priceless boon and preferred something else. Accepting all the coveted freedom which America herself promised to give is not an act of disloyalty." He continued by arguing that he "was personally more interested in genuine freedom than in its trademarks," and concluded by shrewdly observing that "the reality of independence depends upon the Filipinos themselves."[23]

The Japanese, confusing Laurel's admiration of Japanese institutions with sycophancy, probably minimized erroneously his nationalist hostility to Japanese imperialism. He was clearly their best candidate under the actual circumstances, but he, in turn, seems to have been willing to cooperate primarily because he was convinced that Japan lacked the power to sustain the Greater East Asia Co-Prosperity Sphere for any protracted length of time. He saw that American pressure would compel an eventual contraction, but he thought it would happen more slowly than it actually did. "The war is still raging," he wrote in 1943; "after defeating Germany, how long will it take the Allies to bring their war with Japan to a decisive end? Assuming that it takes the Allies six years to defeat Germany, it is reasonable to assume that it will take four years or more to finish the war with Japan. Let us say six more years will elapse before the conclusion of the war."[24]

If he assumed that the war would drag on to 1949, it was possible to reason further that America might be willing to negotiate a settlement with Japan short of total victory. Considering the unwillingness of America to commit the requisite force to Asia prior to 1941, this argument had rationality if not accuracy. He saw that America's primary interest was in the European theater, and he gambled perhaps that war-weariness would deter America from waging the savage battles necessary to drive Japan back from its perimeter fortifications throughout the Pacific. Laurel and others with him knew little of MacArthur's strategy of island-hopping, and they knew nothing of the atomic bomb. Unfortunately for him, he also misjudged the American response to war and the irrational attraction of total victory for most Americans.

If his construct had been accurate, however, it was not an unwarrantable further assumption to foresee some sort of negotiated settlement of the Philippine question. Since the Tydings-McDuffie Act had originally proposed a treaty guaranteeing Philippine neutrality after independence, the idea had been discussed periodically. Quezon's Corregidor plan to resurrect this scheme was only one example of the currency of this idea. If such a plan were resurrected, Laurel, as president of an already "independent" republic, would be in a strong bargaining position with the returning Commonwealth government-in-exile, which, of necessity, would have to make some sort of settlement. This compromise solution seems to have appealed to him as late as October 1944, when he noted that "'war serves as a catalyzer,' speeding up transformations in social and political life which under peace-time conditions may require years, or even generations to carry out." Pointing out the "transitory character" of his government, he noted that the war would have to end some day. "Born out of a war," he concluded, "the Republic may have to effect further radical adjustments to the shape of things to be, following this world-wide upheaval."[25] While events unfolded very differently, Laurel seems to have reasoned that he could alter materially any postwar Philippine society.

Laurel's prewar career had been somewhat circumscribed, despite his widely recognized brilliance and administrative ability. He first came to public attention in 1909 when at the age of eighteen he stabbed a man in a fight over a girl. Convicted of "frustrated murder" in the Court of First Instance, he defended himself successfully before the Supreme Court, where, on March 15, 1912, his action was labeled as legitimate self-defense.[26] This episode, like the similar self-defense of Ferdinand Marcos in later years, helped his career by marking him as a brilliant young man. In the following years he drove himself hard to achieve a superb record, first in Manila and later at Yale. By 1923, when he became secretary of the Interior at only thirty-two, he was already a leader of the new elite.

His rapid rise was abruptly halted when he became entangled in a fight with Governor General Leonard Wood. The conflict turned on Wood's refusal to heed Laurel's accusations against an American police officer named Conley, against whom charges of malfeasance were brought. Laurel led a cabinet revolt on this issue, but it failed. The Cabinet, which had resigned en masse to support Laurel, gradually drifted back into office sans Laurel, who never regained his position at the vanguard of the oligarchy. Laurel was considered to have been "very bitter" as he "saw many men, undoubtedly inferior to him in intelligence, occupying the limelight as leaders of the Filipino people." He felt that he had been sacrificed to the ambitions of others who were willing to freeze him from power for firm opposition to the Americans in contrast to the compromise of the others.[27] This experience, coupled with allegedly unhappy years at Yale, where he felt slighted and mistreated, generated frustrations which became exposed during the war. Laurel saw little prospect of ever achieving the presidency until the war, and the power-vacuum created during the occupation opened opportunities for ambitions all but abandoned. Roxas' decision not to accept the Japanese offer of the presidency gave Laurel his chance to live in Malacañan Palace.

Laurel was receptive to the Japanese request to serve. Patriotism and ambition, ideological belief and pragmatic possibilities, heroism and cowardice all merged in his decision.[28] The Japanese, ignorant of his motivation, were delighted they had managed to find someone of Laurel's stature and brilliance to lead the nation to independence. To them the reason for his acceptance was less important than the fact of it. The Japanese quickly organized a Preparatory Commission for Philippine Independence, the PCPI, and appointed Laurel as president of it.[29] While six standing committees were appointed to write the new constitution, real power was vested in the Committee on Drafting, of which Laurel was also chairman.

On July 2, 1943, Colonel Utsunomiya, chief of the Political

Affairs Section of the Military Administration, called on Laurel, who was still in the hospital recuperating, and the other members of the PCPI were summoned to his bedside. Utsunomiya, in a report to Tokyo, reported that both sides agreed to retain "at least superficially" the format of the Commonwealth constitution. He conceded to the Filipino request that the constitution be redrawn not later than one year after the end of the war, because anything which would encourage Filipino support without inhibiting primary Japanese goals was desirable. Noting Filipino anxiety that the draft of the constitution not be presented as a *fait accompli* by the Military Administration, Utsunomiya encouraged the Filipinos to draft a new and improved constitution. Laurel, who was almost the exclusive spokesman for the Filipinos, accepted this opportunity.[30]

The formation of the PCPI was the sign the propagandists were waiting for. Frequent free newspaper extras were distributed, and there were many radio specials, all designed to whip up enthusiasm among the people. Great publicity was given to a second visit by Tojo, Major General Sato Kenryo, superintendent general of Military Administration in Tokyo, and Greater East Asia Vice Minister Yamamoto Kumaichi. The unpublicized purpose of the visit was to allow Tojo an opportunity to meet Laurel and to see if Tojo approved the selection of him by the local officials. Tojo's on-the-spot approval led to an increased effort to prepare the new government as soon as possible, certainly by the end of 1943.

The discussions over the character of the new constitution increased in intensity after Tojo's visit. Utsunomiya and Laurel met frequently to discuss the draft. The Japanese wanted to simplify the legislative process and to be able to give "internal guidance" from time to time. Laurel in turn wanted to alter the Commonwealth constitution to centralize power, and therefore, he agreed to a weakening of the legislative branch. He argued that the best way to prove to the people that the new constitution was not a puppet document was to make the presidency a real office.[31] The mutually acceptable compromise produced a document which superficially appeared to be a replica of the Commonwealth constitution, while in reality it destroyed the concept of checks and balances.[32] The process of selecting the president, for example, was altered from a direct vote of the electorate to an indirect vote of an appointed legislature. The office of the vice-president was abolished. The power of the presidency was made virtually unassailable in its nearly absolute veto and in its power to declare war. Provincial governors became appointed officials of the president rather than elected officials of the people, thus creating a reciprocal relationship of enormous power for the president. The Supreme Court lost its right to invoke judicial review, and legislative control over appropriations was removed. The Commonwealth constitution's "Declaration of Human Rights" was altered to become the "Duties and Rights of the Citizen," in which some prewar guarantees were circumscribed or abolished outright. "The orientation of the new government under the Republic is one of centralized control for service to the people regardless of any obstacle," said Laurel. "Without political consolidation we cannot hope to accomplish the desired integration of our political, economic, and social life."[33]

This new constitution was promulgated on September 4, 1943, when the twenty members of the PCPI signed it publicly on the balcony of the Metropolitan Water Works building in Manila. The five-minute ceremony was followed by a "general popular assembly," summoned to ratify the work of the leadership. The membership of the assembly was drawn from the Kalibapi organization. It approved the new constitution unanimously and then adjourned within two days. Laurel was heralded as the "man of the hour"; the constitution was praised as a Filipino-inspired document. The Military Administration asserted that it planned to step aside with independence, and Director General Wachi, who had enigmatically commented that "Japan will hold the position of a protector, . . . but the Philippines will not be a protectorate," attempted to publicize Japanese sincerity in promising to yield power.[34] The Japanese, however, merely attempted to make their channel of control more subtle. On September 8 the South Seas Bureau of the East Asia Ministry filed a plan urging the appointment of Japanese "consultants" to every agency of the Philippine government.[35]

As part of this Japanese plan to seem to be withdrawing, the Military Administration had Vargas issue Executive Order No. 198, which provided for the "submission of the Constitution of the Republic of the Philippines to the Filipino people for ratification or rejection."[36] On September 9 his Executive Order No. 201 provided "for the election of delegates to the national assembly. . . ."[37] Both orders were actually an elaborate ruse designed to make it appear as if the new government were receiving a national mandate. The selection of a national assembly was based on Japanese approval rather than on election. Forty-six provincial governors and eight mayors of chartered cities were automatically appointed to this chamber. Another fifty-four were, in theory, chosen by the local Kalibapi organizations, but, in reality, they were selected from

Manila. This carefully screened body was the only group of Filipinos allowed to pass judgment on the constitution and on Laurel for the presidency.

Among the fifty-four selected Kalibapi delegates, nine were prewar senators, eighteen were congressmen, and six were former governors. Of the fifty-four governors and mayors already serving under the Vargas commission, nineteen had been legislators in the prewar era. Virtually all twenty of the PCPI had ranking positions in the Commonwealth government, as did the other cabinet officers of the Vargas Commission, who did not serve on the PCPI. The result, as the Japanese hoped, was that the new assembly appeared as a continuation of the Commonwealth regime. It was actually claimed to be a marked improvement, since it allowed a formation of a government of all the talents without any of the waste of the democratic process. The *Tribune* rhapsodized that the new "one-party regime" was "peaceful, inexpensive, [and] efficient. By and large, the new system can be seen to produce better results than the old one did. And it does not lend itself easily to corruption, unnecessary feuds, noisy bickerings of no value, and other evils of the old system."[38]

Vargas, shunted to the side, was requested to nominate Laurel for a show of solidarity. In front of the assembly he said, "the leadership of our people and the presidency of the Republic should be entrusted to the best available Filipino under the prevailing circumstances. That Filipino, in my sincere belief, is Dr. Jose P. Laurel."[39] The following day the assembly elected Laurel to the presidency and Aquino to the speakership by unanimous votes. Laurel was hailed as "the only Filipino . . . who can make a success of independence."[40] An Inauguration Committee was appointed with Vargas as chairman, Roxas as vice-chairman, and with Alunan, Recto, Paredes, Aquino, Yulo and others as members.

Frenetic activity followed Laurel's formal selection. By September 30 Laurel had arrived in Tokyo accompanied by Aquino and Vargas. This trip, which received enormous publicity throughout the Japanese-controlled areas of Asia, was demanded by Tokyo to permit Tojo to instruct Laurel on what he wanted. Behind the ceremonial banquets and Imperial audiences at which decorations were bestowed on Laurel and the others, Tojo informed the Filipino leadership that he expected a declaration of war against the United States. Laurel, rather naively, recalled that this request caught him off guard. He "did not expect this instruction" and was "not prepared to meet it on the spot." After reciting the "Pater Noster" silently, he said "politely" that he "could not comply with the request." He admitted that he had "never been a popular leader, the three powerful leaders of the country being Messrs. Quezon, Osmeña and Roxas," and that he "would be a leader without any following because the Filipinos were opposed to such a step. . . ."[41] The Japanese yielded at the time because they did not want to abort the possibility of success by heavy-handedness. However, they maintained constant pressure on Laurel to declare war, finally persuading him to agree.

The date of independence was set for October 14, 1943. The precipitate action of the Japanese was based on their desire to fulfill the promised offer of independence within the year and their need to bolster the sagging morale of both the Japanese and the conquered peoples throughout the Sphere. Independence was the Japanese answer to the promises of the Anglo-American Atlantic Charter. Consequently, with as much fanfare as possible, they inaugurated the new regime before a reputed half-million Filipinos. On the morning of October 14, the Military Administration legally proclaimed its own dissolution, and in front of such dignitaries as Diet Speaker Okada Tadahiko, Marquis Sasaki Yukitada, Major General Arisue Seizo, and the local Japanese officialdom, Laurel was sworn into office as president of the Republic of the Philippines.

Laurel's intention to overhaul Philippine society and its standards by taking advantage of the occupation was clearly expressed in his inaugural address. Noting the need for "awakening the moral consciousness" of the nation, he called for "a new type of citizen who would be ready and willing to subordinate himself to the larger and more vital interests of the State." He stressed that the new constitution guaranteed each citizen a "*modicum* of personal liberty essential to his enjoyment of relative contentment and happiness. But of more transcendent importance than his privileges, are the duties which the individual owes to the State." Laurel stressed that obligations had precedence over rights, "in consonance with the fundamental idea that man does not live for himself and his family alone but also for the State and humanity at large." He defined the new citizen as one "who knows his rights as well as his duties, and knowing them, will discharge his duties even to the extent of sacrificing his rights."[42] The comment of the local pundits on the inauguration, punning on the names of Aquino, Duran, and Laurel, was "Aqui no Duran Laureles."

The Japanese government in Tokyo "recognized" the new republic at seven that evening. The newly appointed ambassador,

Murata Shozo, donated a large quantity of cotton, rice, and quinine as a gift of the Japanese people.[43] Laurel's first act as president was an appeal for recognition by the other nations of the world.[44] The Axis powers of Germany, Italy, Bulgaria, Croatia, and Hungary, as well as Thailand, Burma, Manchukuo, China (Nanking), and Spain (conditionally), all moved to follow Japan's lead. The appeal had been directed primarily at America in the hope of embarrassing Roosevelt and distressing Quezon. Laurel had asserted that Philippine independence gave "irrefutable proof" that Japan did not want to subjugate the Philippines. He urged America "to recognize and respect our independence" in order to prevent greater suffering and destruction. He asked "America to prove to the entire world the sincerity of her protestations of friendship toward us by not placing obstacles on the path of the new Republic. All we ask is that we be allowed to work out our own salvation in our own way."[45]

This appeal had its desired effect. Quezon had been chafing in Washington about the Japanese promise for independence. On January 25, 1943, some nine months earlier, Quezon had drafted but did not send a memorandum to Roosevelt in which he asked for immediate independence from the United States, in order that America could avoid the Japanese propaganda charge of "plagiarizing the magnificent gesture of the Japanese." On September 8 Quezon did appeal to Roosevelt to beat the Japanese offer despite the possible charge from Manila of aping.[46] Quezon also got his close friend, Millard Tydings, to introduce an independence bill in Congress to counter the possible effect of the Japanese propaganda offensive. The *New York Times* editorially commented that this Quezon plan was "of no particular dignity," and Henry Stimson sagely got Quezon and Tydings to modify their initial request for immediate independence.[47] The Laurel appeal for recognition reopened the wounds suffered on Corregidor, and prompted Roosevelt to respond sharply in order to minimize Quezon's unhappiness.

Roosevelt, broadcasting by radio to both America and the Philippines, attacked the "puppet government" for its "hypocritical appeal for American sympathy which was made in fraud and deceit and was designed to confuse and mislead the Filipino people." Roosevelt stressed that the only Philippine government was that of the Commonwealth and that America would never consider any act of the Laurel republic as lawful or binding. He again promised "all the resources of the United States . . . to drive the treacherous Japanese from the Philippine Islands, to restore as quickly as possible orderly and free democratic processes of government in the

Islands, and to establish there a truly independent Philippine nation."[48]

In his speech Roosevelt had attacked Laurel for signing "a military alliance with Japan" after his inauguration. This treaty was the price the Japanese extracted for agreeing not to demand an immediate declaration of war against the United States from Laurel. The treaty guaranteed the rights and privileges which the Japanese wanted. It demanded cooperation from the Laurel government, a blanket approval for the retention of all Japanese military facilities, continued control of the transportation facilities, mining rights, the waterfront, and legal permission to move Japanese troops freely on Philippine soil. The Japanese got permission to retain control of the news media and government corporations, though these concessions were not included specifically in the treaty.[49] Most importantly, the Japanese persuaded Laurel to agree that "the High Contracting Parties shall closely cooperate on matters political, economic, and military for the successful prosecution of the war of Greater East Asia." The principle modality was to be that the "Philippines will afford all kinds of facilities for the military actions to be undertaken by Japan; [they] . . . will closely cooperate with each other to safeguard the territorial integrity and independence of the Philippines."[50]

While the political and military provisions were most important in the long term, economic questions were most pressing in the short term for both the Japanese and for Laurel. The Japanese had arrived in 1941 with high economic expectations, since the archipelago was naturally fertile. While their prewar economic planners had focused on Indonesia and Malaya, they clearly hoped that possession of the Philippines would be an economic boon. Unfortunately, however, they discovered that the lopsided development of the sugar industry by the Americans distorted beyond profitable use the nucleus of prewar Philippine wealth. Of the population 12 percent was involved in some way in the sugar trade, and sugar, with copra, dominated every aspect of the archipelago's economic system. The total prewar investment was about 600,000,000 pesos.[51] The Japanese, though, had no real use for this giant sugar industry; they were supplied from their Taiwan colony.

This basic reality was of profound importance to the whole occupation, since their lack of interest in this commercial crop led immediately to a collapse in production and a resultant dissolution of the nation's most vital prop. Sugar production slipped so drastically that by the end of the war sugar sold at prohibitive black market prices. Japanese planners, instead, hoped to utilize the former sugar land to develop vitally needed fibers for Japanese mills. The loss of the American and Indian cotton markets, which had supplied Japan before the war, hurt the Japanese economy badly, and it was the scheme of the planners that they could fulfill the old Spanish dream of a large commercial cotton industry in the Philippines. The new crop was to spring up through the stubble of the cane fields.

This project, directed by Murata and his most able aides, carried top priority. A five-year plan had been drawn late in 1942, in which it was estimated that a total of 1,500,000 piculs of ginned cotton could be grown on 450,000 hectares of land.[52] Sixteen cotton districts were designated—nine in Luzon, four in Negros, one in Panay, and two in Mindanao—and nine major companies were assigned to develop them. A Philippine Cotton Association was formed to regulate and to coordinate the plans.[53] On paper it looked feasible, and as a construct it held promise. In reality it was a disaster, failing as it did to aid the Japanese war effort and producing as it did untold hardships on the Filipinos.

The necessary stability was lacking, as were the required time, labor, and capital. The Japanese, despite their famed technological skill, had failed to give sufficient prior attention to the development of higher yield seeds, especially fertile in the Philippine climate and in soil which had grown sugar for years. Neither hybrid seeds nor pest control were developed, and the necessary machinery did not exist. The war further compounded these problems. During the fighting, the fields had been burned and the work animals killed. Even in the areas spared actual bloodshed, the dislocation had been severe, and the guerrilla movement increased dislocation, as it appealed to the Filipinos not to help the Japanese.[54]

Unlike Korea, Taiwan, and Manchuria, which had all been integrated relatively slowly and peacefully into the empire, the Philippines had to be absorbed under adverse and abnormal circumstances. Economic planning followed rather than preceded military action. Local officials improvised by necessity.[55] The effort to integrate the Philippines was only a small part of the pressure on the Japanese throughout Asia. Even if Japan had been able to devote all her physical resources to this process, she probably would have found her economic base too small for the undertaking; committed as she was to achieving this while waging a total war across all of Asia, her chances of success were infinitesimal. Although Japan started the war with the world's third largest maritime fleet of six million tons, she lost over five million tons of that fleet within three years.[56] The collapse of this transportation in itself aborted any real possibility of producing a viable, interlocking, economic sphere. Enforced isolation actually paralyzed the several Southeast Asian economies, since the necessary flow of commercial crops in exchange for industrial produce dried up.

The weakness of the Philippine economy was further exacerbated by tensions within the Japanese occupying forces. Although the essence of the Sphere concept was that the money market, finance, and trade "should be based on the spirit of 'Hakko Ichiu' [the spirit of universal brotherhood]," the army policy was in practice just the opposite. Instead of using the funds of the "sphere collectively and effectively," the army command used them to finance the war effort.[57] On January 10, 1942, the army had authorized a military peso declared equal to the Commonwealth peso, which along with the use of the yen was banned in the Philippines.[58] The army had also reaped an enormous short-term gain in seized bullion, dollars, and pounds, which it had remitted to Tokyo. Philippine fiscal institutions were crippled, isolated, and denied any hard currency with which to trade for the support of the Philippine economy.

Fiscal collapse multiplied the dislocation caused by the termination of the sugar market. The Japanese-sponsored peso, devoid of bullion support, soon sold under its par value. A thriving black market developed in Commonwealth pesos, which commanded a high premium throughout the war. The Japanese peso acquired the Filipino nickname of "Mickey Mouse" money, and the Japanese army, over the sharp protest of the civilian authorities, increased the output of the presses. On July 18, 1943, for example, the army promulgated Proclamation (kojuki) No. 8, announcing an additional series of one, five, and ten-peso notes to augment those already in circulation.[59] It has been estimated that between 6,623,000,000 and 11,148,000,000 pesos were issued by the Japanese during the occupation.[60] The actual amounts printed will never be known, however, since field commanders had their own presses. The resultant inflation did not cost the Japanese army hardship because it used coercion to purchase supplies at a fixed price. The effect of this policy on the Filipinos, however, was catastrophic.

The efforts of the civilian administrators were nugatory. Their attempt to generate economic activity failed despite their flurry of activity. They created a Manila Banker's Clearing House, opened a Southern Regions Development Bank (Nanpo Kaihatsu Kinko), and supported Philippine credit institutions. However, even with inflation, these institutions did only a fractional amount of their prewar business. The Philippine Agricultural and Industrial Bank, which had an important role as a stimulus in the prewar era, had little to do during the war.[61] New industrial development dwindled to almost nothing. In 1943 the total new aggregate capital investment was 16,440,000 pesos in spite of inflation, and the net gain to employment was only 10,491 jobs.[62] Existing production also lagged as lack of parts and materiel in addition to Japanese military requisitioning crippled activity.

The Japanese government was unable to send sufficient supervisory personnel to fill the technical and managerial gap created by the internment of American and English businessmen. The National Power Corporation, for example, became a part of the Taiwan Electrical Power Corporation (Taiwan Denryoku Kakushiki Kaisha), but it was constantly deficient in trained manpower. The local Japanese business community was called upon to fill the gap through the technique of the "association," in which the few properly trained officials attempted to give direction to others. The army retained control of the monopolies in prime commodities: salt, tobacco, soap, paper, cotton, lard, and matches.[63] None of these measures proved to be successful, and the economy soon became comatose.

The proportions of this problem required the prime attention of the Filipino leadership, which was caught in an intolerable squeeze. Government revenue declined to a fraction of its prewar levels, severely inhibiting governmental action.[64] Tax delinquency, guerrilla opposition, and disappearance of customs revenue all contributed to the economic decline. Government salaries were drastically cut, despite the inflation, as the bureaucracy was trimmed.[65] More than fifty offices were closed, and others were reduced. The Bureau of Census and Statistics was cut from a prewar size of 373 men to 137 employees; the National Development Corporation, which had had 196 employees earning 263,880 pesos in December 1941, was reduced to 72 employees earning only 86,765 pesos by March 1943.

The chronic underemployment which had existed in the Philippines before the war was greatly aggravated by the occupation. Manila was swollen with unemployed, and the contraction of the government service often cut off the one source of revenue for extended families. Despite government palliatives, a hungry and hostile unemployed group, which the *Tribune* admitted to be about one-fourth of the city population and was probably much more, presented one of the great challenges to the Filipino leadership.[66] The severe reduction in government spending also weakened the strength of the public sector of the economy, on which the urban, Westernized part of the nation depended for its existence. While the Japanese civilian authorities saw that not only the concept of the Sphere but also the viability of the Filipino government was jeopardized by this economic collapse, the field command was only mildly concerned about the economic debacle.

The black market became the only market, as food grew increasingly scarce.[67] Most Filipinos, especially the urban dwellers, discovered that their daily business was the struggle for physical survival. For the few who were in a position to sell to the Japanese or to make money on the black market, the great effort was to hide the profits and hedge against inflation. The government urged the people to "develop the technique of social pressure, the virtue of self-help, and of collective action," but eventually Laurel had to make bribery, black-marketeering in food, and "racketeering" crimes punishable by death.[68] Laurel went even further, establishing by Ordinance No. 7 special courts and prosecutors to handle such crimes. Draconian in nature, this ordinance abolished habeas corpus and permitted these drum courts to "impose a longer term of imprisonment, or imprisonment for life or death where not already fixed by law, taking into consideration the nature and gravity of the offense, the perversity of the means employed by the accused, and the effect on the social and economic life of the people as a result of the commission of the crime."[69] A punitive deterrent like this had only very limited success.[70]

The prime demand on the Laurel government, therefore, was to stave off economic chaos by meeting the most pressing problem, that of threatened starvation. The Philippines, which had been a chronic importer of rice in the prewar era, in part because of the distortions of the sugar industry, had entered the war with a serious food shortage. A drought in 1940 and a series of floods in 1941 had damaged the crop reserves, requiring the purchase of about 450,000 bushels from Burma in 1941. The destruction caused during the Japanese invasion, coupled with the demands made by the two armies, which requisitioned all the grain available, created an acute crisis. The cultivator's lack of confidence in the Japanese peso aggravated the problem, since many refused to allow their crop to come to market, preferring instead the more risky but profitable black market. The guerrillas also limited the supply or diverted a part of it for their support.

As early as May 14, 1942, just one week after the fighting

ceased on Corregidor, Vargas had issued Executive Order No. 40, "initiating a national campaign for the cultivation of idle lands to produce food crops."[71] Rice rationing soon followed; the National Rice and Corn Administration (NARIC) and the neighborhood organization (DANAS) were jointly utilized to improve distribution. A Foodstuff Control Association was created to purchase food entering Manila and distribute it at fixed costs, while a City Farm Credit Corporation was created to cultivate about 10,000 fallow hectares around the city.[72] Publicity was given to the *horai* strain of rice grown so successfully by the Japanese on Taiwan.

However, while both Filipino and Japanese civilian officials were struggling to ease the crisis, the Japanese field command was aggravating it. As the Japanese merchant marine grew weaker, the occupation forces became increasingly dependent on Filipino production of cereals. Despite Japanese disclaimers to the contrary, Philippine rice was shipped to the front by the army whenever the slightest surplus could be gathered. Of necessity the army commanders had to become self-sufficient, viewing an adequate grain supply as a military necessity.[73] The army either seized the crop outright, despite protests of the local farmers, or paid for it in newly minted pesos, which never reflected true market value. Floods in 1943 tightened the supply even further.

By the time Laurel became president, the domestic economic situation was critical. He knew that if he could not alleviate the situation and improve the living conditions of the people, any other reforms he might want to implement would be futile. His government had to confront the food shortage or abandon any hope of ever gaining popular support. Right after his inaugural he attempted to strengthen NARIC by authorizing it to pay a price which reflected more accurately the real value of the crop. At the same time he strengthened its punitive powers, threatening Filipinos who refused to comply with a 10,000 peso fine or ten years in jail. He also attempted to increase production, and to reorganize more effectively the bureaucratic apparatus, by creating a new super agency of cabinet rank, the Food Administration.[74] When these reforms did not work, Laurel abolished NARIC because it had lost the confidence of the people, and he created BIBA, an organization almost identical in everything but name.[75]

Inextricably intertwined with the economic crisis was the confrontation between the Laurel republic and the guerrillas. At first Laurel attempted to woo the guerrilla movement into supporting the new regime. Four days after his inaugural, he proposed amnesty legislation, which carried through the assembly by unanimous vote. It offered "full and complete pardon to all those citizens" who were "responsible for the crimes and offenses of sedition, illicit association, engaging in guerrilla activity, . . . spreading false rumors, and for all crimes and offenses political in nature."[76] An amnesty board of Commonwealth generals was appointed to grant pardons within a sixty-day period. The critical provision, however, was that the guerrilla swear allegiance to the new government by recognizing "the supreme authority of the Republic" and by maintaining "true faith and allegiance." The former guerrilla had to swear to defend the new constitution and to obey all its laws "as a law-abiding citizen," promising to perform this obligation "without any mental reservation or purpose of evasion."[77]

Laurel's attempt at accommodation was a demand that the guerrilla renounce his allegiance to the Commonwealth government, to Quezon, to MacArthur, and to America and to accept as valid Laurel's claim that he now spoke for the only legal and independent government of the Philippines. While his government claimed that enormous numbers of guerrillas accepted this condition and signed the amnesty, Laurel encouraged a further polarization of Filipino allegiance by challenging the guerrilla movement directly. Laurel himself believed that it was folly to battle the Japanese, since they wielded so much power. He felt that whoever believed that the Filipinos could drive the Japanese away "by *guerrilla* warfare must be either a fool or a renegade."[78] He saw the guerrilla movement as harming rather than helping the nation. "However strong they might become in numbers and in arms," he wrote, "they cannot possibly influence the outcome of this war one way or another. In these days of mechanized warfare, the forces that are pitted against each other are, ultimately, those of industrial production and resources." Laurel next indicated the very crux of his thinking. "To be sure," he continued, "it is not easy for a self-respecting man to change convictions overnight even after objective realities have rendered such convictions irrelevant," but he felt that the new symbols of the constitution and the "hoisted flag" made this the only reasonable course.[79] Peace, order, compliance, and allegiance were not only essentials to the success of his new government, but they were also the ingredients which prevented society from collapse and anarchy. Since respect for law prevented chaos, it was a force of vital importance in preserving the nation during military occupation.

The majority of the nation did not share this valuation with

Laurel. The rational pragmatism with which he viewed Japanese force was irrelevant for others whose emotive response and web of allegiance dictated that the struggle be continued. The guerrilla activists and their passive supporters throughout the archipelago were a disparate group, differing on many things except the basic unifying issue of allegiance. The Hukbalahap, which became one of the most successful guerrilla operations throughout the country, was a radical peasant movement in central Luzon with a political and social outlook sharply different from other guerrilla units led by Filipinos of a nonradical persuasion.

Men joined the guerrilla movement for a complex of reasons. Motivation was both noble and base, and often these two strains were combined. Men who were unemployed and without hope of employment joined more readily; severe economic dislocation, starvation, and misery abetted participation. Avarice and greed were also motives for action. Some guerrillas were really bandits who plundered for themselves under the guise of guerrilla membership. It is important to notice that guerrilla participation was frequently triggered by local political rivalries, in which sometimes each faction struggled to outdo the other in guerrilla activity or in which sometimes one faction joined the guerrillas because the traditional rival family at the local level cooperated with the Japanese and with the central Manila government. Membership in guerrilla movements permitted men to settle old grudges and feuds. Violence could be cloaked under the mantle of patriotism and justified accordingly. Participation could take on an ideological tone, as it did in the Hukbalahap, who opposed not only the Japanese but the landlord as well. Thus, the guerrilla movement was a means of social conflict in which the peasant was able to attack the landlord when he was most vulnerable. The landlord was isolated from his traditional means of control, impoverished by the collapse of normal agriculture, and frequently labeled with the pejorative "collaborator." The Hukbalahap used the opportunity of the war to assume effective control of the central provinces of Luzon, instituting agrarian reforms and destroying as completely as possible the prewar structure of the community.

Despite this wide range of motivation, however, the common thread of allegiance to Quezon and to MacArthur, to the Commonwealth and to America never disappeared. Every guerrilla unit shared the excitement of MacArthur's promised return. Redemption was the dream which compelled men to keep going despite the savage reprisals of Japanese armed might. Most units acceded to the

short-wave supervision of MacArthur's command, followed his instructions, complied with his requests, coordinated, as instructed,
with neighboring units, and participated as a part of a total system
stretching throughout the archipelago. Guerrilla control of an area
was proportional to the size and militancy of the nearest Japanese
garrison. It was a military objective of each guerrilla unit to deny to
the Japanese as much of the crop as possible, to harass Japanese
concentrations, and to weaken Japanese morale in any feasible
manner.

The guerrilla challenge was met by the field commanders with
severity as the military situation turned against Japan. As a reconquest attempt by the Americans became a real possibility, the combat officers saw their first obligation as preparing their troops to
fight. Over the staunch opposition of such civilian advisers as Ambassador Murata, the army turned increasingly ruthless by using
indiscriminate retaliatory destruction for every guerrilla offense. For
every Japanese ambushed the policy was usually to execute at random ten Filipinos. The Japanese in Manila complained that such a
policy widened the gulf between the Japanese and Filipinos and
negated their efforts at friendship, but, of course, the officials in
Manila were not the men being ambushed. The general staff increasingly ignored the political impact of their operations.[80]

The Japanese lacked sufficient troops to suppress such widespread resistance. Their concept of counterinsurgency was still
rudimentary, and the guerrilla movement was really a prototype of a
national liberation front. The plan implemented was piecemeal
saturation of a particular area by a large number of troops, who
attempted to trap and eradicate the hard core of guerrilla resistance.
It rarely worked, since the guerrillas usually were able to melt into
the population. Despite offers of bribes and rewards, few Filipinos
ever revealed the information necessary for the capture of the key
people.

To gain peace and order the Japanese decided to increase their
use of the Philippine Constabulary. Laurel was pressed to lend his
prestige toward a strengthening of this possible second tier of defense for the Japanese. He was well aware of the unpopularity of
using Filipino troops against other Filipinos, but he yielded to these
Japanese demands, in part because he felt he had no choice and in
part because of the blatant challenge the guerrilla movement leveled
at his regime. In early November 1943 he increased the size of the
Constabulary to 40,000, establishing regional training schools to
improve the quality of the service. He also gave General Francisco

the rank of vice-minister of the Interior in charge of the Constabulary.[81] On December 23, 1943, he issued Executive Order No. 23, which both increased the size of the Constabulary and eased the requirements for membership. Former officers in the Philippine army or Commonwealth Constabulary were to be given immediate commissions in order effectively to "accelerate the pacification campaign."[82] The propaganda media were directed to dramatize the new Constabulary. The *Tribune,* for example, in showing a picture of a trainee getting "battle training," commented in the caption that the trainees were "shown undergoing training on how to advance toward an enemy position."[83] While the enemy was never defined, the meaning was clear.

On February 4, 1944, Laurel appointed two commissioners to direct the pacification drive in the southern part of the country. Both Paulino Gullas in the Visayas and Paulino Santos in Mindanao were to exercise general supervision and administrative control of the provinces, cities, and municipalities in their respective areas as quasi-military administrators.[84] In April Laurel created the Order of Tirad Pass for Constabulary personnel who showed high gallantry. The Order, named after the famous military defense of the Insurrectionaries against the Americans, was a further attempt to strengthen the pride of the service. While all but one of the awards were posthumous, the government made it widely known that it was providing for the families of the fallen. On July 14, 1944, Laurel issued Proclamation No. 20, which threatened the severest punishment to guerrillas who destroyed any Japanese military facilities.[85]

In spite of these and other similar efforts, the Constabulary was never an effective force. The Japanese were loath to arm these men, since they feared, with good reason, that the arms supplied would slip into the hands of the guerrilla units. The Constabulary usually felt close affinity for the guerillas, and even in those areas where local tensions pitted one faction as the guerrillas and another as the Constabulary, the Constabulary usually tried to do as little as possible. There were tacit understandings that the Constabulary would not take patrols into the guerrilla areas and would, in turn, never be ambushed by the guerrillas. Constabulary troops were always slipping into the ranks of the guerrillas, and few were willing to die in battle or in front of a postwar firing squad.

The Constabulary's lack of activity was reflected throughout the bureaucratic structure of the Manila government. Dissatisfaction, inflation, underemployment, guerrilla sympathies, and anti-Japanese sentiments all combined to undermine government efficiency. Almost alone, Laurel attempted to keep the wheels turning. With incredible energy he plunged into activity, so that by January 1944 he had assumed executive responsibility for the key portfolios of the Interior (Home), Economic, and Education departments. As a result he directly controlled the Executive Bureau, the Bureau of General Auditing, the Civil Service Board of Examiners, the Bureau of Information, and the Bureau of Printing in his capacity as president. As secretary of the Interior, he had direct authority for the provincial, municipal, and local administrations, the Constabulary, the Board of Review, and the Bureau of Religious Affairs. As administrator of other agencies he personally controlled the Bureau of Commerce and Industry, the Food Administration, the government-owned corporations, the government purchasing agency, the Bureau of Census and Statistics, the Bureau of Public Instruction, the University of the Philippines, the Bureau of Private Education, Physical Education, Oriental Culture, the National Library, and the National Language Institute.[86]

Laurel was also president of the Kalibapi, which he tried to strengthen with the Junior Kalibapi, the Woman's Auxiliary, the New Leader's Institute, and the Labor Institute. By the spring of 1944 the government claimed 1,500,000 members. On May 1 Laurel issued Ordinance No. 17, which reorganized the Kalibapi from a "service organization" into a "nonpartisan political organization." The new aim was to "uphold, maintain, defend, and protect the Republic of the Philippines at all times."[87] Speaking of this reorganization, Aquino perhaps reflected Laurel's motivation when he said that "the Philippines is still too weak to guarantee that the Americans would not take back these Islands, and as Japan has made great sacrifices to drive the Americans away, she naturally feels she must defend the Philippines at all cost and thus perpetuate the Republic implanted here."[88] The Kalibapi became increasingly a centralized authoritarian party with paramilitary potential.

In every aspect of activity the Laurel regime was never free from the reality that American military momentum was increasing in the Pacific and that the Japanese were preparing for a defense of the archipelago to protect the Japanese home islands from invasion. Physical famine, guerrilla opposition, bureaucratic inertia, and Japanese brutality all reflected this fact. Early in 1944 Laurel and the Japanese got the assembly to pass Bill 186 [Act 39], which declared a "state of emergency" similar to that which Quezon had got before the war and which authorized the "President of the Republic of the Philippines to promulgate rules and regulations to safeguard the safety, health and tranquility of the inhabitants of the Philippines."[89] Based on Article three, section thirteen, of the new constitution, the act granted Laurel a further increase in executive power.

The deteriorating situation raised the question of conscription, despite frequent Japanese disclaimers that they did not need or want any Filipino troops. General Wachi had said in mid-1943, for example, that "with her 100,000,000 people as a potential source of manpower and with the nation solidly behind the prosecution of the war to a successful end, Japan need not rely on the countries under her influence in Greater East Asia for men to crush the Anglo-American combination. . . ."[90] Rumors were rife, however, and people were uncertain about the disclaimers. Since Laurel had promised only a year earlier that the Filipinos would run a government free from "the Japanese Military police, without military garrisons, without the intervention of any foreign government," people were not convinced when he promised that his government would "render every aid and assistance to the Imperial Japanese government short of conscription of Filipino manhood for active military service."[91]

The anxiety was increased when on September 21, 1944, the first American air raid over Manila forced Laurel to the brink of war. The next day he declared martial law and created, by Proclamation No. 29, nine military districts, each with a governor who would "suppress treason, sedition, disorder and violence."[92] The Japanese, it will be recalled, had yielded to Laurel's plea during his Tokyo visit to avoid a declaration of war and had decided to wait for "a convenient time after independence" to get the declaration.[93] They now felt that the time had come.

On September 22, 1944, Laurel issued Proclamation No. 30, the most critical document of his administration. He began it by stressing the historic quest of the Filipinos for independence, which, he claimed, had been attained finally in 1943. He noted that he had appealed to the nations of the world for amity and had made a special request to the United States. "Notwithstanding this appeal," he continued, "the United States of America and Great Britain have attacked from the air certain parts of the Philippines thereby violating the territorial integrity of the Republic, and causing death, injury to its citizens and destruction or damage to their property." He declared that "every self-respecting sovereign state" is honor bound to protect its independence and integrity and recalled the pact of alliance with Japan. "Now, therefore, I, Jose P. Laurel, President of the Republic of the Philippines, do hereby proclaim that a state of war exists between the Republic of the Philippines and the United States of America and Great Britain, effective September 23, 1944, at ten o'clock in the morning." Laurel concluded by calling upon every Filipino "to show his unswerving loyalty and to give his support to the government" in order to unite the country.[94]

The proclamation was followed by a meeting of the provincial governors called by Teofilo Sison, who reminded them of their legal obligations to the republic. He stressed the provisions of the treason clause, Article 114 of the Revised Philippine Penal Code, and warned them to obey the instructions of the central government.[95] On November 14 Laurel promulgated Executive Order No. 100, in which the government required compulsory labor for "construction, reconstruction, repair of roads, bridges, and other public works including airfields, port works, and other military establishments."[96] Filipinos had first been pressed into manual labor for the aid of the Japanese military effort nine months earlier, when the government required one day a week from all able-bodied males and females between sixteen and sixty.[97] The *Tribune* had then noted, overoptimistically, that there were "more than 250,000 Filipino laborers now working on various military projects" to extend "full cooperation to the Japanese army and navy."[98] The degree of aid and comfort that these two labor decrees gave the Japanese is impossible to measure, but they indicate, both before the declaration and afterward, that the Japanese could get what they wanted from the Laurel regime.

While Laurel never committed Filipinos to fight openly against the return of the Americans, he did almost everything short of that. Probably more valuable to the Japanese than the labor gangs was the invisible support gained by the espousal or seeming espousal of their cause. At a time when every guerrilla unit was calling on Filipinos to arise and strike the Japanese, Laurel's government committed its prestige to the Japanese side. Laurel was unable or unwilling to prevent the Japanese from doing what they wanted. After the war he wrote that "a small country is a small country and a weak people is a weak people. We had no choice and everything depended on the result of the war."[99] The Japanese had the power to dominate Manila, even if they lacked the strength to suppress the guerrilla movement throughout the provinces. Laurel yielded upon demand because of his original gamble, in which he conceded that Japanese hegemony was the price to be paid for the opportunity to restructure those aspects of Philippine life over which he did have control as president. Having taken that original step, however, he discovered, perhaps with alarm, that the path that he was required to follow was more precipitously downward than he had anticipated initially. Probably only too late did he realize that it was impossible to keep his balance when the Japanese pushed him.

Laurel had taken the gamble because, it appears, he felt condescension for the will of the people. His model was the philosopher king, and he believed that "the whole history of government shows that public affairs would be better administered and the welfare of the people better subserved in the hands of a moral and intellectual aristocracy. The people cannot both be governors and governed at the same time; a statement affirming the contrary would be a contradiction in terms." Laurel, the oligarch, was convinced that "a good and efficient government, a benevolent government, may exist and continue indefinitely to function with admirable harmony, when men of superior moral and intellectual endowments are in control of the state."[100] He seems to have been guilty of intellectual arrogance. Because of his elitist views, he thought that he knew better than the people which values were worth protecting and which were not. His disregard for the anti-Japanese decision of the nation, however, was a costly mistake to have made. As his regime was the object of so much hostility, he was isolated from the people for whom he had such grandiose plans. To have succeeded in his gamble to rework the society while it was under the crisis of occupation, he would have had to divorce his government from the onus of collaboration. In failing to do so, he was trapped between a hostile guerrilla movement reflecting the will of the majority and an unsympathetic Japanese military occupation, which increasingly abused the people he was pledged to defend. His situation was intolerable, though perhaps predictable, and whatever he dreamed of accomplishing vanished elusively in the mirage of false expectations.

CHAPTER VI

Dual Government Returns

This is the way the world ends
This is the way the world ends
This is the way the world ends
Not with a bang but a whimper.
—T. S. Eliot

The United States paid dearly for its military weakness in the Pacific at the outbreak of the war. It was not until early May 1942, just when Wainwright was surrendering the last remnants of the Fil-American forces in the Philippines, that Japanese forward momentum was retarded elsewhere in the Pacific. The battle of the Coral Sea cost the Japanese navy 100,000 tons of vital vessels. The American navy also finally succeeded in breaking the Japanese naval code and was thus prepared for the major Japanese attack on Midway in early June, which had disastrous consequences for the Japanese. In August 1942 the battle of Guadalcanal began, and by the time it ended in February 1943 American productive wealth had already doomed Japan and her Co-Prosperity Sphere. The multitiered defense perimeter, which had seemed so formidable on Japanese maps, was penetrated effectively by the "leap-frog" technique of island-hopping. After Saipan and Guam were reconquered in 1944, it was only a matter of time and Allied effort.

The American navy proposed an attack directly against Taiwan, rather than against the Philippines. Arguing from its conviction that the Japanese military had lost its cohesion and was but a fragmented series of isolated commands, it urged Roosevelt to authorize this penultimate example of island-hopping. MacArthur, on the other hand, was adamant about the military and psychological need of liberating the Philippines before proceeding to attack Taiwan and eventually Japan itself. Refuting Admirals Leahy, King, and Nimitz at a top-level strategy meeting with Roosevelt at Pearl Harbor, Mac-

Arthur "argued that it was not only a moral obligation to release this friendly possession from the enemy, . . . but that to fail to do so would not be understandable to the Oriental mind." He also felt that "to by-pass isolated islands was one thing, but to leave in your rear such a large enemy concentration as the Philippines involved serious and unnecessary risks."[1]

MacArthur's opinion prevailed. His concern that the United States would be *walang hiya* if it ignored the Philippines led to a policy which brought to the Philippines a critical Japanese-American confrontation. The Americans tried to fulfill their obligations to repay Filipino loyalty by returning; they honored *utang na loob*, though, as it turned out, at a terrible price in Philippine lives and property. The Japanese had expected this major American attempt to reconquer the Philippines and had prepared accordingly. The Philippine defense plan, euphemistically called *Sho* (Victory), entailed a final and total commitment of Japan's remaining naval resources from all over Southeast Asia in order to prevent an American landing. Supplies were so greatly limited and fuel oil so scarce that the navy knew that there was no point in saving ships, since they would never again be able to put to sea as a fleet unless the Americans were stopped.[2]

The Japanese assumed incorrectly that the attack would come in Mindanao, but every effort had been made to strengthen the whole archipelago. The size of the total garrison was well above three-hundred thousand men, and able commanders were dispatched to Philippine commands from all over the Japanese Empire. Tominaga Kyoji came from Tokyo to command the Fourth Air Army, as did Muto Akira who assumed the position of chief of staff. On September 29, 1944, the Imperial General Staff ordered the legendary "Tiger of Malaya," Yamashita Tomoyuki, to replace Lieutenant General Kuroda Shigenori. He arrived in the Philippines a scant two weeks before MacArthur's attack to discover a large but somewhat inefficient force, weakened by isolation from materiel and harassed by an openly hostile people. The Japanese army sucked the countryside dry in its ruthless effort to prepare for the American attack.

The attack, which had the elements of a classical heroic epic, came in mid-October.[3] Two generals, each at the peak of his fame, confronted each other across a vast stage of air, sea, and land. The greatest battleships ever built bombarded each other from over the horizon, and the Japanese nearly succeeded in destroying the American armada by committing as sacrificial lambs her few remaining aircraft carriers naked and shorn of planes. The battle lines, which stretched for hundreds of miles across sea and land, reverberated to the resonant boom of bombs and guns as the Japanese fleet closed in on Leyte Gulf from three directions. For a while the fate of this colossal invasion was in doubt as the Japanese fleet nearly broke through to shell the American troop ships, but through fortune, firepower, and superior communications the Japanese were turned back in their attack. Over two-hundred thousand American troops of the Sixth Army were committed to the Leyte invasion, which took place near the city of Tacloban on October 20, 1944.[4] Soon after the beaches had been secured, MacArthur waded ashore to fulfill his pledge to return. With him was Osmeña, who succeeded Quezon in exile. Two Filipino governments were once again on Philippine soil, each dependent on the military power of one of the adversaries. Dual government and the dilemmas of allegiance had returned with MacArthur.

The Commonwealth government-in-exile was, like most exile governments, not really a government at all. While in theory a cabinet existed as a functioning unit, the exile government was primarily the vehicle for Quezon and Osmeña. It cloaked them with the appurtenances of office, continued the legal claim of the Commonwealth, and served as a propaganda force, publicizing the plight of the Filipinos to the American people. Essentially, it was a symbol of the past and the hope for the future, serving as the continuing focus for loyalty of the majority of Filipinos in the archipelago.

Roosevelt had made every effort to flatter Quezon and to dignify the government. He insisted that Quezon be given an honored place in the councils of war and peace and was responsive to Quezon's sensibilities. Well aware of Quezon's initial turmoil about going into exile, Roosevelt guessed how unhappy he was in exile and without power. Mortally sick with tuberculosis, Quezon, in turn, watched idly as Roosevelt, the master practitioner, manipulated people, including himself. Throughout the war he grumbled at the Europe-first policy of the American government, which seemed especially inexcusable because of the American failure to give adequate protection initially to the Philippines. He continued to hold America accountable for playing fast and loose with Filipino affections, resenting the fact that the war effort prevented him from complaining more vocally. His evacuation had not only removed him from his own locus of power but also raised the nagging issue of whether he had discharged his obligations most successfully. The charge of the Japanese that he had taken "French leave" needled him, and it was with some defensiveness that he explained that he could only be of service by "being free from the clutches of the enemy."[5]

Quezon was also concerned about his constitutional position. According to the amended Philippine constitution, Quezon's term of office was to expire on November 15, 1943. This fact had been one of the tacit reasons why the Japanese had rushed independence for the Laurel government. Quezon himself felt it imperative that he retain office despite the constitutional prohibition, but others were less sure. Secretary of the Interior Harold Ickes, long a friend of Osmeña, felt the United States should not alter the legal requirements despite Quezon's fame. He noted that "Osmeña is capable and loyal and has enjoyed a popularity among the Filipino people equal to that of Quezon."[6] The issue was complicated by the intense personal quality of Filipino politics. Quezon and Osmeña had engaged each other in the past with the result that the rational aspects of the argument were obfuscated by the personal confrontation. At one point Quezon in the style of le Roi Soleil exploded against Osmeña, "Look at that man. Why did God give him such a body when I am here struggling for my life? I am Manuel L. Quezon—I am the Filipino people—I am the Philippines."[7]

Fortunately for Quezon, Osmeña seemed to feel during the war that *l'état, c'était* Quezon. After being subject to heavy pressure from Quezon, he decided that Philippine unity and the prosecution of the war effort could best be achieved by standing aside. He was persuaded that the Commonwealth constitution ought to be suspended by the action of the United States government. Despite the opposition of Ickes and others, Roosevelt approved this course and Senator Tydings introduced for the Administration Joint Resolution No. 95, which retained Quezon as president until normality returned to the Philippines and an election could be held.[8] This measure, which passed the American Senate easily enough, ran into difficulty in the House, where the Republicans opposed it as a means of registering their protest against Roosevelt's own long tenure of office. Walter Judd felt that the tactics of the proponents of the resolution were "a little like Hitler," but the resolution passed despite the opposition of 104 Republicans and three Democrats.[9] Roosevelt signed the measure into law three days before Quezon's term was to have expired, but the victory was pyrrhic for Quezon, since by late 1943 he was a dying man. Despite his heroic effort to preserve his health long enough to return with MacArthur in triumph, he died at Lake Saranac in New York on August 1, 1944.

Sergio Osmeña inherited a difficult situation. He had neither the time nor the personnel to alter the government-in-exile. He was forced to accept the Quezonian stamp of the cabinet for lack of options, despite the intense ill feeling that had just divided this same group a few months previously on the succession dispute. Although he had a legitimate claim to the presidency in his own right, the character of wartime propaganda forced him to assume a caretaker role, in which his job was to complete Quezon's unfinished work. Consequently, he was forced to accept things he might not otherwise have chosen. Since Philippine polity has always been an intensely personal relationship of patron and client, it normally has required that a leader build his own organization of loyal followers with whom he has a reciprocal *utang na loob* relationship. Osmeña's isolation from the Philippines made it impossible for him to inherit Quezon's mantle. He had to establish his own connections as quickly as possible.

Osmeña felt compelled, therefore, to leave Washington almost immediately in order to join MacArthur for the reinvasion. He was certain Quezon would have been at MacArthur's side, and he could do no less. Whereas Quezon was clearly the leader who would have automatically become the key figure in a postliberation Philippines, Osmeña knew that his great rival for Quezon's position, Roxas, was already organizing his supporters in his quest for the presidency. If Osmeña could not get back quickly as the returning hero, he would be in great trouble politically. He was thus forced to reject the advice of Harold Ickes, who warned him that "the country will be entirely under military command, and you as a civilian leader will be powerless. . . . Your people will expect many things from you that you will be unable to give them. Be wise. Stay in America." Ickes foresaw that Osmeña, unlike Quezon, would be eclipsed by MacArthur, but Osmeña could only reply, "My place is in the invasion. Otherwise, the Filipinos would say, 'Where is our government? Where is our President?' They might even think I was afraid." "Very well," Ickes replied, "but don't blame me later on."[10] Psychologically and politically, Osmeña had to bring dual government back so that his government would inherit postliberation power. He could not allow MacArthur to be the sole repository of the loyalty originally given to Quezon and MacArthur jointly.

MacArthur's fame had reached enormous proportions. His own dramatic flair, coupled with the impact of wartime propaganda, made him, after Quezon's death, the most popular and powerful political force in the Philippines. Carlos Romulo, who had done much to build up this mystique, summarized the Filipino attitude when he said before the American Congress that "to America he [MacArthur] is the hero strategist who held the Stars and Stripes in its prideful place in the Far East. To us in the Philippines, he is you. He is America."[11] MacArthur neither was America nor did he win the war single-handedly, but many Filipinos, with their desire to personalize abstractions, believed in him as self-proclaimed surrogate. Filipinos only half-jokingly claimed that when MacArthur returned to Leyte he walked on the water, while everyone else waded ashore in the water. Osmeña's great dilemma was that he could neither compete with Quezon, a dead hero mourned by the people, nor with MacArthur, a living symbol already revered as a demigod.

Osmeña had no choice. He had to accompany MacArthur and to watch him make the "return" his own personal triumph. "I have returned," proclaimed MacArthur on the Leyte beach. "By the Grace of Almighty God our forces stand again on Philippine soil— soil consecrated in the blood of our two peoples. We have come, dedicated and committed to the task of destroying every vestige of enemy control over your daily lives, and of restoring, upon a foundation of indestructible strength, the liberties of your people." Announcing that Commonwealth government was "firmly reestablished on Philippine soil" and proclaiming the hour of redemption to be at hand, MacArthur summoned the Filipinos to "rally to me. Let the indomitable spirit of Bataan and Corregidor lead on." He urged the nation to "strike at every favorable opportunity. For your homes and hearths, strike! For future generations of your sons and daughters, strike! In the name of your sacred dead, strike! Let no heart be faint. Let every arm be steeled." MacArthur concluded that "the guidance of divine God points the way. Follow in His Name to the Holy Grail of righteous victory!"[12]

Osmeña, who had years before been nicknamed the "sphinx" because of his taciturn personality, was overwhelmed by the insoluble tasks MacArthur immediately turned over to him. Without permitting Osmeña the time to structure his new government, MacArthur forced the few returning Commonwealth officials to handle what was obviously beyond their capacity. MacArthur claimed that "like all American professional soldiers," he believed "that civil power of government should be paramount to any power wielded by the military." He restored to Osmeña "the right to govern in that part of Leyte" which he had recaptured. He "called the President [Osmeña] to the wrecked and devastated provincial capitol building three days after the landing," and said that on behalf of the American government, he was restoring to Osmeña constitutional

administration. He announced that he would "in a like manner restore the other Philippine cities and provinces throughout the entire
land" as soon as his troops had secured them.

MacArthur could not have been oblivious to the difficulties he
was creating for Osmeña. Confusing, perhaps intentionally, the
importance of a civilian government's control of its own military
forces with the complex dependence of the Commonwealth government on American support (entirely a military dependence,
while the Philippines was a combat area), MacArthur abandoned
the messy problems of reconstruction to the fiction which was the
Commonwealth government. Osmeña had no staff, no money, and
no room for maneuver. MacArthur reminisced that Osmeña did not
expect this sudden resumption of civilian control. Claiming that he
"had not discussed it with any of them beforehand," he rather un-
kindly commented that "President Osmeña looked upon his trip to
Leyte as a ceremonial visit, and that he fully expected to go back to
the United States and continue to administer a government-in-exile
until the war was over, or at least until military operations in the
Philippines were concluded."[13] In fact, MacArthur seems to have
done just what Ickes warned Osmeña would happen. He seems to
have taken the glory for himself while avoiding sullying his hands
with the thorny problems of reconstruction. He foisted upon Osmeña the myriad problems of governing a devasted, bankrupt, and
divided land with only the semblance of a government.

If Osmeña's political situation was critically compromised, he at
least was on the winning and overwhelmingly popular American
side. Laurel in Manila was in a worse situation. The attack on Leyte
brought back to the Philippines the overt problems of dual government, ending at the same time the Japanese pretense that Laurel's
republic had an independent posture. Even more than MacArthur,
Yamashita's immediate concern was the battlefront. He left to
Laurel only those governmental functions which he had neither the
time nor the inclination to perform. Whereas Osmeña, at least in the
beginning, had to be concerned only with the few thousands liberated in Leyte, Laurel had responsibilities to millions of Filipinos
across the islands still held by Japan. Osmeña, who had access to the
superb American logistical system, could gain some emergency food
supplies, while Laurel had to combat a paralyzed, inflated, and
plundered agricultural sector. By December 1944 the Japanese were
pumping five-hundred peso notes into the swollen money market.
Since the American return was expected, few would accept the Japanese pesos. People either used hoarded stocks of Commonwealth

pesos, jewelry, or machines to buy provisions on the black market, or, if they were unlucky and poor, they starved. It took suitcases full of Japanese pesos to buy bread or rice.

Laurel's attempt to solve the food crisis absorbed increasing amounts of his attention, but it was unsuccessful. Five months before the Leyte landing he pressured Roxas into accepting a post as a food czar. At that time and with an eye on the probable postwar struggle with Osmeña for power, Roxas said that he heeded the call because he believed that "no Filipino can decline, under the circumstances now obtaining, to do what lies in his power to ameliorate the suffering of thousands of people due to the insufficiency or maldistribution of food supplies."[14] Roxas reversed the existing restrictive policy in favor of one in which food could move freely and be sold at prices more competitive with the black market.[15] Simultaneously, an effort was made to find hidden caches and prosecute speculators relentlessly.[16] When these efforts proved unsuccessful, Laurel abolished Roxas' position and created yet another set of agencies, one in September and the other in November, in a futile quest for a workable solution.[17] Roxas went back into retirement while Laurel vacillated frantically in his unsuccessful search.

Laurel's position was further undermined by his increasing loss of support from the Japanese. Despite the declaration of a state of war, it was clear to them that he had failed to rally a large percentage of the nation to the new republic. As early as May 1943 the Japanese had begun a quest for Filipinos who were clearly willing to give loyalty to the Japanese cause when they organized the Sapilnip, an organization based on former residence in Japan.[18] The Japanese attempted also to attract the society's discontented, paying special attention to the former Sakdalistas and Ganaps.[19] Whenever potential spies, informers, and agents could be found, they were encouraged and rewarded. All these efforts were combined into an organization known as the Makapili (an abbreviation for the Tagalog, Kalipunang Makabayan ng mga Pilipino, the Patriotic League of Filipinos). Organized hurriedly just after the Leyte landings, the Makapili was a direct threat to Laurel's position with the Japanese.[20] Benigno Ramos apparently proposed a coup d'état to Yamashita's chief of staff, Muto Akira, which the Japanese rejected as unnecessary and dangerous.[21] Laurel, aware that his power was badly eroded by the Makapili, was pressured to incorporate some Makapili into his cabinet.[22] While he was willing to permit Pio Duran to hold a sensitive post—he became inspector of martial law for the Third, Fourth, and Fifth Districts—he refused to incorporate

Ramos and Ricarte. The compromise reached was that Laurel became "the highest supreme adviser" of the Makapili, but this was
mainly a face-saving device. The Japanese were able to train about
five-thousand Makapili by early 1945. Whereas they had mistrusted
the Constabulary, the Japanese trusted these avowedly pro-Japanese
sympathizers and armed them freely. Most Makapili fought courageously for the Japanese; as a group their allegiance had polarized,
which placed them in sharp contrast to the great majority of the
nation, who saw them as traitors.[23]

Osmeña's return began a period of great anguish, as Filipinos
on both sides of the battle line began to consider the meaning of
collaboration. The Makapili were easily adjudged as traitors because
they had openly proffered their allegiance to Japan. But could the
term treason be applied when political collaboration by Filipinos
whose allegiance was to their nation was under scrutiny? While two
rival governments existed behind two foreign armies, and each demanded obedience and allegiance from the people, the leaders of
both governments were committed to the same basic national aims.
The governments of Laurel and Osmeña were both served by the
same oligarchic elite, which only divided into these two hostile units
by the accident of history. The problem of possible culpability is
elusive. The two governments, rivals for loyalty for a brief period,
were interlocked personally by reciprocal bonds predating the war.
The community of goals, experiences, and kinship blurred the rigid
lines required by war. Hostility between Osmeña's and Laurel's
governments was somewhat artificial.

To the Americans the collaboration issue was simpler. Americans viewed those who collaborated as traitors, attacking them as a
pernicious category of the enemy. From the American point of view
this simplistic definition worked. Roosevelt, Ickes, and most people
without experience in the archipelago saw the collaboration issue as
one in which the leadership had failed to discharge the demands of
continuing loyalty to the Commonwealth government and to the
United States of America rather than to its own people. The basic
American policy, which was predicated on the assumption that such
obligations were more important in war than in peace, posited a
postwar purge for those whose loyalty had been found wanting.
Roosevelt frequently stated that "those who have collaborated with
the enemy must be removed from authority and influence in the
political and economic life of the country."[24] This policy, which was
similar to the one implemented subsequently in Japan, avoided assessment of an individual's innocence or guilt. It was a pragmatic

attempt to resolve a social crisis without questioning an individual's motivation. The policy avoided a verdict on each case, leaving that more difficult problem to subsequent court action.

Since the United States was still sovereign after liberation in the Philippines, this policy might have succeeded if it had been applied as forcefully as in Japan. But it was highly dubious that, given the nature of the Fil-American relationship, such a ruthless implementation would have been possible. The issue was, in any case, academic, because when Osmeña and MacArthur returned to the Islands, a formulated means of executing such a plan did not exist. The American government was so busy at war that no one had developed Roosevelt's guidelines into policy. When Osmeña became president he discovered, "much to his dismay," hopeless confusion and inertia in Washington. Trying to gain some direction from the American government, Osmeña found that "Stimson and Hull were friendly and vague; Ickes pontifical and vague; Tydings mildly interested and vague. All agreed that something should be done regarding the issue of collaboration. . . . But they had no program and all insisted that only the White House could produce the needed action."[25] However, Roosevelt, tired, harried, and ill, was too busy to meet with Osmeña at length, and the policy remained inchoate. Osmeña waded ashore without any clear directives, forced instead to attempt the reconciliation of the ill-defined American policy with the realities of Philippine life. Without external direction and support, his task was nearly hopeless.

Had MacArthur sympathized with the basic Roosevelt policy, Osmeña might have succeeded in administering the American policy. During the war, MacArthur's position had been one of anger at the collaborators, who, he felt, had aided the Japanese war effort. Moreover, since MacArthur tended to confuse America with himself, he regarded disloyalty to the United States as a personal breach, a type of *walang hiya*, of the oligarchy to him. On December 29, 1944, shortly after his reinvasion, he issued a "proclamation providing for military measures to be taken upon the apprehension of citizens . . . who voluntarily have given aid, comfort and sustenance to the enemy." Proclaiming that "military necessity requires that such persons be removed from any opportunity to threaten the security of our [American] military forces or the success of our military operations," MacArthur decreed that he intended "to remove such persons, when apprehended, from any position of political and economic influence in the Philippines and to hold them in restraint for the duration of the war." The statement concluded, however, with a critical alteration by MacArthur of the vague Washington policy. He declared that after the war he would release those apprehended "to the Philippine government for its judgment upon their respective cases."[26] MacArthur, by limiting American intervention to the duration of the war, thrust the resolution of the issue back on Osmeña.

Had Quezon lived long enough to return with MacArthur, the problem might have had a different resolution. Quezon, secure in his primary position within Philippine society, might have had more maneuverability. He might have used the threat of a political purge to reestablish his personal relationship by practicing "politically selective absolution in his own interest."[27] Quezon, by dispensing grace, could have increased the sense of *utang na loob* owed him by those pardoned. Since the Washington policy was vague and MacArthur was his *compadre,* he could have resolved the dilemmas of allegiance and loyalty by exploiting the fact that he was the living symbol of the nation. His strong confidence in the hand-chosen lieutenants he had left behind, coupled with his oligarchic valuation of the need for the elite, would probably have resulted in a presidential amnesty designed to heal the wounds of the society as quickly as possible.[28]

Quezon, the president of all the people, could have achieved this by the force of his reputation; Osmeña, the president by the accidents of fate, could not. Osmeña was not the symbol of the state; he was only a member, albeit a famous one, of the elite who had experienced the good fortune to be spared the dilemmas of collaboration through American evacuation. He lacked the stature to ordain by fiat how to restore the Philippines. If he had remained in the Islands, he knew that the Japanese would have tried to get him to serve as president instead of Laurel, and while he was courageous and steadfast throughout his life, he must have wondered how he would have responded under that kind of stress. Two of his sons were alleged to have been active collaborators, and they would have to be tried.

Osmeña must have sensed vividly the irony of history which had taken him to the United States and finally fulfilled his life-long ambition to be president, only to vitiate it by bringing him back to the Philippines as judge of his peers rather than as their leader. Instead of a joyous reunion with his life-long friends and disciples, he was forced to pursue them as enemies of the Commonwealth. An oligarch himself, Osmeña was firmly convinced of the importance of his group for Philippine society. He shared with those still serving in the Laurel government in Manila a common framework of values built mutually over the decades. Indeed, the bonds of reciprocal kinship, *utang na loob,* and friendship, which linked him so intimately with those across the battlelines, made it almost impossible for him to conceive of that Manila group as traitors. The return to Leyte was in part a nightmare in which the terms of "traitor" and "collaborator" were jumbled virtually out of recognition.

Yet somehow during those first lonely days on Leyte Osmeña had to evolve a policy on collaboration which would do justice both to his *compadres* in the oligarchy in Manila and to that enormous segment of the nation which had actively supported the guerrillas, the Commonwealth, and America. He had to evolve a policy of reconstruction which could heal the schism within the nation and yet also fulfill the Washington demand that collaboration be punished. Like other Filipinos, he had to confront the moral problem of whether there had been a violation of some code; the masses had apparently opted one way and the elite had seemingly opted in the other direction. A month after the Leyte landing he broadcast his first statement on collaboration, indicating his dilemma and his tentative solution. Noting that "it was not possible for all to evade the enemy" and that "the fate of the immense majority was to bear the manacles of enslavement," he reminded the people not to "be forgetful of the loyal civilian population" in the general "praise of the guerrillas."

Osmeña stated that "not all public officials could take to the hills to carry on the heroic struggle. Some had to remain in their posts to maintain a semblance of government, to protect the population from the oppressor to the extent possible by human ingenuity and to comfort the people in their misery." Osmeña acknowledged that the realities of the occupation were "cruel and harsh." Expressing his own elitist attitude, he commented that had the prewar elite not served, "the Japanese would either have themselves governed directly and completely or utilized unscrupulous Filipino followers capable of any treason to their people. The result would have been calamitous and the injuries inflicted to our body politic beyond cure." Osmeña, like his colleagues in Manila, saw the oligarchy as the last bulwark preserving Philippine institutions and preventing nameless chaos.

Osmeña's solution to this dilemma was exactly opposite to the American approach. Whereas the American policy suggested a purge of everyone who held office before any judgment of innocence or guilt, Osmeña's idea was the reverse. "Every case," he proposed, "should be examined impartially and decided on its own merits."

Osmeña felt that the wartime office holders fell into three categories: "those prompted by a desire to protect the people, those actuated by fear of enemy reprisals, and those motivated by disloyalty to our government and cause." Osmeña, perhaps overconfident that motivation could be easily categorized, believed that "the motives which caused the retention of the office and conduct while in office, rather than the sole fact of its occupation, will be the criteria upon which such persons will be judged."[29] The American policy posited general culpability until the individual could establish his innocence; the Osmeña policy posited individual innocence until treasonable motivation could be assessed.

This policy was first tested on Leyte when, on November 2, 1944, Osmeña established a Board of Inquiry under the chairmanship of General Basilio Valdes, one of the cabinet in Washington.[30] The board, which conducted loyalty investigations as a kind of grand jury charged with determining indictments for a later trial, received attention as the likely precedent. Of the 145 cases reviewed, the case of wartime Governor Bernardo Torres received the greatest publicity. Torres in his defense claimed that he "had one basic principle. It was to establish a government that would protect the people, guide the people during the crisis, and make this government a cushion against Japanese oppression." Claiming that he had secretly aided the guerrillas, Torres challenged the board to determine how anyone else in his position could have done differently.[31] The board quickly discovered that assessing motivation was the most difficult of all possible tasks. Torres further complicated the problem by raising a host of procedural and legal objections which bogged the board down into a morass. Since it became clear that despite the strong popular and guerrilla hostility to men like Torres there would be no orgy of lynching, it was to Torres' advantage to retard any trial as long as possible. The longer the delay, the cooler the people's passions would become; the cooler the passions, the less risk of a conviction in court.

Throughout this period the American military was overwhelming the Japanese forces. American logistical superiority crushed the Japanese defense, despite fanatical resistance. By the end of 1944 Leyte was secured. It was obvious that an invasion of Luzon was only a matter of time, and this exigency prompted General Yamashita to withdraw his command and the Laurel government from its exposed position in Manila to the more defensible summer capital of Baguio. With secrecy the Laurel government was moved on December 22, 1944, almost three years to the day that Quezon and

Osmeña had been forced to slip out of Manila for Corregidor. Only Leon Guinto, Quezon's former secretary of Labor, was left behind as mayor in Manila, as Vargas had been. On January 6, 1945, Yamashita announced that "the Imperial Japanese Forces will carry out their operations taking into consideration that the capital of the Republic and its law-abiding inhabitants should not suffer from ravages of war."[32] Yamashita, like MacArthur, realized that Manila was indefensible, and for the second time, Manila was declared an "open city," though Guinto's Military Order No. 4 instructed every Filipino to support the Japanese forces short of conscription in order to protect Philippine territorial integrity.[33]

Yamashita, expecting MacArthur's attack to come at Lingayan Gulf, as had General Homma's attack three years earlier, built his defense plans around a withdrawal into the central mountains of Luzon rather than into Bataan and Corregidor. He considered it his duty to tie down as many American troops as long as possible to delay any possible invasion of Japan. Tragically, however, his order for withdrawal to the mountains was ignored or unreceived by about 30,000 marines and sailors, who, stranded without ships, decided to fight for the city of Manila rather than retreat or surrender. Because of the separation of the services under the Japanese constitution, these men were not under Yamashita's command. His failure or inability to prevail upon the local naval commanders to follow his strategy and evacuate the city resulted in the destruction of Manila. Atrocities perpetrated by the Japanese fighting for the city rank as one of the great crimes of World War II, though the degree of Yamashita's culpability is still intensely contested.[34]

The Fourteenth American Army Corps reached Manila on February 3, 1945. The city was declared secure exactly one month later. One thousand Americans, sixteen thousand Japanese, and tens of thousands of Filipinos perished in this savage struggle, which was fought room by room, closet by closet. MacArthur, aware of Yamashita's general defense plans, was totally unprepared for the fanatical Japanese defense of Manila, expecting instead that the city could be cleared easily and without much damage. "GHQ SWPA [MacArthur's headquarters] had even laid plans for a great victory parade à la Champs Elysees," that MacArthur was to lead in person.[35]

MacArthur's detractors have argued that the destruction of the city was an unnecessary byproduct of MacArthur's ego. They have claimed that by closing in on the city and ringing it, he encouraged the Japanese trapped there to fight. It has been argued that had he skirted the city and forgotten his plans for a triumphant return, like De Gaulle's through Paris, the Japanese marines would have been more likely to slip through to Yamashita's lines. Whether the Japanese would have stayed in the city even if they had not been trapped there is idle speculation for military historians. What actually happened is the reality which influenced subsequent Philippine developments. Manila was about 80 percent destroyed, ranking behind Warsaw as the most damaged city of World War II. Even more importantly, the destruction of the city touched the lives of every Filipino, since as in most underdeveloped countries, the modern sector of the economy was overwhelmingly located in the city. Manila held the precious resources of the nation, including universities, hospitals, libraries, port facilities, banks, newspapers, factories, government offices, tourist hotels, government records, and all sorts of vital operations unappreciated until they were destroyed. The death and injury rate to this urban population was not only a tragic sacrifice of human life, but it was also a crippling blow to the society, since it cut most heavily into the meager professional and middle-class groups upon whom modernization depended. Perhaps ironically, only the wartime oligarchy survived this carnage intact, since it had been evacuated to Baguio en masse.

On February 27, while the fighting still raged through the city, MacArthur brought Osmeña to Manila. Assembling a gathering at Malacañan Palace, which had fortuitously survived because of its noncentral location, MacArthur restored responsibility for governing the Commonwealth despite the chaos. Announcing emotionally that the Philippines was "again at liberty to pursue its destiny," MacArthur turned to Osmeña and told him that his "capital city, cruelly punished though it be, has regained its rightful place—Citadel of Democracy in the East." At that point in the ceremonies, MacArthur's "voice broke" and he "could not go on." He swept out of Malacañan, leaving Osmeña behind with all the problems. For Osmeña the tribulations had only just begun.[36]

For Laurel and the other members of his government, the tribulations had not yet ended. Powerless and isolated in Baguio, this group lived more on anxieties than on food. On March 19, when the fighting was almost over, Tokyo ordered that Laurel be flown to Japan to establish the Japanese variant of a government-in-exile. On March 22 Laurel, Aquino, Osias, and General Capinpin left secretly, arriving in Japan June 27 after a long stay on Taiwan.[37] The rest of the wartime government in Baguio, however, was left to its own devices, especially after the fighting became critical during the spring of 1945. As the American troops moved closer to Baguio, groups of these leaders began to slip away from Japanese surveillance and to escape toward the American forces. The first group included Paredes and Sison; the second, Roxas, Yulo, De las Alas, Paez, Sabido, and Sanvictores; and the third, which escaped on April 16, included Recto, Alunan, Abello, and Francisco.

The capture of these men by the Americans received widespread publicity from the press throughout the world. The significance of the wording of the dispatches was lost to most people outside of the Philippines, however. The statement from MacArthur's headquarters said that "among those freed is Brigadier General Manuel Roxas, former Speaker of the Assembly. Four members [Yulo, De las Alas, Paredes, and Sison] of the Philippine collaborationist cabinet have been captured. They will be confined for the duration of the war as a matter of military security and then turned over to the government of the Philippines for trial and judgment."[38] The hidden significance of this statement, which radically altered postwar Philippine politics, was that MacArthur had by fiat distinguished Roxas from the rest. Roxas was freed, restored to his rank of general on MacArthur's staff, and given MacArthur's personal pardon, while all the rest were summarily interned.

MacArthur claimed that he knew that Roxas was innocent, that Roxas had helped the guerrilla movement, and that he personally was able to speak for Roxas' character.[39] While this was in large measure accurate, MacArthur willfully disregarded legal procedure, leaving men like Yulo interned in a penal colony awaiting possible charges for treason. The glaring quality of Roxas' special treatment raised a chorus of protest. MacArthur's headquarters explained that, unlike all the others, Roxas alone had held a commission in the United States army and was therefore an American army officer rather than a Filipino collaborationist. This justification conveniently ignored men who, like General Francisco, also had held commissions in the American army but who were interned anyway.

MacArthur must have been well aware that by freeing Roxas he was pardoning, liberating, and encouraging Osmeña's great potential rival for the presidency. MacArthur's imprimatur was a sign clearly and correctly read throughout the archipelago as signifying support for Roxas over Osmeña. Because Roxas had been a member of the oligarchy living in Manila through the war, his liberation was also seen by the rest of the oligarchy as the wedge for their own political rehabilitation. As General Aguinaldo expressed it, "Roxas became the hope of those who faced prosecution for treason, and among them were the most powerful political leaders [and himself]."[40] Since Roxas was given a push toward the presidency, he would be expected to show clemency if elected, and at least force Osmeña toward a more concessionary policy if defeated. Thus, while the American Counter-Intelligence Corps, the C.I.C., was arresting some six thousand Filipinos, MacArthur's special handling of this one key Filipino was vitiating effectively much of the original Washington policy.

Osmeña, who was well aware of the political threat he faced upon his return, had attempted to persuade Washington to curb MacArthur's power. He wanted former Governor General Frank Murphy to return to the Philippines to counterbalance MacArthur's authority.[41] He recognized that, unless there was an American of stature in Manila, he would be in great trouble, especially after MacArthur had intervened so openly for Roxas. Osmeña had never had the kind of intimate relationship with MacArthur which Quezon maintained. It was an open secret that MacArthur did not think Osmeña could handle the job of reconstruction successfully, indicating privately that he could not "work with Osmeña."[42]

Osmeña's efforts to get support from Washington were largely futile. Frank Murphy declined to leave the Supreme Court to return to Manila. Ickes in Washington hurt Osmeña's position by feuding unsuccessfully with MacArthur without substantively improving Osmeña's bargaining position. MacArthur, on the spot, used his authority as supreme commander in what was still a military zone, his expertise based on years in the country, and his political capital as conquering hero to determine policy. Osmeña's last hope evaporated when Roosevelt died in April 1945. Osmeña, who had been trying to attract Roosevelt's attention for months, finally managed to visit with him at length just before he died. This meeting at Warm Springs led to a full discussion of reconstruction, including the collaboration issue. Osmeña apparently convinced Roosevelt that the situation would soon be hopelessly out of control if Roosevelt did not impose his policy directly. Roosevelt, who was able to give consideration to the Philippines for the first time in months, apparently agreed to support Osmeña by intervening, but he died a few days later, before action was taken at subsequent planned Washington meetings.[43] Truman, overwhelmed by the multitude of problems he had inherited, had no time to determine his own thinking on collaboration. By default he abdicated authority to MacArthur in Manila.

Washington's disinterest did not mean that Osmeña was free to abandon the wartime policy of a purge. Indeed, Washington's tendency was to avoid a rethinking of the problem by reiterating vehemently earlier decisions. Osmeña was compelled to resurrect a government free from the taint of collaboration. In his initial speech at the ceremonies at Malacañan restoring civilian government, he had declared that he would only "enlist the assistance of all those possessing not only proven ability and loyalty but also the confidence and trust of the people."[44] This proved to be no easy feat. The people who had proven their loyalty—the guerrillas—had never had a chance to prove their ability to govern in a peacetime environment. The people who were experienced in governing were those whose loyalty was in question. On March 8, 1945, Osmeña was able to construct a cabinet which met these requirements, but at the price of bringing into high position men who had never achieved full oligarchic status in the prewar era. Osmeña was forced to weaken the monopoly of power held by the prewar elite, and, as a result, further alienated himself from his prewar peers.

While he was able to fulfill the Washington policy at the higher levels of government, he had little choice in staffing the civil-service grades of the bureaucracy. These officials, who had continued to serve throughout the war, were so vitally needed for the tasks of reconstruction that they had to be restored to their jobs. Initially, Osmeña's Information Bureau stated that under the pressure of circumstances the government was compelled "to reemploy temporarily officials and employees who had remained in the public service under the Japanese regime. Should they be found to have collaborated with the enemy, said persons would be separated from public office immediately."[45] It soon became obvious, however, that their restoration to civil-service rank was tantamount to complete pardon, except in those rare cases where malfeasance or disloyalty charges existed for nongovernmental activities. In effect, the Philippines neither debated nor resolved the postwar European dilemma over the rank in a governmental bureaucracy at which trial for wartime action should begin. The Philippines needed the cogs of governmental machinery so badly that the moral discussion over the fulfillment or refusal by a governmental servant and common citizen of orders from above never took place.

A debate which did rage, however, was when, where, and how Osmeña would call a legislature. Since MacArthur had restored civilian government immediately, Osmeña was required by the Commonwealth constitution to call Congress as soon as possible, rather than to continue to rule by Executive Order. Upon assuming control of Manila, Osmeña had called "upon all the duly elected members of our Congress who have remained steadfast in their allegiance to our Government during the period of enemy occupation, to be in readiness to meet in Manila as soon as conditions permit for the reestablishment of the Legislative branch."[46] However, the determination of the steadfastness of the members could not be determined by the chief executive. The president did not have the authority to decide upon the seating; that was a jealously guarded constitutional right of each House itself. In late 1941 a new Congress had been elected along with Quezon and Osmeña, but, because of the occupation, it had never been summoned and sworn in. Since this was the last valid expression of the electorate and since a new election was impossible immediately, because of the total disruption of the society, there existed the question of whether this body should be the one called into session by Osmeña.

MacArthur and the recently liberated Roxas thought that this was the best solution, especially since Roxas had been elected a senator in the 1941 election. Osmeña, attempting to fulfill Washington's purge policy, was less sure. Because of the wartime cooperation of the prewar elite, technically there would not be a quorum if the 1941 Congress were called. The C.I.C. had detained too many to permit the formation of a legislature under the Commonwealth constitution. Moreover, since MacArthur had made it quite clear that the American army would detain Filipinos only as long as the Philippines remained a war zone, there was an excellent chance that, once these wartime officials were released on bail pending civilian trial, they might have to be seated, in case Osmeña chose to call that Congress. Since Congress had the constitutional authority to determine its own membership, calling Congress would probably violate Washington's injunctions. Finally, summoning that Congress would give his arch rival, Roxas, both a major forum to attack Osmeña's administration and an independent political source of power through Congressional appropriations and patronage.

Osmeña's supporters, aware of Roxas' political strength, attempted to find reasons why Osmeña could not call the 1941 legislature. It was argued that the legal time limit for this Congress had expired, denying it the right to speak for the will of the people. An attempt was made to prove that some of the senators, including Roxas and the guerrilla leader, Carlos Garcia, had violated the Commonwealth provisions prohibiting legislators from holding military or civilian posts of an executive nature during their term as legislators. It was argued that since the will of the people had been violated by the wartime activity of many of those who were elected in 1941, they were no longer fit to speak for the people. Osmeña was even urged to appeal to the United States Congress, which had the technical power to alter the Commonwealth constitution as it had done over the succession question, to extend presidential authority until a new election.[47]

Osmeña may have pursued this last possibility in his meeting with Roosevelt at Warm Springs, but with Roosevelt's death MacArthur was the political force with which Osmeña had to live. MacArthur wanted the 1941 Congress called, and it was summoned to meet on June 9, 1945, despite technical objections. Of the ninety-eight congressmen, only seventy were present; eleven were dead and seventeen were still detained by the American army. Of the twenty-four senators, only thirteen were present; two were dead, two, Cuenco and Rama, were still out of Manila, and seven, Recto, Yulo, De las Alas, Tirona, Sebastian, Paredes, and Madrigal, were detained by the Americans.[48] At the first meeting Roxas was elected president of the Senate while Elpidio Quirino became pro tem and Jose Zulueta became speaker of the House. Roxas also became chairman of the influential Committee on Appointments, and with this new power he began to review all of the appointments Osmeña had made on an acting basis. Roxas became the second most powerful man in the country.

Osmeña had appointed the outspoken guerrilla leader, Tomas Confesor, as acting secretary of the Interior, and Tomas Cabili as acting secretary of National Defense. These two men, both with powerful guerrilla support, emerged as the most influential men in the postwar Osmeña cabinet. Each was a potential rival to Roxas as a successor to Osmeña, and each was vehemently opposed to the wartime collaborators. In a famous speech at the Lotus Theater in Manila on April 1, 1945, Confesor warned "these collaborators, these pro-Japanese agents, that they can not fool the Filipino people." Noting that "their leadership has been repudiated" in every "nook and corner" of the country, he asserted that "by their leadership they have cast their country and their people into tragedy and disaster. . . ." Striking a vitriolic tone, he maintained that he and his supporters were not afraid of them during the war or after it. "If I were a collaborator," he said, "I would not for a minute cross the gates of Malacañan to whisper to someone therein that I did collaborate because I wanted to save my country from catastrophe. What I should do would be to hang my head in shame and recite the confiteor. In this manner, I would ennoble myself and perhaps win the respect of my fellow men." Confesor, challenging his audience to survey the carnage around them in Manila, asked rhetorically whether the collaborators had in any way mitigated the nation's suffering. Confesor wondered "where in the world did the soldier of a civilized country rip open the womb of a prospective mother except in the Philippines during the Japanese régime, while collaborators were singing paeans of praise elevating unto the heavens the goodness of the Samurai?" Confesor asked whether the collaborator could "conscientiously affirm that the rape of Manila would have been more hellish if there had been no collaborators?"[49] Confesor attacked Roxas as a collaborator and the defender of collaborators. These were powerful charges on an emotional subject, and they posed a direct threat to Roxas.[50]

Similarly, Cabili also was a threat to Roxas, since he claimed that "men who wear the uniform [Roxas] must be willing to pay the price. The army is no place for divided loyalty. It is a place for men. If I had collaborated, I would not have the courage now to request reinstatement."[51] On March 17, 1945, he had issued General Order No. 20, which challenged Roxas' position as a general reinstated personally by MacArthur. His order prohibited any Filipino soldier who had been called into the American army in 1941 from remaining on active duty, if he had "accepted appointment or performed service in a military or civil capacity in any activity controlled by the Japanese or by the so-called puppet 'Philippine Republic.'"[52] The order, which attempted to strip Roxas of his rank, failed because Quezon's and Roxas' friend, Chief of Staff Valdes, immediately ordered Roxas onto inactive status, which made him liable to censure under the articles of war only if he had committed a felony.[53]

Roxas struck back in his position as chairman of the Appointments Committee by rejecting for permanent appointment both Confesor and Cabili. Skillfully using his new power, Roxas managed to force Osmeña into a conciliatory attitude rather than one risking an open split with him. Osmeña agreed to appoint both men to the rehabilitation mission going to Washington in order to keep Roxas in the monolithic Nacionalista party which he, Osmeña, had done so much to preserve over the previous forty years. There was still only one major party, in theory, and as president he was titular head of it. For the nation, the party, and himself, he chose to yield to Roxas on these two key appointments. He appointed Alfredo Montelibano as secretary of National Defense, but left the most vital post of secretary of the Interior vacant.

The war continued while all this political infighting was taking place. It was not until June 28 that MacArthur could report the island of Luzon secured, calling the campaign "one of the most savage and bitterly fought in American history."[54] On July 5 Mac-

Arthur was finally able to issue Communiqué No. 1185, which declared the whole Philippine campaign "virtually closed."[55] During the final phases of the Philippine operation, MacArthur and his staff had been preparing for the projected monumental attack on Japan itself. No one expected the stunning effect of the atomic bombs on the Japanese leadership. The crisis atmosphere in MacArthur's Manila headquarters remained until the surrender.

During these last months of the war, the fiction of the Laurel government persisted. Some propaganda efforts were made to dramatize Laurel in Japan, but the war was so clearly being lost that few in Japan had the time or energy to give the Laurel republic any attention. On August 17, after Japan's surrender, Laurel, still correct, proclaimed the dissolution of his own government. From Nara, Japan, he tersely announced that "in view of the reoccupation of the Philippines by the United States and the reestablishment therein of the Government of the Commonwealth of the Philippines . . . , the Republic of the Philippines has ceased to exist."[56] Laurel and the others then cabled the newly arrived Americans in Tokyo of their whereabouts and proceeded to internment.

On August 22 MacArthur's Manila headquarters announced that effective September 1 the last remnants of military control of the Philippines would cease, including military help in the public services of health, education, welfare, and reconstruction.[57] MacArthur and his staff suddenly had a new job in Japan, and they attempted to clear up their obligations in the Philippines with a rush. On August 23 the Commonwealth government received all jurisdiction over the interned Filipinos.[58] On August 30 MacArthur's C-47, the "Bataan," landed at Tokyo, confronting him with a new world to conquer. The challenges and problems of remaking Japanese society appealed to a man who believed that there was no job he could not handle. His will would be done on earth if not in heaven.

All of a sudden a lull fell upon the Philippines. MacArthur's departure left the archipelago with an aching void. The Filipinos had suddenly lost their hero. The country had lost the single most potent source of power. The painful task of reconstruction had to be accomplished without the glamour and grandeur of MacArthur's rhetoric. MacArthur's shift of arenas took the spotlight off the Philippines, leaving the Filipinos in the gray shadows. They resented the loss of excitement and attention. Life grew dull. Reality overtook romance. When the lights went out, the play had not ended; in fact it had just begun.

CHAPTER VII

The Tribulations

A vile race of quislings—to use the new word which will carry the scorn of mankind down the centuries—is hired to fawn upon the conqueror, to collaborate in his designs, and to enforce his rule upon their fellow-countrymen, while grovelling low themselves.
—Winston Churchill

Peace revealed the archipelago to be more severely damaged than anyone had thought possible. The 1944-45 crop had yielded only 60 percent of normal, much of which had been destroyed or consumed by the two armies. Transportation was at a standstill; industrial production had collapsed. The hub of Manila was even more battered than it had seemed during the fighting. Many people were homeless and most were starving. Medical and sanitation facilities were destroyed, and many Filipinos who did not show war wounds suffered from dysentery, malaria, and, occasionally, cholera. Law and order had collapsed, while a new black market grew tremendously under the inflationary stimulus of American goods. Because American troops were the one immediate source of hard currency and food, the pimp, the whore, and the thief were the only people with steady employment. Philippine per capita production was perhaps lower in 1945 than in 1899. While the population had increased by about three million from 1937 to 1946 the combined index of physical production had fallen to 38.7 percent of the 1937 level. Damage was in excess of several billion dollars.[1]

This economic chaos formed the background to the postwar collaboration debate. Physical survival was the paramount crisis, and all other considerations had to be judged in this context. Before any purge of the wartime leadership could be implemented, the nation had to determine whether it could risk turning the job of reconstruction over to untried hands. The wartime elite alone had experience derived from decades of government service. In the poverty-stricken, underdeveloped, and destroyed Philippines, these men were a national asset which could not be ignored.

The death and destruction of the previous few months had left the nation in a state of shock emotionally, as well as physically paralyzed. The trauma of the fighting blurred the delineation of those loyalties which had been so intensely polarized just a few months before. Since virtually each person suffered his private grief, the pain was still present, but wartime vengeance no longer seemed an effective solution. In chaos, the society recoiled from hate and closed ranks in an effort to begin life anew. The horrors of the war, especially to those around Manila, were repressed as too grim to remember. The busy tasks of reconstruction served as a sponge, absorbing energy and pain. It was not the optimum time for Philippine society to have to confront the human imperfections of an imperfect world.

Nevertheless, that was exactly what the American collaboration policy demanded of Osmeña and the society. While Christian charity, physical carnage, and psychological withdrawal all combined to lessen hostility toward the wartime oligarchy, the Washington policy compelled the movement of the wheels of justice to bring these men to trial. On June 8, 1945, Osmeña had issued Executive Order No. 53, in which he created a "national board of inquiry to investigate charges of disloyalty to the governments of the Commonwealth of the Philippines and the United States of America." Based on the model established on Leyte, the board was to investigate the "legal problems and matters of policy." It was also charged to "investigate the conduct of those public officials or employees who served during the enemy occupation and who may be recalled to duty."[2]

The Japanese surrender, which established peace throughout the Pacific, prompted Osmeña to create the People's Court. On August 20 Osmeña was faced with the impending release of Filipinos detained only for the duration of the war by the American army according to MacArthur's orders. Osmeña sent a message to the Philippine Congress recommending the creation of a "Special Collegiate Court" to try "political prisoners."[3] MacArthur's alteration of the original Roosevelt policy required that the Philippine government be prepared to handle the thousands of cases within the normal peacetime regulations of government prosecution. The government had limited time in which to prepare and bring in indictments against those whom it might want to accuse of a crime. Constitutional safeguards, which legitimately protected every citizen from government abuse, placed an incredible strain on a judiciary as disorganized and damaged as the rest of the society.

The Osmeña proposal for a People's Court over which would preside prewar judges who were free from any wartime taint and whose prosecuting arm would be the solicitor general immediately became a major political issue between the Osmeña and Roxas forces. Two Roxas men, Congressmen Francisco Ortega and Senator Elpidio Quirino, had attempted to counter the Osmeña bill by submitting a rival measure which proposed more constricting limits on the authority of the special court. On August 23 MacArthur, as expected, ordered the release of all interned Filipinos, maintaining that his right to detain these people no longer existed.[4] The American army claimed that the release in no way indicated either innocence or guilt; it asserted that those released might still have to stand trial in Philippine courts. Many of those released, however, either willfully or mistakenly claimed that their release indicated that the Americans thought they were innocent. Many thus claimed that they were subject to double jeopardy when later indicted, despite the clear American disclaimer on the reasons for the release.

By August 23 Osmeña's version of the People's Court bill was rushed to the House floor. On that same day, however, Quirino and Roxas had managed to push their version through its second reading in the Senate.[5] The Osmeña-Roxas confrontation, begun over the Confesor and Cabili appointments, turned into a struggle over the People's Court. On September 3 Roxas won a round when he forced Osmeña to issue Executive Order No. 65, "providing for the provisional release on bail of political prisoners, prior to the institution of the corresponding criminal cases against them. . . ."[6] Roxas effectively used the charge of dictatorial tendencies against Osmeña to obtain this bail order. It not only freed on bail the wartime oligarchy, but also potentially altered the congressional balance, since those who had seats in the 1941 Congress had claim to their seats. Under the Commonwealth constitution Osmeña would have to receive congressional approval for suspending the bail provisions; lacking this strength in the Roxas-dominated Congress, he was compelled to yield to Roxas, even though he was strengthening Roxas' potential votes in the Congress.

Osmeña won the second round when he returned to Congress, for revision and amendment, the Roxas-supported version which had passed the Senate. His veto message singled out what he considered to be an inadequate provision regarding the special prosecutors. "Such exclusion of members of the Bar," he commented, "would so reduce the field of choice as to hamper considerably the discharge of my duty . . . in line with the spirit with which the People's Court is intended to be created." Osmeña continued by warning the Roxas group that the "public forum, both at home and abroad" was watching their deliberations over collaboration. With an eye to the scrutiny which future generations would make "when we shall no longer be alive to defend ourselves," Osmeña warned that "our good name, nay, the good name of our country—which, I am sure, we all want to keep untarnished—demands the removal of any possible cause for misunderstanding on this matter."[7]

Osmeña was correct in saying that people abroad were watching the struggle over the creation of the People's Court. It was during the first weeks in September, when MacArthur's presence and staff were no longer controlling the situation or the flow of information, that officials in Washington began to realize that the wartime collaboration policy was in serious trouble. Belatedly, Washington tried to exert influence. The day after Osmeña vetoed the Roxas version, Ickes attempted to strengthen Osmeña's hand during a radio broadcast on the C.B.S. network celebrating Osmeña's sixty-seventh birthday. Ickes noted that "this wanton war" had "killed and maimed many of the best and worthiest Filipinos. It has tested in the terrible crucible of war the spirit of each Filipino. With few exceptions the people of the Philippines have proved themselves to be staunch, fearless and devoted." Ickes further commented that "except for a few," the Filipinos "refused to yield to the temptation offered by their enemies, or to cringe before the samurai sword of their momentary invader. I am certain that from their common anguish there will emerge a stronger and more confident Philippine people." Ickes claimed to be confident that the Filipinos would "firmly, coldly and relentlessly cast out those few timid, craven, and opportunistic helots who basely collaborated with the cruel enemy who sought to enslave their people." Ickes concluded with a direct appeal to Osmeña. "Finally, to President Osmeña, I say: 'may your heart continue strong, your eyes clear, and your arm sturdy for the great job that lies ahead.' "[8]

A few days later, on September 11, Ickes sent Osmeña a cable to make sure that he and his government had got the point clearly. It bluntly stated that "both official and press reports indicate that a substantial number of persons who adhered to the enemy and gave him aid and comfort through their service in the puppet governments during invasion are now holding important offices in various branches of the Commonwealth government including judiciary. I am informed that you intend to release numerous persons against whom evidence was collected by the United States Army." Ickes then reminded Osmeña of Roosevelt's policy "that those who have collaborated with the enemy must be removed from authority and influence over the political and economic life of the country." Noting that the Commonwealth was to fulfill this policy, Ickes deemed it essential "that this task be completed before the holding of the next Commonwealth general elections and I would call the attention of your government to the probable reluctance with which funds may be appropriated for relief rehabilitation and support of the Commonwealth government if it becomes generally believed that that government has failed diligently and firmly to convict and punish those guilty of collaboration."[9]

The telegram was a major blunder. Its contents soon leaked out and embarrassed Osmeña greatly. Ickes revealed only a dim awareness of the political and social realities of the archipelago. Since MacArthur was known to support Roxas, the division of American policy became evident. Ickes' blackmail threat to withhold aid made Osmeña seem a stooge for the Americans. Ironically, it further weakened him by apparently withdrawing some of Washington's support. Cast unhappily in the role of an unsuccessful lackey, Osmeña had to answer Ickes. Sharply denying Ickes' allegations, Osmeña noted that the prisoners he was releasing had been detained beyond the legal limits permitted under Philippine law. He further commented that a People's Court would "try all persons accused of collaboration." He defended his policy of reinstating officials who had committed no hostile act and, in effect, was forced to assume a nationalist response to what was heavy-handed meddling by an American.[10]

Osmeña was caught in a cross fire. Despite his telegrammed response to Ickes' charges, Washington pressure increased. He was forced to promise that he would speed what the *New York Times* called the "Quisling trials," though he was well aware of the domestic damage his buckling to American pressure was causing politically.[11] At the same time he was being attacked in the Philippines as soft on the "collaborators" because two of his sons were implicated. Senator Mariano Cuenco of Cebu called for his resignation because he could not do justice while his sons were involved, and it was Roxas who rose on the Senate floor to defend Osmeña's integrity.[12] Attacked for whatever he did, Osmeña was unable to stand still and not powerful enough to move forward alone.

After considerable backroom political negotiation, he finally reached a compromise with the Roxas forces, creating a "People's Court and an Office of Special Prosecutors for the prosecution and trial of . . . crimes against our national security committed during the war."[13] Osmeña claimed that this act (No. 682) would be able "to deal with political offenders with the utmost dispatch and with guarantees essential to a fair and impartial hearing."[14] However, this claim was made more to appease Ickes than to state facts. The Roxas group had won a number of concessions inhibiting the potential of the court. Only fifteen judges, divided into five divisions of three each, were authorized. A strict six-month time limit was established for filing the indictments against the approximately 5600 cases turned over from the American army to the Commonwealth government. The appropriation of money to the People's Court was so limited that funds existed for only twenty-five prosecutors. Each prosecutor, therefore, had six months to prepare approximately 225 cases. Each prosecutor working a six-day week had to prepare roughly nine cases a week. Since transportation and communication were paralyzed and records were lost or destroyed, this rigid time and staff limitation weakened the potential effectiveness of the prosecution enormously. The actual trials would of necessity drag on for decades if there were only five courts with three judges sitting on each case.

The staffing of the prosecution and courts raised additional problems. Osmeña's prime task was to find someone to serve as solicitor general. This man had to have a clean record himself, had to be dedicated and skillful as a lawyer and administrator, and had to be willing to risk the censure of the elite for bringing the wartime oligarchy to trial. After some search Osmeña prevailed upon Lorenzo Tañada, a lawyer trained by Felix Frankfurter, to accept the post. Tañada realized he faced formidable opposition under the severe restrictions of what he called the "weak and rotten" People's Court Act. Aware of Osmeña's awkward position, Tañada knew that his only hope of success lay in using the dossiers prepared by the American Counter-Intelligence Corps and in relying on American legal and financial support. However, the aid he needed had to come from MacArthur's staff, and it was not forthcoming. The jeeps, airplanes, and assistance of the American judge advocate's personnel was diverted to the war tribunals in Tokyo. MacArthur's legal staff was ordered not to become involved, and Washington's policy was further undermined by MacArthur's Tokyo headquarters.[15]

In late September Truman's high commissioner, Paul McNutt,

belatedly reported to Washington that "by inattention to civil affairs we have allowed the enemy collaborators to come into control of the legislative branch . . . and to force Osmeña, who is weak and aging, to compromise with them. For our part, we do not wish to be placed in the position of granting independence to a Philippine government composed of enemy-collaborators."[16] For the first time, Truman became personally concerned about the way this issue was drifting. In the course of discussions about possible remedial steps, Truman wrote Attorney General Tom Clark, noting that while many in health and education "remained at posts of duty with an evident intention to sustain the physical and cultural welfare of their people, . . . regrettably, a number of persons prominent in the political life of the country assisted the enemy in the formulation and enforcement of his political policies and the spread of his propaganda." Truman's instructions, which had whole sentences taken verbatim from Ickes' telegram to Osmeña and clearly showed the influence of Ickes on this issue, requested that Clark "send experienced personnel to the Philippines" to discover and to recommend what action would be appropriate for the United States to take.[17]

Truman's sudden concern for this issue was soon known in both the United States and the Philippines. In late November the *New York Times* reported that the attorney general was sending a key assistant, Thomas Hennings of St. Louis, to Manila to investigate.[18] A few weeks later it was announced that Walter R. Hutchinson, another member of Clark's staff, would make the investigation instead.[19] Hutchinson flew to Manila where he met with Tañada, Secretary of Justice Ramon Quisumbing, Colonel George Bishop of MacArthur's intelligence staff, and many other Filipino and American officials. His presence in Manila and the possibility that on the basis of his report the American government might intervene openly in the collaboration issue was a critical factor influencing events in the Philippines that winter. Virtually every decision taken by the Filipino leaders, who jockeyed for position throughout the winter, was to some extent influenced by Hutchinson's awaited report.

On October 1 the People's Court had begun its first case: "The People of the Philippines, Plaintiff v. Teofilo Sison, Accused—Criminal case No. one for treason." On October 27 Sison pleaded not guilty before the three judges, and for the next five months, while people waited in Manila, attention focused on this first case and potential precedent. Sison, as a second echelon official in the wartime governments, was clearly the test by which future prosecution and defense arguments would be determined. The case received tremendous publicity as a result.

By the time the Sison trial began, it had become clear that Roxas, with MacArthur's tacit approval, had decided to make an open break with Osmeña and splinter the hitherto dominant Nacionalista party of Quezon. As independence approached, problems proliferated. A new relationship with the United States had to be structured; a new pattern of economic legislation including trade, tariffs, American investment, parity rights, rehabilitation, and restoration had to be evolved. Roxas considered Osmeña as lacking the drive and the personal contacts necessary to get even a moderately acceptable settlement of these issues. Osmeña had failed to move the American Congress into action, despite a series of trips to Washington. Roxas, convinced that Osmeña was unable to evolve solutions for the numerous other issues including a postindependence security agreement, veteran legislation, and a new sense of dynamism for the nation, resolved to challenge Osmeña at the next election.

This challenge to Osmeña's claim as Quezon's successor had its origins in the prewar era. In the postwar period it was spurred by Osmeña's apparent inefficiency and weariness and by the explosiveness of the collaboration issue. Everyone who dealt with Osmeña came away with the impression of his age and ambivalence. While party stalwarts struggled to preserve the Nacionalista party either by getting Osmeña to step down in favor of Roxas or by getting Roxas to agree to be vice-president, the two sides were increasingly hostile to each other. By December the *New York Times* reported an "irreconcilable" split between the two men.[20] Roxas took over one of the small splinter parties, the Liberal party, from its leader, former Congressman Prudencio Remigio.[21] Using this vehicle, he split the Nacionalistas and thus the oligarchy. While his action was based on a combination of factors, including his belief that he could give more dynamic leadership, his disenchantment with Osmeña's policies, his own ambition, and his knowledge of MacArthur's support, Roxas in part became the spokesman for the group who had collaborated. He gained the active support of those who were under accusation in a way that might not have happened had the collaboration issue been absent in the forthcoming election. He was able to carry a potent segment of the oligarchy with him out of the Nacionalista party because of this issue.

While Osmeña retained the outer symbol of the Nacionalista party name, he lost to Roxas the inner living core of functionaries. Osmeña was forced to look elsewhere for political support. He was forced to depend on former guerrillas and lesser officials who had lacked prewar power and who lacked the lifetime of reciprocal political relations with local functionaries throughout the country. As the prosecutor of the wartime elite, he bore the onus for continuing the division of the society between guerrilla and collaborationist. Lacking options, he had to welcome fringe groups into his inner council, with the direct result that he alienated many hitherto neutral Nacionalista oligarchs and drove them toward Roxas. The awkward obligation to prosecute the collaborators made Osmeña something of a traitor to his own group and isolated him from his peers. After years in the United States his personal reciprocal bonds with his followers had slipped, and he showed neither the energy nor the inclination to take to the hustings to reestablish them. While his supporters attempted to utilize patronage to rekindle the dormant fires of political support, he himself did not pursue actively the necessary symbiotic relationship required in the patron-client bonds.

Osmeña's isolation led him to accept support from all wartime guerrilla groups including the powerful leftist Hukbalahap. The Huks represented both a communist threat and a manifestation of peasant unrest against the traditional social order. Nearly autonomous during the war, the Hukbalahap refused to disband after the war ended. They were divided politically, one group urging a direct use of violence to achieve revolution, and the other urging an alliance with Osmeña to reach power peacefully. They attempted to develop both possibilities; initially the moderate element won out. Through the Democratic Alliance, a political arm of this peasant unrest, they attempted to use the collaboration argument to embarrass and weaken the wartime elite. When Ickes had cabled Osmeña, the Democratic Alliance in a cable to Ickes was "sincerely gratified" by Ickes' "forthright clarification" of the collaboration issue, especially "in view of pernicious attempt of [the] powerful collaborationist clique led by Roxas to sabotage plans to bring [the] collaborators to speedy trial before [the] People's Court."[22] The Huks could offer Osmeña solid electoral support in central Luzon, but at a high price for him elsewhere.

His dilemma was clear. In order to find support he was forced by the collaboration issue into a working relationship with the whole spectrum of nonoligarchic groups within the society. But in this move, especially by his acceptance of leftist support, he alienated many uncommitted Filipinos who shared with the oligarchy a deep-seated fear of radical leftist movements. The oligarchy stood for security to these people. Society was already so disrupted that the elite, as a group, represented one of the few surviving links with an earlier and simpler past. Few were aware of this consciously, but as it became clear that prewar normality would never return, people began to crave such normality more passionately. The Hukbalahap threatened to split the fabric of Philippine society even further, and the specter of civil war was so horrendous that many rallied to Roxas and his followers, despite the taint of their wartime actions. Initially, the Huk threat challenged only a relatively few landlords in central Luzon directly, but indirectly it menaced every aspect of the traditional order. Many Filipinos confronted with that choice opted for Roxas to help protect the established order. The Huk movement, by consciously maintaining the polarization of society between landlord collaborators and peasant guerrillas, forced many uncommitted Filipinos to change their scale of priorities, especially on collaboration. The delineation of the postwar world altered the perspectives formed during a wartime situation.

Osmeña, caught in this vicious circle, increasingly lost his traditional appeal to the great moneyed families who underwrote election campaigns. Sympathetic to Osmeña personally, these families feared he had become the pawn of the radical left, which was their avowed enemy. They became unwilling to gamble on this risky course when Roxas, a known economic commodity, was promising major success through his good connections with MacArthur. The economy needed help, and they wanted to control the flow and manner in which this aid would be spent. Many of this economic elite, compromised by charges of economic collaboration, had additional reason to fear Osmeña because of his commitment to prosecute collaborators. Consequently, these families tended to support Roxas financially, with the result that Osmeña was pushed further and further away from the center of gravity.

Roxas very shrewdly capitalized on this shifting climate. He emphasized his connections with MacArthur. He had his aides publicize him as an economic wizard. He stressed his resolute anticommunist leanings and his utter hostility to radicalism. He minimized collaboration by confronting it directly and by blurring the question of wartime motivation. In his acceptance speech to the Liberal party when it nominated him for the president, he said on January 19, 1946, that he was the sworn enemy of collaboration. He did not believe, however, "that a man, merely because he occupied a public office during the Japanese occupation, is necessarily a collaborator or traitor." He defined someone as guilty "who can be proven to have voluntarily given aid, comfort, and sustenance to the enemy," and he stated that he stood "four square" by the proposition that anyone who could be found guilty "should be condemned by the courts to the severest punishment and many of them should be hanged." Roxas shrewdly claimed that he wanted "to remove the question of collaboration from politics." He knew that if the issue could be neutralized politically it might be neutralized judicially also.[23] The Liberal party platform promised "to prosecute mercilessly those guilty of collaboration," but ten of the sixteen national Liberal candidates for senator had held wartime positions and three of the remaining six were accused of making money off the war.[24]

Roxas tried to shift the focus away from what the wartime leaders had actually said and done to whether they could be held accountable if they had been forced into service under duress. He projected the war leader as the highest kind of hero, willing to accept an unpleasant job rather than run to the hills and leave the people in the lurch as, he implied, the guerrilla leaders had done. His own record was ideal for such an appeal, because he could legitimately claim that he served only with great reluctance when famine threatened. Roxas used his own record of wartime behavior as an exemplary model, and many of the wartime leaders who had been more vocal received indirect assistance from this policy.

Nine days after Roxas' nomination, Hutchinson submitted his "confidential" preliminary report to Attorney General Tom Clark and High Commissioner Paul McNutt. The report, which was never made public, stated frankly that "the present situation is one of our [America's] own making. After liberation of the Philippines, our army and navy intelligence had . . . developed substantial cases against practically all of the collaborators. But instead of disposing of the cases in the same manner as the other United Nations, we gave the basic and gigantic problem of collaborationism over to the Commonwealth government, harassed by problems of rehabilitation and itself, not entirely free of collaborationists in its component units, its congress, its army." Hutchinson continued by urging that it was "American duty and American principle to implement the case of the American and Filipino peoples against the collaborationists." Hutchinson urged that the key collaborators be brought to trial for treason to the United States, if for nothing else, and he urged that "there must not be permitted any loopholes of escape for they are America's Quislings." He felt this was an obligation to "the thousands who have died in a sacred, democratic cause."[25]

Hutchinson's solution was legal rather than political. Unaware of the dynamic of Fil-American relations, he urged the United States "to adopt a policy to enter into and participate in the trial and disposition" of all the treason cases under one of three methods.

Most attractive to Hutchinson was a war crime tribunal which would have Filipino judges and prosecutors but which would have American support by treaty right after independence to guarantee trial of all the cases. Hutchinson felt that "this would have universal support among the Filipinos." His second alternative was "an extra-territorial court in the Philippines to commence hearings at as early a date as possible in cooperation with the officials of the Philippines. . . ." Hutchinson wanted the United States to have the rights "to investigate, arrest, prosecute, and convict persons" charged with treason. This alternative, he felt, would "have support among the rank and file of the Filipino people." His third solution was to change venue by trying all those charged with treason before American courts in the United States. Hutchinson stated that "this likewise would receive the approval of the Filipino people. . . ."[26] He urged immediate United States legal and financial aid for Tañada and his staff. He felt that a jury system would not work and questioned whether even the three judges could be protected from political pressure.

He noted that "there appears to be little or no consideration being given to the prosecution of members of the Philippine National Congress who served under the Japanese and who now retain their position. . . ,"[27] and that only the ranking members of the prewar legislature such as Recto, Yulo, Paredes, and De las Alas were still denied their seats and were out on bail with a good chance of being seated soon. He concluded that Osmeña "has not publicly taken a position that would lend strength to an all-out prosecution of collaborators; in fact, his administrative position has been described as one of appeasement."[28]

Hutchinson reported that "the entire plan and program . . . for investigation, arrest and trial of known collaborators" bogged down because "the problem was not attacked and pursued to conclusion by the United States military forces immediately after our re-entry into the Philippines"; instead, he remarked, it was turned over to Osmeña, who was unable to handle it. He observed that the whole question had been "so discussed in the newspapers, and by politicians so as to obscure the real crime, that of committing treason, and thereby lessening in the minds of many people, including some of the present government, the enormity of the offense." Hutchinson predicted that unless the United States acted, "a general amnesty will be declared by whoever wins the election thereby freeing many if not all leading collaborators. This probability is almost a certainty if Roxas is elected."[29]

The Hutchinson report was sent to Washington, where it received close attention by high officials during the late winter of 1946. While no one in Manila knew its recommendations, it clearly magnified the political tensions already sharpened by the Roxas-Osmeña split. Another factor which increased tension because of its unknown outcome was the Sison trial. This case had been watched closely throughout the late autumn and winter, and the People's Court was expected to hand down a decision during the late winter. Both the Hutchinson report and the Sison decision would have an obvious and perhaps overwhelming effect on the election, and until these two unknown factors were assessed, the political future remained clouded.

Teofilo Sison was a charter member of the modern oligarchy. Born on February 29, 1880, he had served as governor of Pangasinan, secretary of the Interior, secretary of National Defense, and secretary of Justice. He had been one of the signers of the provisional Council of State in early 1942 and had served as minister of Justice and Home Affairs in the Laurel republic.[30] His case had been chosen as the test because his wartime actions raised the basic dilemma underlying every future political trial before the People's Court. The American Counter-Intelligence Corps report stated ambivalently that Sison may only have "accepted these appointments in order to steer his country through a critical period and not because of any desire to further Japan's program. . . . Among Americans he was one of the most highly regarded Filipino political leaders. . . . The fact remains, however, that he has very definitely helped their [the Japanese] cause by holding high positions in the collaborationist government."[31]

Sison was charged before the People's Court with twenty-six counts of treason. The first was merely for holding office during the wartime administrations. The prosecution maintained that "the act of accepting, holding and performing the duties and functions of the aforementioned positions . . . clearly shows the defendant's treasonable adherence. . . . Hence, said act constituted an overt act of treason."[32] The second charge concerned the oath to the Kalibapi, which Sison took and which began, "On my honor, I solemnly pledge to be loyal to the Japanese Military Administration. . . ." The third concerned the "letter of response" of January 23, 1942. The prosecution urged that duress was not a defense in signing that letter, since Dr. Jose Fabella and Alfonso Mendoza had suffered no ill effects from their refusal to sign.[33]

Charges four and five dealt with the "Manifesto to the Philippine People" of February 26, 1943, and the "Appeal to the Philippine People" of May 31, 1943. Charge seven concerned Laurel's Proclamation No. 30 declaring a "state of war" to exist. The indictment alleged that since Sison was, at the cabinet and Council of State meetings, called to discuss this proclamation, his failure to oppose its issuance or to resign constituted his tacit approval. The tenth count dealt with Sison's circular letter of November 1944, which he sent out as inspector general of Martial Law for Laurel. This circular, which gave instructions to local officials regarding "treason, sedition, and other crimes," had in the opinion of the prosecution the natural effect of deterring Filipinos from harassing the Japanese and from extending aid to the Fil-American forces of liberation.[34]

Most of the other counts cited specific speeches which Sison was alleged to have made. Some could be established by two witnesses to the overt act and others could not, but until it was clear how lenient the People's Court would be on the witness rule, every charge was filed. Charge nineteen alleged a private meeting between Sison and some local judges at which Sison urged them to cooperate with the Japanese. Charges twenty and twenty-two concerned his control over other government employees through his position as secretary. He was accused of threatening his staff that the first people to be fired would be those who did not show pro-Japanese sympathies, and he was indicted for circulating a letter in June 1944 in which he threatened to withhold salaries unless the employees under his control took an oath to the Laurel republic.

Charge twenty-four accused him of ordering the recruitment of forced labor on October 12, 1944, in his capacity as inspector general of Martial Law, by sending a series of telegrams to the provincial authorities. The prosecution stressed the "military purposes" for which these recruits were openly used, and it argued that even if the labor force was proven never to have given the Japanese aid and comfort, Sison was accountable for the intent rather than the fact.[35]

Sison, who was defended by three prominent Manila lawyers, Jose Hontiveros, Mariano Albert, and Jose Aruego, offered a seven-point defense. First, he made a general denial of his guilt in any of the charges against him. Second, he claimed that during the occupation, prewar allegiance was suspended because of the triumph of Japanese military might. He maintained that the Vargas and Laurel governments were the only de facto governments. Third, he argued that words, whether oral or written, could not be treason, because at worst they constituted mere sympathetic expressions. Conviction on a charge of treason, he claimed, required two witnesses to an overt physical deed. Fourth, he propounded a theory of duress which permitted him to justify his actions because of the threat of Japanese force. Fifth, he asserted that he was only executing the instructions which the leader, Quezon, had left before his evacuation to Corregidor. Sixth, he said that he had acted because he was concerned for the health, welfare, and protection of the Filipinos, for whom he felt love and obligation. Finally, he asserted that he had secretly supported the resistance movement by contributing to the guerrillas and by remaining secretly loyal to the Allied cause.[36]

In rebuttal Tañada attempted to refute each of Sison's defense arguments. He claimed that allegiance was permanent, and as a result the treason statute, Article 114 of the Revised Penal Code, remained in force during the war. Tañada said, "What was suspended during enemy occupation was the exercise of . . . sovereignty, but this fact would not prevent the United States and the Commonwealth . . . from punishing the citizens of the Philippine Islands for treason . . . when they returned and expelled the Japanese invaders."[37] Citing the examples of Laval, Petain, and Quisling, Tañada referred to the Belgian case, *Suditeur Militaire a. G. van Diaren,* and the South African case, *Ladewyk Johannes de Jager* v. *Attorney General of Natal,* to gain legal precedents for his claim of continuing sovereignty. He quoted the South African decision, which had stated that "the protection of a state does not cease merely because the state forces, for strategical or other reasons, are temporarily withdrawn, so that the enemy for the time being exercises the rights of an army of occupation." Tañada emphasized the clause which stated that "the actual redress of what has been done amiss may be necessarily postponed until the enemy forces have been expelled."[38]

Tañada also argued that the overt act need not succeed provided the enemy's cause would have been aided if it had met with success. The prosecution attempted to refute Sison's defense claim of Quezon's alleged instructions by maintaining that, even if Quezon had actually given such orders, he had no authority to do so. Every government employee had, as a citizen, a direct obligation to the constitution which transcended any loyalty to a superior no matter how famous or distinguished. It was argued that Quezon had no power to issue orders which contradicted the obligations the citizen owed to the constitution.

To Sison's claim that he acted to protect the general welfare the prosecution replied bluntly that "war is a highly practical affair, and consequently, what matters are deeds and results and not thoughts. Personal motive or purpose, therefore, no matter how laudable it is, cannot condone the offense." The judges were urged not to allow Sison "to take shelter behind the nice metaphysical distinction that although he [Sison] knew perfectly well that he was assisting and advancing the interest of the enemy, he did not intend to do so, but only meant to help the people."[39] The court was further reminded that in a society of law, protection for all lay in the prior construction of codes. Thus, any man who disregarded the established codes had to run the risk of social censure.

The prosecution also attempted to refute the argument of duress. It listed for the judges men who had managed to leave office without suffering any penalty and stated that the fear of punishment must be immediate and well-founded for the defense of duress to be valid. It emphatically rejected the concept of "collective duress," in which a whole group within a society could claim fear of reprisals.[40] Similarly, it rejected Sison's claim that he had aided the guerrillas, noting that whatever efforts he had made were not sufficient to qualify as an extenuating circumstance.

Finally, the prosecution argued that Sison had no defense in denying the authorship of the speeches he was alleged to have made. While conceding that Japanese propagandists might have altered his words, the prosecution argued that Sison could not deny the total weight of the evidence presented against him. It cited the recently decided American case of *Cramer* v. *the United States* (65 S.C. 918) to substantiate its claim that no court could ever divine a man's motivation. Noting that it was impossible to prove conclusively what a man was thinking, it argued that a man must be judged by his words and his actions, because no other valid criteria existed.

Sison's final defense in his summation before the judges was a fervent appeal of his innocence. He said that "if it is a crime to have feigned collaboration with the enemy, to be of service to my people, then I am ready to serve the penalty meted out to me by the respected tribunal of Philippine justice."[41] He thrust onto the three-man panel the dilemma of the occupation; he stood before the judges as a distinguished servant accused of the most dreadful of social crimes. If he was found innocent, who of the wartime leaders was guilty? If he was found guilty, how could any of the others establish their innocence? If he was guilty, what punishment would fit the crime? As the case reached its conclusion, attention shifted to the three judges who had to ponder and to decide.

The judges had to make their verdict on the basis of a provision in the penal code which defined treason in terms of American precedent. The statute, which was written during the American occupation, was transferred directly from American law and was ill suited to the Philippine colonial context. The three judges had to determine Sison's fate on the basis of a clause written in 1789 to satisfy a specific American situation; as they were to discover, its applicability to a twentieth-century collaboration trial was tenuous.[42] The statute (Article 114) read that "any person who, owing allegiance to the United States or the Government of the Philippine Islands, not being a foreigner, levies war against them or adheres to their enemies, giving them aid or comfort within the Philippine Islands or elsewhere" shall be punished with either life imprisonment or the death penalty. It went on to state that "no person shall be convicted of treason unless on the testimony of two witnesses at least to the same overt act or on the confession of the accused in open court." Therefore, unless there had been some other criminal offense, the only charge which could be brought against a collaborator was the capital offense of treason, with its exceptional requirements for proof. Since there was no lesser provision in the statutes, it was an all or nothing situation.

The American Supreme Court, shortly after the United States acquired the Philippines from Spain, had ruled in the *Diamond Rings Case* (185 U.S. 176) that the Philippines had "come under the complete and absolute sovereignty and dominion of the United States, and so, became territory of the United States over which civil government could be established. Their allegiance became due to the United States and they became entitled to its protection." As a consequence, technically it was an equal crime to commit treason against either the United States or the Philippines. However, in a colonial context did the treason provision remain if the United States had failed to give the protection which the Filipinos were entitled to receive? Moreover, given the nature of Philippine nationalism, mature and about to receive independence, could there be treason against the United States if the Filipino's loyalty to his own nation put him at variance with the technical statutory provision demanding loyalty to the metropolitan power? If the accused could substantiate that he had been loyal to the Philippines at the cost of treason to the United States, could he be convicted of a capital crime for malfeasance to the United States? Despite Hutchinson's claim that the United States should intervene to try the wartime leaders for treason to the United States, it was dubious that this assertion had force. Either the People's Court would find Sison guilty of treason to the Philippines and convict him on those grounds, or it would find him innocent. Modern nationalism virtually excluded any other possibility.

In early March, after an agonizing wait, the three judges handed down their decision. All three found Teofilo Sison guilty, sentencing him to life imprisonment and fining him fifteen thousand pesos.[43] Two judges, Pompeyo Diaz and Jose Veluz, wrote in their majority decision that they had delved into the records and found them "replete with evidences of the accused's guilt." They turned to the law and found "therein nothing which will mitigate its rigor."[44]

The third judge, Antonio Quirino, had originally voted for the death penalty.[45] In his concurring opinion he wrote that "all told, the overt acts proved and enumerated in the foregoing, constitute a deep, unbroken stream of adherence which leaves no doubt as to the sympathies of Teofilo Sison." Quirino failed "to notice any streak of duress as this term is understood in order to constitute a legal defense." He wrote that "mere imaginary fear borne of the experience of others is certainly not the kind of duress contemplated as a defense of treason." Quirino equally rejected the defense based upon Quezon's instruction, noting that Quezon's instruction, "if it was given at all, is as much talked of as it has been misunderstood. As interpreted by the defense, it does not lend credit to the late President."

Quirino wrote that "the phrase 'for the good of the people' means and should mean the *ultimate* good; not merely the temporary relief from want and harm." He felt that the phrase "of the people" should refer not only to the living but also to the "generations yet unborn." Quirino asked the rhetorical question, if "collaboration had redounded for the good of the people, would such constitute a valid defense? The answer is obvious," he continued, "Suffice it to say that Petain, Laval and Quisling, and other no lesser figures from many lands, have all repeated the catchy selfsame plea." Quirino conceded that it "penetrates the innermost recesses of the heart and touches the finest chords of human feelings," but he noted that other countries had still extracted the "supreme penalty of death and dishonor" from the accused. Quirino argued that "the country must be preserved; the government must have unstinted loyalty"; and "national dignity and honor must be maintained at any cost."

The concurring opinion continued by rejecting Sison's argument that he had remained loyal, merely fooling the enemy. Quirino wrote that "loyalty is not merely vocal. Loyalty, to be true and to be believed, must be active and demonstrative, not passive and indifferent." Accepting the prosecution argument, Quirino insisted that "the success or failure of a treasonous venture is immaterial in the prosecution of treason. What is penalized is not the result of the act, but the act itself."[46]

The decision was a bombshell. It greatly strengthened the Osmeña forces, and set the Roxas forces back on the defensive for the first time. A week later, Bishop Cesar Ma. Guerrero was indicted for treason on thirteen counts, and two days after that, Laurel himself was indicted on one-hundred and thirty-two counts.[47] Suddenly, the whole political outlook had changed as Roxas' association with other wartime leaders appeared a distinct liability. Osmeña's strengths seemed greater than they had a few weeks before. People suddenly started to remember that he still held control of the Nacionalista party, with all of its rural strength based on tradition and habit. Osmeña's fame throughout the country, stretching back more than four decades, suddenly seemed to enhance his electoral chances. The Sison decision gave the Nacionalistas a potent weapon to attack the Roxas forces, and rumors of the strong anticollaborationist quality of the Hutchinson report indicated that Osmeña's strength in Washington rather than Roxas' strength with MacArthur would be the critical determinant.

The attack on the wartime leadership intensified. The opinions of the judges were publicized, and the wartime leaders were asked publicly in what ways they had mitigated the suffering of their countrymen. The nation was told that the claim of the collaborators to this effect was actually a perversion of the truth, which was that they had aided themselves. The nation was also asked whether there was a legal or moral right to claim that a person should be considered innocent because someone else would have done that same act anyway. The Japanese were bound to find some Filipinos willing to hold office, but did they have to be the most famous members of the elite?

These arguments, which had been used again and again by the guerrilla units, were now picked up by the Osmeña forces as a means of embarrassing the Liberals. The people were told that the longer the war lasted, the worse the civilians' suffering. Therefore, to the degree that the wartime elite helped the Japanese this elite had to bear the consequences of prolonging the war. If they were able to command respect from the people because of their prewar positions, they aided the Japanese by releasing at least some troops which might otherwise have had to be committed to the Philippine operation. By definition, it was argued, the more famous the collaborator, the easier the occupation for the enemy.

It was further argued that the national leadership had to accept the liabilities as well as the emoluments of office. The Osmeña supporters conceded the difficult position in which the elite found itself, but the responsibility of political trust placed greater risks on the officeholder than the average citizen had to bear. With a clear eye to the forthcoming election, it was claimed that public officials had to protect the prestige of their office before considering their personal interest. Although it was an unpleasant reality, the society might be compelled to remove officials to protect the integrity of the office. The theory expounded was that even an innocent official had to be willing to step aside if there was the slightest question of the propriety of continuing in power. The Filipinos were asked whether any of the wartime officials had shown that willingness. The people were reminded that one of the first things the 1941 Congress did upon reconvening in 1945 was to vote itself 31,600 pesos per member back pay for the war years. It was argued that had the wartime leadership stepped aside, it could have proven that it had acted patriotically and not selfishly, but that since the obverse was happening, it was the duty of the electorate to refuse to return these officials to postwar power.

While these arguments gained credence following the Sison conviction, the Osmeña forces maintained the upper hand for only a very short time. The momentum was stopped when Washington acted on the Hutchinson proposal. Despite the strong plea by Hutchinson for active intervention in the collaboration question, Truman rejected this plan and thus finally abandoned the wartime Roosevelt policy of an American-enforced purge. Truman's statement, reached after some sharp internal debate, declared "that there is no necessity for any change in our established policy of leaving the disposition of civil collaborationists in the Philippines to the civil authorities there."[48] Truman's decision, which was influenced by "the strong recommendation of General Douglas MacArthur," was based on the changed world situation of the approaching cold war. Its net effect was to minimize the collaboration issue for Osmeña despite the Sison conviction. The Truman decision left Osmeña pursuing a collaboration policy about which he had always been ambivalent. The decision lifted some of the cloud hanging over the Roxas forces, since it meant that Washington was less hostile than before.

For Truman to pursue the Hutchinson suggestions would have been to withdraw a vital element of Philippine sovereignty just prior to independence. It would have been an open admission that the United States did not think the Filipinos were able to handle the problem, and that they could not be trusted. Moreover, to reassume jurisdiction after such a long wait would be to shift the focus from the crime of treason against the Philippines to that of treason against the United States. Philippine nationalism would inevitably seize upon this invasion of sovereignty and convert the collaboration issue into a question of national maturity. Hutchinson was naive to think that any American intervention just before a Philippine election would be welcomed. Indeed, it was most probable that American intervention would guarantee the election of those very men whose conviction the United States had originally desired.

The American opportunity to intervene was lost when the policy planners in Washington failed to evolve a strategy before Osmeña returned. A clear American policy, formulated and executed not by the local military commander but by the President in Washington, might have kept Osmeña out of the quagmire of collaboration. It would have run the risk of making national martyrs of the wartime leaders, eliminating the possibility of their implication in crimes against Philippine society. It would, however, have permitted the United States to purge them for at least a brief time. The postwar political alignment would have altered, and Osmeña's hand would have been strengthened. The United States failed to impose its solution and at the same time allowed the wartime leaders to claim effectively that they were nationalists hounded by the metropolitan power. Charging that they had been patriots who had served the Philippines at the expense of America, the collaborators altered the debate from collaboration to latent anti-Americanism.

Tensions between the Americans and Filipinos had shown a marked increase in the months after the war ended. The large number of American troops, suddenly inactive, caused constant friction. The postwar American economic concessions were considered woefully inadequate. Many Filipinos felt that America had been *walang hiya* for failing to repay the debt of gratitude, the sense of *utang na loob*, which America owed the Philippines for wartime support. The provisions of the various agreements seemed niggardly, revealing the seamier side of American economic imperialism. The blackmail threats, like those of Ickes, to withhold the rehabilitation funds unless the Filipinos yielded to American wishes was an affront to Filipino dignity. American mistreatment of Philippine pride and

American insensitivity to the demands of the *compadre* relationship between the two countries saddened and embittered Filipinos.

Had the Hutchinson recommendations been adopted, Truman correctly saw that the Fil-American relationship would have deteriorated even further. Having withheld economic sovereignty from the Filipinos, the Truman administration could not deny judicial sovereignty without making a complete sham of the promise of political independence. The legal problems of collaboration could not be dissociated from their political effects, as Hutchinson proposed. The Americans missed the chance to do what they thought was correct. Thereafter, they could only hope that the People's Court would come to consider the events in a way akin to their own. The Sison case gave evidence that this might occur. Truman felt that his best course would be to gamble that the Sison case was the precedent. Any other policy contained too many risks.

This decision was greatly reinforced by the changing American policy objectives throughout the world. The emergence of a major communist threat in Europe, China, and also the Philippines, coupled with the growing American concern to contain communism everywhere, led the Truman administration to see the Philippines in a new light. The American desire to avenge by trying the collaborators receded as the United States began the cold war. The Philippines had to be America's showcase of democracy in Asia after independence as well as before it, and Truman gradually realized that the Hukbalahap threat was at the least embarrassing and at the most potentially disastrous to American power and prestige. Since the China situation was deteriorating rapidly with the effective communist insurgency throughout this period, American planners were alarmed at how ill-prepared the Philippines, with its dowry of carnage and civil war, would be for independence.

MacArthur in Japan, McNutt in Manila, and many in Washington advocated a series of measures designed to bolster the embryonic nation and to guarantee that it would not go communist. The new priority scale embodied in these measures did not put collaboration high on the list. The new policy, in fact, advocated massive support of the traditional oligarchy to enable it to restore order, to lead the fight against communism, and to assure stable leadership in independence. This required that the collaboration question—a divisive issue within the oligarchy—be allowed to fade. As in the early American era, when the United States backed the traditional order rather than the radical reformers, once again the United States supported the establishment against the radical reformers of Philippine society. Washington, considering the Hukbalahap to be the international conspiracy of communism, ignored the noncommunist, indigenous, albeit radical, quality of peasant unrest.

The American insistence upon viewing this complex movement in simplistic terms led the United States government to reverse its wartime valuation of collaboration. The oligarchy as a whole, rather than any wartime division of it, became important. American money and prestige started to flow to the very men that Roosevelt had wanted to purge only a few years earlier. Washington began to see Roxas not as the collaborationist candidate but as an economic wizard who was anticommunist and who could be depended upon to keep the Philippines staunchly on the American side in the global struggle with communism. Osmeña, in turn, was distrusted more, especially after he accepted support from the Hukbalahap and the Democratic Alliance. Caught in a web by trying to fulfill Washington's policy, Osmeña, ironically, was driven into a situation in which the Americans turned against him because of his pro-American efforts. The effect of the American shift in policy, which was visibly demonstrated by the Truman statement, was to befuddle further an already befuddled collaboration question. The American concern with the communist threat silenced many of the noncommunist but antioligarchic voices in the Philippines, since the new postwar realities made a middle position untenable. It became increasingly difficult to be antiestablishment without being labeled as a sympathizer of the Hukbalahap.

This gradual change was reinforced by the behavior of the wartime oligarchs, who demanded throughout the postwar period that society restore them to power. They refused to approach the nation as humble supplicants begging forgiveness for their wartime actions. They themselves did not doubt the compelling need of society to return them to their prewar positions, maintaining, as a result, their traditional status of dominance, even under indictment. Shrewdly aware of the dynamics of Philippine social structure and of their own historic role in that structure, they denied categorically that they had committed any acts of which they need be ashamed. They denied that there had been any alternative for them. Without apology or penitence they told the people that no one, especially the Americans, could appreciate "the bargaining, the evasions, the temporizings and the show of apparent cooperation" which they and all Filipinos had to make in order to placate the Japanese.[49] Quintin Paredes said later that the saddest thing was that many of those who "benefited by our conduct that had exposed us all the time to dangers, are our most uncompromising accusers, in thinking that they are the only patriots, and all the rest are traitors."[50] Laurel noted that there was "heroism" in collaboration.[51] Jose Ma. Veloso attacked the "advocates of the policy of unmitigating revenge and reprisal, hate and hostility [who] are sowing the seeds of dissension. Such seeds, allowed to grow, will cause the eternal damnation of our people."[52]

Washington's new policy, in addition to the strong defense of the wartime leadership, left Osmeña in a weak position and tended to nullify his brief advantage from the Sison conviction. Truman's statement relieved some of the tension for the wartime elite by indicating that with the passage of time, the collaboration question would recede. America's new priorities required retention of the established Filipino leadership, and Osmeña, with his new nonoligarchic supporters, was somewhat on the fringe. Roxas, capitalizing on the numerous issues at play in the forthcoming election, became the man with a future. The bandwagon began to move in his favor, and Osmeña was unwilling or unable to stop it. Osmeña refused to campaign, running on his name and reputation. Roxas took to the hustings and permitted the Filipinos to participate in one of their favorite activities, the political rally, for the first time since Quezon's campaign of 1941.

The elections, held on April 23, 1946, gave Roxas a solid but not overwhelming victory. By gaining 54 percent of the vote he carried most of the Liberal party into office with him. For the first time since 1907 neither the Nacionalistas nor Osmeña held peacetime power. All sorts of imponderables, including an American decision to prosecute the collaborators, might have altered the outcome of the election. For whatever reasons, the nation voted for the men who had stayed in Manila rather than for those who had taken to the hills or to Washington.

Osmeña cabled Roxas his formal concession on April 29. The day before, when the election was already assured, Roxas had broadcast to the American people by radio. Talking about the charges leveled against him as the collaborationist candidate, he said that "these charges have been completely and unequivocally repudiated by the Filipino people who were here and in the best position to know the significance of my actions." Roxas asserted that he considered himself "completely cleared of all taint of collaboration." He claimed that he had been "fully vindicated by the highest and fairest tribunal that can pass upon such matters," noting that if "there had been any semblance of truth to these charges, the Filipino people would have completely rejected" him.[53]

Two weeks later the validity of the electoral mandate was

endorsed by MacArthur, who met Roxas, on his way to Washington, in Japan. Speaking of Roxas as "a staunch patriot and a most fitting representative," MacArthur stated that "the recent election, which selected Roxas for the presidency reflected the repudiation by the Filipino people of irresponsible charges of collaboration made in foreign countries by those who lack an adequate knowledge of the circumstances."[54]

The political explosiveness of collaboration did not end immediately. At the opening session of the newly elected Congress, called on May 25 to certify Roxas' election, the anti-Roxas forces, led by Tomas Confesor, walked out over a procedural issue. This boycott postponed the certification of Roxas as president until May 28. This three-day flurry arose when Confesor challenged the seating of three senators still under indictment for treason as collaborators. Confesor claimed that these men did not have the right to take their seats and that under the Commonwealth rules the certification of a president required a majority of the total number of senators rather than a simple majority of those present. Maintaining that sixteen senators were required to form a quorum and that the three indicted senators could not vote, he argued that Roxas could not be certified without the approval of the minority Nacionalistas. A comparable seating dispute took place in the House, but there the indicted collaborators were seated in order to use their votes to prevent the Hukbalahap leader, Luis Taruc, from taking his seat.[55]

These procedural efforts failed. They represented the last gasp of the political fight over collaboration.[56] The guerrillas, both moderate and radical, were denied power on a group basis, though individual leaders were incorporated into the elite structure. This sapped much of the legal opposition to the oligarchy, forcing dissident elements to resort to violence to make their protest felt. Taruc, barred from his seat on the charge of election irregularities, led the Huk movement into a violent phase. By resort to violence he was forced to assume an extralegal, and therefore illegal, stance. As in previous times, the elite coalesced as the national symbol of unity and stability. With chaos and further unrest as the alternative, most Filipinos rallied to support the traditional order in its fight with the radical Hukbalahap. This decision had the blessing of the American government, summed up in a *New York Times* editorial which stated that "the time would seem to have come for the Filipinos to collaborate with each other."[57] It was, therefore, only a matter of time before the courts began reflecting the political decisions of the nation. The Sison conviction became the exception which proved the rule that justice cannot be dispensed in a vacuum.

CHAPTER VIII

The Trials

Treason doth never prosper;
What's the reason?
Why, if it prosper, none dare call it treason.
                                        —John Harrington

On July 4, 1946, when the Philippines became an independent republic, the Americans ended their venture into colonialism. Roxas, who had already been inaugurated as president of the Commonwealth, was reinaugurated as president of the republic. With great pomp the Stars and Stripes was furled as MacArthur and lesser American luminaries watched the symbolic occasion. The Philippine flag was raised alone to full staff amid general rejoicing, as Roxas pledged that the new nation would preserve her historic, intimate ties with America in the years to come. He pledged to rebuild the country, maintain peace and order, preserve democracy, and oppose communism. The American government had succeeded in fulfilling the original policy objectives of McKinley, Theodore Roosevelt, and Taft. The Philippines became independent without the birth trauma of hatred for the metropolitan power; the self-liquidating quality of American imperialism had smoothed over what was a friction point elsewhere in the world. The tacit alliance between America and the evolutionary elite had worked. Just as the initial bargain had blunted the hostility of the Insurrection in 1901 by turning imperialism into altruism and hostility into friendship, the Truman decision not to intervene in the prosecution of the collaborators launched the new nation under the firm command of the American-supported oligarchy. This success, which was achieved at the price of social reform, left a legacy of violent agrarian discontent. The Hukbalahap validly accused the elite of collaborating with the Americans at the expense of the peasant.

This postwar reaffirmation of the traditional alliance between the elite and the Americans did not resolve the problem of collaboration, but it did much to guarantee that the verdict would be an acquittal. Shortly after independence Roxas "ordered the collaboration issue out of politics and into the courts, where it must be decided."[1] It was obvious, however, that the People's Court was very sensitive to the political, social, and economic events around it. At the time of independence the People's Court had tried only ninety-one cases of the approximately 5600 cases on the docket (1.6 percent), and most convictions were under appeal. When the defendant was also accused of some criminal act accompanying his wartime actions, the court had a relatively easy time. If he were to be found guilty, he could be convicted for felonies other than treason. However, where the accusations were for political or economic collaboration alone, the court floundered in a quagmire.

The prosecution, in particular, was in a quandary. The Huk challenge and the American-supported oligarchic response left men like Solicitor General Tañada in no-man's-land between the two opposing sides. The Huks, by continuing to attack the elite for its wartime behavior, made the prosecution arguments appear to support the Huk claims. The cross fire rendered Tañada's position untenable; he was trapped and had no way of standing his ground. Forced to retreat, the prosecution felt increasing restraint in handling the political cases. Tañada searched in vain for allies. He appealed to United States Attorney General Tom Clark for support, but was denied any assistance. Clark wrote that his response was "governed by the statement issued by President Truman on March 16 of this year, in which he announced that the United States would not intervene in the trial of the collaborators in the Philippines." Noting that "the reasons which the President gave for this policy apply with even greater force today," Clark felt "obliged to decline" Tañada's "kind and generous invitation."[2]

Roxas, eager to appear resolute in meting justice fairly, had reappointed Tañada as solicitor general; however, the Roxas victory over Osmeña weakened enormously the strength of this office. It was clear to everyone that Roxas gave Tañada less support than Osmeña had done and that the authority of the solicitor general was severely compromised. On October 21, 1946, Tañada, chafing at his isolation in the administration, indicated his discontent in a stinging letter to Roxas. He complained vehemently about his lack of actual support from Roxas. The crisis was precipitated when Tañada learned of a meeting at Laurel's home. There the indicted wartime leaders met to plan a common defense strategy together with Roxas' top advisers, "such as Messrs. Jose Yulo, Sergio Bayan, Jose Paez,

Rafael Corpus, Arsenio N. Luz and Leon Gonzales against whom no treason charges are pending, . . ." In his letter to Roxas, Tañada wrote that "the apparent intimate alliance between your [Roxas'] closest advisers and those accused of treason may easily lead the public to suppose that your administration is indifferent to the prosecution of collaborators."

Abandoning his diplomatic language, Tañada stated frankly that "current rumors about the alleged weekly visits of Mr. Abello, your executive secretary, to Dr. Laurel during the latter's detention at Muntinglupa [prison] and about the frequent attendance at Malacañang's official or social functions of Messrs. Recto, Aquino and others whose cases have yet to be heard, . . ." had already "caused such general uncertainty and confusion as to considerably hamper the preparation of the cases for the government." Tañada, noting the "universal impression" that Roxas was, "to say the least, indifferent to the question of collaboration, . . ." asked if there had been "a change in policy"; if there had been, he wanted to know of it. Tañada stated that his own position on collaboration "has ever been clear and open." Observing that he had "the heavy duty to make a preliminary determination of the guilt of the detainees before prosecuting them in court," he had "reached the conclusion that upon the basis of the evidence . . . and of existing law, they are guilty of treason."

Tañada felt that the collaboration issue was "of transcendental importance and that the discovery of the active participation of your [Roxas'] trusted advisers and of other high government officials in the preparation for the defense of Dr. Laurel and his fellow defendants in the People's Court," left him "no choice but to request a statement of the administration's policy with regard to the prosecution of the political collaborators."[3] The statement was not forthcoming, and Tañada resigned shortly thereafter. Since the oligarchy had survived, the inner centers of power never closed to those Tañada felt were guilty. The relationship between those against whom formal charges had been lodged and the others who were never indicted was so intimate that the establishment of a common front was inevitable. Two subsequent solicitors general were to battle against this intimate connection.

Roxas' victory affected not only the prosecution but also the judges, who were as sensitive to the situation as anyone. From the inception of the People's Court it had proved extremely difficult to find judges experienced enough to hear a complex treason trial and impartial enough to administer justice. These men had to be free of any personal taint of wartime cooperation with the Japanese, and, equally important, they had to be free of prior obligations to those who were to be tried. Since the judges were also part of the elite, and since the reciprocal quality of Philippine social structure interlocked people in a web of relationships demanding the obligations of *utang na loob,* it was exceedingly difficult to find men who did not owe favors to the indicted.

Staffing the bench was even more difficult after Roxas was elected. The judges became nervous about their own future careers, thus hesitating to challenge the president too openly. They also were sensitive to the factors influencing the electorate—the Huk menace, the economic crisis, the shift in the American attitude. Finally, the composition of the court changed with Roxas' appointments. On June 6, 1946, Roxas' nomination of Eusebio Lopez was confirmed by the Liberal majorities in the Congress.[4] Whether Roxas intended it or not, Lopez, while serving as one of the judges, became a bitter critic of the People's Court. In *People* v. *Osias,* Lopez petitioned his fellow judges to dismiss the case because Osias had been elected to the senate while under indictment. Lopez argued that in a democracy "the people, as the Pope in the church, never make mistakes."[5] His fellow judges voted down this legal nonsense, but Lopez' lack of judicial restraint proved a constant problem to the other judges.

Lopez had his own theories, which he expounded frequently. He wrote: "It is cruel and inhuman to maintain the theory that the treason law of the Commonwealth was in full force and effect during the period of enemy occupation. . . ."[6] He argued that because a man was caught between two conflicting demands for loyalty he was able to determine allegiance as a function of chronological circumstance. During an attempt to disqualify him from a place on the People's Court, he defended himself by arguing that "even in those states of the American Union where bias and prejudice are made statutory grounds of disqualification, bias and prejudice, to be a cause of disqualification, must refer to the mental attitude or disposition of the judge towards a party to the litigation, and not to any views that he may entertain regarding the subject-matter involved. . . ." In other words, Lopez argued that he could not be disqualified because he happened to think that the accused in general were innocent of the charges. He believed that "leaders have a right to the presumption of patriotism, unless the contrary is proved, . . ." arguing that "no treason law, however stiff and exacting and cruel, has ever made a country great. . . . The strength of a country depends on the loyalty and devoted patriotism of its citizens, and the world has yet to find a treason law that will create patriots." With remarkable candor Lopez maintained that "courts and judges should not be bound by old and obsolete doctrines that hamper growth and progress." Seeing his role as peacemaker, he was moved by a "sincere wish to help clear [the] Philippine atmosphere of misunderstanding and of mutual charges and recriminations that have sprung out of the horrors of war."[7]

Lopez' theories about the role of a judge raised havoc in the People's Court. Even if a conviction could be gained there, the defendant had the right of appeal to the Supreme Court. Since there was little legal precedent within the Philippine system, most convictions were, in fact, appealed. Five of the eleven members of the Supreme Court—Chief Justice Manuel Moran, Ramon Ozaeta, Cesar Bengzon, Manuel Briones, and Ricardo Paras—had held some position during the war.[8] The Supreme Court was a bastion of the oligarchy, closely related literally and figuratively to the political elite under indictment. To have expected these men to convict their *compadres* was to have expected the impossible. Washington was naive, given the dynamics of the situation, in thinking that Filipino judges could mete out impartial justice to Filipino politicians. The policy, which had crippled Osmeña's return, collapsed in execution.[9]

The courts became entangled in a thicket of procedural disputes, which further complicated their substantive tasks. One issue, which dated back to the inception of the court, was the objection by the accused against the use of documentation seized by the American army. The American army had impounded relevant material and turned it over to the solicitor general's office after the peace. These documents became the nucleus of the prosecution's case because of the limitations of time and staff. If these seized documents could be barred from court because they were ruled to have been taken illegally, the prosecution would lack enough additional evidence to bring many cases to trial. The American army had based its original actions on military authority within a zone of combat. Under martial law the individuals had little recourse. With the return of peace, the question remained of the right of Americans to turn such material over to the solicitor general's office without the consent of the owners.

The test case was *Alvero* v. *Dizon* (GR No. L-231). Alvero's case, which had been the thirty-third case to go before the People's Court, was appealed to the Supreme Court on the grounds that he had been tried with illegally seized evidence. Alvero claimed that, even if his papers had been taken with a search warrant, they would be inadmissible at his trial because the constitution protected him from giving evidence against himself. The prosecution, in turn, argued that the documents had come from the war zone, that they had been taken legally even without a search warrant, and that they were valid in the Philippine courts. This early challenge to the legal validity of a postwar trial was denied by the Supreme Court, though the accused never conceded admissibility of the seized evidence.[10] The Supreme Court subsequently ruled in *Hilario Camino Moncado v. The People's Court* (GR No. L-824) that documents seized even after the peace were admissible as evidence.

The courts were also called upon to resolve the bitterly disputed issue of whether allegiance to the United States had been suspended by the enemy occupation. During the war Laurel had said that "it was the duty of America to defend her sovereignty here and when she could not defend that sovereignty, why should we Filipinos defend it? We have done our duty."[11] After the war he wrote that "if the U.S. had been prepared to repel the Japanese invasion, there would have been no military occupation of the Philippines; and without military occupation there could have been no collaboration." Laurel concluded from this that in the last analysis collaboration was "attributable to the unpreparedness and fault of the United States."[12] Laurel, Recto, Paredes, and others frequently argued that under international law the Philippine obligation of allegiance to the United States terminated with the Japanese victory.

The validity of this defense was tested before the Supreme Court when Anastacio Laurel petitioned for habeas corpus on the grounds that allegiance had been suspended by the occupation: *Laurel v. Misa* (44 *Official Gazette* 1176). The decision, which was handed down on January 30, 1947, divided the court. One justice, Ricardo Paras, in his dissent, supported the appeal, writing that "during the long period of Japanese occupation, all the political laws of the Philippines were suspended. . . ." Paras held that "no treason could have been committed during the Japanese military occupation . . . because Article 114 of the Revised Penal Code was not then in force. . . ." Paras maintained that "if the Filipinos did not obey the Japanese commands and feign cooperation, there would not have been any Filipino nation that could have been liberated. . . ," for he believed that "everyone who took advantage of the peace and order prevailing during the occupation for the safety and survival of himself and his family, gave aid and comfort to the enemy."[13]

The rest of the court ruled differently. Rejecting Anastacio

Laurel's petition, the court stated that "there is no such thing as suspended allegiance, the basic theory on which the whole fabric of petitioner's contention rests." Drawing a distinction between allegiance and the more simple obedience to law, which each citizen is bound to honor, the court ruled that "the adoption of the petitioner's theory of suspended allegiance would lead to disastrous consequences for small and weak nations or states . . . , for it would allow invaders to legally recruit or enlist Quisling inhabitants of the occupied territory to fight against their own government without the latter incurring the risk of being prosecuted for treason."[14] As in the Alvero case the court was not willing to allow this kind of legal argument to become a procedural means by which every case on the docket would have to be dismissed.

Another procedural issue which went to the Supreme Court was the question of the right of bail. Early in the postwar period, on November 16, 1945, the Supreme Court had ruled seven to one, in the case of *Pio Duran* v. *Salvador Abad Santos* (GR No. L-99), that bail could be denied the defendants of a treason trial. Pio Duran had petitioned the Supreme Court because section nineteen of the People's Court Act had stated that "the aforesaid political prisoner may, in the discretion of the People's Court, after due notice . . . be released on bail even prior to the presentation of the corresponding information [indictment], unless the Court finds that there is strong evidence of the commission of a capital crime." The People's Court judge, Salvador Abad Santos, had refused Duran the right of release on bail because he claimed that Duran's membership in the Makapili was common knowledge, and there was sufficient likelihood of a conviction to warrant his refusal to grant bail.

At that time the Supreme Court supported the People's Court as well as Abad Santos' contention that a conviction for treason would be almost automatically a "capital offense." Pio Duran was denied release on bail. However, after Roxas' election, the courts reversed themselves and permitted release on bail to everyone indicted for political collaboration. Even Laurel and Vargas, charged with more than a hundred counts of treason each, were released. The shifting social and political climate altered the legal judgment that collaboration was a "capital offense" in which conviction might mean the death penalty. Time and events softened attitudes, which, in turn, softened the rigor of the law.

This changing outlook was reflected in the court's growing sympathy to the issues of "duress," "justifying circumstances," and "exempting circumstances." The prosecution had argued in each of the cases that duress had to be direct, immediate, and intense to be a valid argument for possible acquittal or leniency, and the People's Court in its Sison decision had accepted this contention. The basic claim of all those indicted was, in Quintin Paredes' words, that force was "omnipresent during the occupation. It was not necessary to exercise it at the point of the gun."[15] After Roxas' political victory, the courts became responsive to this defense argument.[16] In *People* v. *Godinez* (45 *Official Gazette* 2524) the Supreme Court ruled that working for the Japanese during the occupation could be justified by the claim of duress. The People's Court in its conviction had ruled that there was little imminent danger to Godinez, who had served as a marine pilot in the waters around Cebu. The People's Court accepted the prosecution contention that some of Godinez' peers who were also naval pilots had refused to serve with no ill effects, and, therefore, convicted him. The Supreme Court, reversing the lower court decision, noted that it "was not demonstrated, however, that these seamen [who did not serve] were surrounded by the same circumstances of herein indictee as to family members, means of evasion, personal relations or conditions et cetera all of which necessarily affected the decision to serve or not to serve. . . ." Accepting duress as a valid defense, it ruled that "those who refused to cooperate, in the face of danger, were patriotic citizens; but it does not follow that the fainthearted who gave in were traitors."[17]

The shift from the verdict of treason to that of faintheartedness exemplified the altering opinion of the Philippine judiciary. The Philippine courts, after Roxas' election, became rigid in their interpretation of the two-witness-to-an-overt-act rule, which appeared in both the American and Philippine statutes. The American Supreme Court, in a completely unrelated case of April 1945, had ruled in *Cramer* v. *the United States* (65 S.C. 918) that the two-witness rule had to be applied exactingly. Since the Philippine courts were still a part of the American juridical system, the American decision became the most recent precedent for Filipino judges. This American decision proved to be a fortuitous dodge, permitting Filipino judges the option of a technical rather than a substantive decision. Rejecting the relatively liberal reading of the treason statute offered by the People's Court in the Sison trial, subsequent Philippine courts fell back on a rigid adherence to the wording of the Philippine treason provision taken verbatim from the constitutional provision written by the American founding fathers in the eighteenth century.[18]

In *People* v. *Adriano* (44 *Official Gazette* 4300), for example, it was held that "it was necessary to produce two direct witnesses to the whole overt act," maintaining that it might "be possible to piece bits together of the same overt act; but, if so, each bit must have the support of two witnesses." The courts came to demand that each witness convince the judges so that if the court believed only one of the two witnesses while doubting the second, a defendant was entitled to dismissal. In *People v. Abad* (44 *Official Gazette* 4901) the court rejected the prosecution contention that where an overt act was single, continuous, and composite, it was not necessary to have two witnesses at every stage. In *People v. Escleto* (47 *Official Gazette* 107) the court specifically reaffirmed that the law was based directly on the American constitution and was "severely restrictive" as a safeguard.

With such a constrictive view of the requirements for conviction on the treason statute the prosecution found it virtually impossible to find two witnesses willing to swear that they heard or saw any specific event. The courts refused to accept any extrajudicial admissions of guilt and rejected all circumstantial evidence, no matter how compelling, unless there was an open confession in court or two witnesses. Each witness had to be willing to testify that he had heard a particular speech and remembered the words exactly. Given the political climate after Roxas' election, few were willing to testify.

The courts obviously had a sacred duty to preserve the rights of any defendant charged with the capital offense of treason. To have failed to protect the legal right of each individual to the assumption of innocence would have been a major miscarriage of justice. The courts were justified in preventing the treason law from degenerating into a catch-all means of prosecuting people for misdeeds which, however deplorable, were not treason. In *People v. Tan* (43 *Official Gazette* 1263) it was ruled that friendship with the Japanese during the war was not punishable under the treason law. In *People v. Roble* (GR No. L-435) it was ruled that emotional or intellectual attachment to Japan was not treason unless it also was accompanied by aid and comfort to the Japanese. In *People v. Butawan* (46 *Official Gazette* 5452) and *People v. Castro* (47 *Official Gazette* 105) it was ruled that service to the wartime constabulary was not in itself treasonable. In *People v. Agoncillo* (45 *Official Gazette* 2874) it was held that selling nonstrategic materials to the Japanese was not treason. In *People v. Perez* (46 *Official Gazette* 4886) the court made it crystal clear that procurement of women for Japanese pleasure was not treason.

It has been argued, however, that the courts hid behind the restrictive provisions of the treason law to avoid having to face the fundamental substantive issue, especially in regard to political collaboration. The courts recognized the explosiveness of elite collaboration and avoided the issue whenever possible. The Sison case, however, proved to be an embarrassing legal precedent.[19] After Roxas' election virtually every argument made in that first trial was reversed in later trials. In the Sison case, for example, the court ruled that he held positions which were "not only highly responsible, . . . but in the opinion of the Court, policy-determining. They were policy-determining because they defined the norm of official conduct." The judges felt that whether "the accused was successful in aiding Japan in furtherance of her designs is a question of no importance because, whether successful or not, the fact that accused discharged, as the evidence overwhelmingly shows, the functions and duties of the high positions to which he had been appointed is the determinative decision."[20]

This early opinion was reversed in the case against another ranking wartime official, when a later court ruled in *People* v. *Alunan* (43 *Official Gazette* 1288) that "although some of the offices and acts, object of the prosecution, have been established in the form and manner prescribed by law, such acts were executed by the accused in the performance of his legal duties, . . . and therefore, cannot be considered as his own acts of aid and comfort to the enemy's cause." The court then expounded in its decision the argument which Roxas had advanced during the election campaign. It ruled that "the mere acceptance of a public office and the discharge of the functions and duties connected therewith during the Japanese military occupation of the Philippines do not constitute per se the felony of treason." Even "admitting that such acts charged against the accused were really of aid and comfort to the enemy," the court argued that "they cannot be punishable in this particular case, because there is no satisfactory proof of the adherence of the accused to the cause of the enemy which is an essential requisite for the conviction of the crime of treason."

Whereas Sison was convicted for his words and actions because he was held to have set the norms, Alunan was pardoned because this later court felt that the opinions a man expressed while in office reflected the office and not the man. The court drew a distinction between his personal involvement with the Japanese and his public posture, and it argued that in treason only the private sentiment, if it could be proved, was grounds for conviction. This policy, which cleft a man's motivation from his behavior, allowed those accused to claim that they had been personally loyal to the Commonwealth, America, and Quezon even though their public position appeared to reflect disloyalty. The court decision validly reflected this dichotomy for most of the wartime elite, but it also established a set of extenuating circumstances by which the elite could claim expiation for wartime actions. The net result was to establish a system in which some members of the society were not accountable for their actions.

The distance which the courts traveled from that first Sison decision can be clearly seen in the case of *People* v. *Guillermo Francisco* (42 *Official Gazette* 2452). The decision, which was handed down five months after Roxas was elected, pardoned the man who was perhaps in the most difficult legal position of any of the top wartime leadership. General Guillermo B. Francisco was one of the most distinguished military men in the Philippines. Born in 1885, he had been graduated from the Constabulary Academy in Baguio in 1908. By 1927 he was a full colonel. Throughout the Commonwealth era he was a key aide to MacArthur and Quezon, second in command only to General Vicente Lim.[21] Shortly after the Japanese invasion of Luzon, General Francisco was inducted directly into the American army. In the process of becoming an American army officer, he took the oath of allegiance to the United States.[22] He fought with the Fil-American troops on Bataan, becoming a prisoner of war with the Japanese victory. Rehabilitated and restored to the rank of major general, he commanded the Constabulary throughout much of the war.

In the abstract the case against Francisco because of his military obligations would seem to have been as solid as against any of the wartime elite. He was liable for court-martial by the United States army, but, because of the political nature of the accusation, was turned over for trial to the People's Court along with all of the civilian cases. The solicitor general's office brought in a twenty-two count indictment, submitting 223 exhibits to establish its case. The court overruled Francisco's objections to the use of this material because most of it was seized by the Americans, but proved to be so restrictive that the prosecution dropped charges two, three, eight, nine, eleven, thirteen, fifteen, and seventeen before the trial. Similar charges to those discarded had been accepted during the Sison trial, but in the interim the subsequent court rulings indicated to the prosecution the impossibility of substantiating those counts.

The court proved even more rigid in its evidence requirements than the prosecution had anticipated. For example, exhibit "P" was a carbon copy of a letter from Francisco to a Major Ausejo which had been found in Francisco's papers. The letter was an appeal to Ausejo to give up his guerrilla activities and come down from the mountains with his comrades. Ausejo testified that he had received such a letter and had sent it on to MacArthur's headquarters in Australia. Since he lacked the original and was unable to swear that the carbon copy was a verbatim rendition of the letter he had received in the mountains, the court rejected any further testimony on count number twelve.

The prosecution placed great emphasis on charge number twenty, which accused Francisco of giving aid and comfort to the enemy by conducting "a pacification campaign intended for the suppression of the resistance movement in the Philippines. . . ." Francisco was accused of trying to make this campaign more effective by spending government funds, "in paying among others the compensation of agents, under-cover men, and informers."[23] The government produced thirteen witnesses and 198 exhibits to help substantiate this accusation, but the court rejected all of them. For example, one witness testified that the signature on an exhibit was Francisco's, but he could not remember if he was actually in the room when Francisco signed that specific exhibit. A handwriting expert testified that the signature was, in fact, Francisco's, but, because there were not two witnesses to the overt act, the court rejected every exhibit and witness. The defense did not deny the veracity of the evidence; it claimed instead that without two witnesses the material was invalid in a treason case.

The majority of the court used the "severely restrictive" provisions of the treason statute to avoid the basic question of possible culpability. Eliminating most of the prosecution's case on procedural grounds, it decided that "there is nothing . . . which shows that the accused had ordered, urged, or advised the Constabulary soldiers to fight or liquidate those identified with such a [resistance] movement. He [Francisco] always referred to the suppression of bandits or lawless elements for the establishment of peace and order. . . ."[24] The majority decision seized upon semantics, claiming that there was a valid difference between those referred to as "guerrillas" and those spoken of as "bandits or lawless elements."

The concurring opinion of Eusebio Lopez not only acquitted Francisco but rejected the possibility that there might have been any malfeasance by Francisco or the others during the war. Lopez could not "believe that the Filipino leaders, who have been trained all their lives in the democratic way under an atmosphere of freedom, could have accepted service under those two governments [Vargas' and Laurel's] without compulsion and coercion." Confusing a man's motivation with the effect of his actions, Lopez maintained that the wartime leaders had to "feign cooperation . . . to convince the enemy that they were sincere."[25]

However, the question remained that if there existed the necessity to go to great limits to fool the Japanese, did there not exist equal risk that these men might also fool some Filipinos? If they succeeded in fooling the Japanese, who were politically sophisticated, was it not conceivable that they might also deceive a large number of politically innocent Filipinos? Finally, was there not an excellent possibility that the Japanese would see through "feigned cooperation," but that many Filipinos might be hoodwinked by the deception? If this were the case, would not the wartime leaders have inadvertently given the Japanese material aid and comfort? Lopez argued that pro-Japanese speeches delivered by the elite "were not sword thrusts directed to the heart of the Commonwealth or the United States; they were shields to protect the people from the brutality of the enemy."[26] However, even if this was the intention of the speaker, he had to be aware that his audience might take his words at face value. As a member of the prewar elite, could any ranking Filipino assume for sure that his audience would discount totally everything he said?

Reversing the assertions of the Sison conviction, the courts evolved the theory that a public official was not responsible for public behavior, provided a disclaimer was explicitly or even implicitly expressed by the accused subsequently. This disclaimer was forthcoming. The wartime elite asserted collectively and individually that it had been motivated only by patriotism and was, therefore, innocent of the charges. After the Roxas victory, the courts upheld this defense as valid. By the autumn of 1946 it was clear to everyone that the risk of conviction for political collaboration was minimal, that prewar authority had already been or would soon be regained by the wartime leaders, and that it would be only a matter of time before Roxas closed the issue by granting amnesty. A few days after the Francisco decision, Laurel was released from jail after winning an appeal for habeas corpus ad subjiciendum.[27] A few weeks later at a bail hearing, Laurel said that "all Filipinos were collaborators." He was confident enough about his future to say that "others may like the United States, but I don't."[28] Release on bail was granted him a few days later.[29] On December 27 he arranged for his trial, which had been scheduled for January 6, 1947, to be postponed indefinitely.[30] By the end of May 1947 he was nominated for the Philippine Senate, and by mid-October 1947, exactly four years after the Laurel republic was inaugurated, one of the first balloons went up suggesting him for the presidency in 1949.[31] A few days later, and just three years after MacArthur and Osmeña had waded ashore at Leyte, Laurel's trial began before the People's Court.[32]

Vargas, though not interested in a political restoration, stalled equally successfully for time. After four postponements Judge Emilio Rilloraza finally ordered the case to trial in June 1947. Vargas' lawyers, who included Laurel, Recto, Paredes, and Vicente Francisco, thereupon appealed to the Supreme Court for a writ barring the People's Court from calling the case.[33] This maneuver was denied, but though the trial began in the first week of July, it was almost immediately recessed until the beginning of September.[34] It was obvious that there would be years of litigation before verdict, and if Vargas were to be convicted, years more before an appealed decision was reached by the Supreme Court.

The prosecution, which had begun work on this trial years before, prepared a massive attack, accusing Vargas of spearheading "the forces of collaboration" and of becoming "the outstanding Filipino exponent of the Greater East Asia Co-Prosperity Sphere, the chief salesman of ideas and things made in Japan, the most outspoken foe of pro-Americanism. . . ." Vargas was accused of transmitting the Japanese message "in a language which his people would better understand and more readily believe in."[35] The prosecution concluded that "when the Japanese entered Manila, two courses lay before Jorge B. Vargas—service to his country or service to the enemy. Service to his country entailed the possibility and risk of suffering, hardship, and the danger of meeting death; service to the enemy on the latter's terms promised possible immunity from harm as well as personal gain and comfort. . . ." Rejecting the claim that Vargas merely "played ball" with the Japanese, it noted that "it may seem harsh to judge him by a rigorous criterion of right and wrong, loyalty or disloyalty, removed as we are from the circumstances which are supposed to have influenced . . ." him. "Yet," it asked, "how else shall we judge a man who, by his own admission, willingly cooperated with the enemy, by the testimony of the Japanese Commanders-in-Chief . . . was highly responsible for the success of their program, and by the unmitigated harshness of the occupation, was entirely unable to avert the disasters which his cooperation was supposed to avert?"[36]

Despite the severity of the accusations, by late 1947 the issues were stale and the acquittal verdict almost assured. Vargas was indicted on 115 counts, but almost all were based on the written record of material which appeared in the *Official Gazette*. The prosecution built its case on the public performance of the man, avoiding the question of his internal motivation. However, the courts had already established the inapplicability of these criteria. It was generally conceded that when the trial actually got underway, the government case would be devastated on procedural grounds. Despite the sweeping indictment presented the court, it was clear that Vargas would never be tried on the substantive issue of possible culpability.

The issue, as had been expected, became academic when, on January 28, 1948, Roxas issued the long-awaited Amnesty Proclamation (No. 51). Even before Roxas' election, Hutchinson had predicted that amnesty would be assured if Roxas won, but Roxas delayed issuing it because it was not needed to protect any of the wartime elite.[37] Sison's conviction was in appeal to the Supreme Court, and no other key officials were in legal jeopardy. Roxas withheld the proclamation in order not to exacerbate the collaboration issue in the United States during a period when the Philippines was vitally dependent on American congressional rehabilitation funds. Moreover, the premature issuance of the proclamation would have given substance to the Huk charge that Roxas was coddling his peers.

This amnesty decree stated that "the majority of the Filipino people now realize that the alleged acts attributed to political collaborators either were not voluntary on their part or, in effect, were performed by them in the sincere belief that it was their patriotic duty. . . ." Deploring the fact that "collaboration has divided the people of the Philippines since liberation in a manner which threatens the unity of the nation at a time when public welfare requires that said unity be safeguarded and preserved," Roxas announced "that the overwhelming sentiment of the people of this Republic is now in favor of resolving this question as speedily as possible by the grant of amnesty to all persons. . . ." Carefully excluding those who "took up arms against the allied nations or the members of the resistance forces, or acted as spies or informers of the enemy," or committed any other felony, Roxas "granted full and complete amnesty. . . ."[38]

Roxas also submitted a request to the Philippine Congress asking for a resolution of concurrence, which he received on February

13, 1948. Such approval was a foregone conclusion, but Roxas was eager to make amnesty seem more than a personal decree if possible. Noting that "collaboration is no longer a political issue among us," he wrote that he had maintained close contact during the war with those who collaborated and had "the conviction that there was no seed of treason in their hearts." Stating that he had desired to grant amnesty ever since he had become president, he acknowledged that he was prevented from doing this earlier because of the "adverse reactions based on misinformation in the Philippines and elsewhere which might endanger the welfare of the Republic. . . ." Roxas maintained that the people had "chosen to vindicate the actions of some of the accused and to forgive and forget the conduct of others," and, therefore, it was the government's duty to erase "the issue of collaboration from among us . . ." in order to "heal the sores that we might still carry in our hearts."[39] The resolution was passed in the House by a vote of forty to eight, with two abstentions, but thirty-one were absent, indicating perhaps that many preferred not to have their vote recorded at all.[40]

When on September 25, 1945, Osmeña had signed the People's Court Act into law, he had said that he was "confident that the People's Court will carry out its judicial tasks without fear and without favor, and that it will punish the guilty and exonerate the innocent."[41] Nevertheless, it was clear that the courts had in fact favored influential political collaborators. Of the 5603 cases originally filed before the People's Court, only 156 had been convicted (0.27 percent), and of those, only one, Teofilo Sison, was prominent politically.[42] During the war the American army had prepared dossiers on each ranking Filipino from information gained by monitored radio and guerrilla contacts.[43] These dossiers, which have been cited throughout this book, served as the basis for the American arrests immediately after reconquest. From this list, I selected 165 of the most influential names to compare with the People's Court records.

The results were startling. Sison was the only man appearing on both lists who was convicted. Fifteen others had their cases dismissed for unspecified reasons, and Benigno Aquino's case was dismissed at his death on December 21, 1947. A few like Francisco and Lavides were acquitted, and eleven more, including Laurel and Vargas, had their cases dismissed by amnesty. Thirteen more were listed by the People's Court as having been bonded, but with no further determination of their cases. Presumably, the solicitor general's office abandoned prosecution. Of those listed by the Americans 122 had no record in the People's Court and were never indicted. These men, who had all been detained by the Americans at the end of the war, returned to full activity with the Japanese surrender. In percentage terms, this cross check meant that 0.6 percent of the wartime leadership was convicted, and 74 percent was never in court. There was no bloodbath in which the mob ruled at the end of the war, and there was no purge either internal or external. The elite remained intact, with a remarkable survival rate, considering the risks of war and the average age of the group. The war diminished neither the size nor the authority of the establishment. The ability of this group to weather the vicissitudes of belligerent occupation attests to the flexibility and perspicacity of this remarkable elite.

CHAPTER IX

The Dilemma of Collaboration

A patriot is a fool in ev'ry age
—Alexander Pope

The elite survived. Incorporating into its membership the most articulate and powerful of its nonradical critics, it sapped the strength of its guerrilla opposition by assimilation. It revealed its strength as a social institution by yielding some of its exclusiveness in preference to risking an alliance of its enemies which might become strong enough to overthrow it. Placed in jeopardy because of its collaboration, it formed over the years a coalition in which former guerrilla leaders became the protegés of former wartime collaborators. By the time of amnesty the Philippines was governed by one elite, although the format of a two-party system survived the Osmeña-Roxas split. This establishment succeeded in defeating the Hukbalahap challenge and has controlled events ever since independence.

To achieve this fusion, which has dominated postwar history in the Philippines, a quarantine of silence has been placed around the collaboration question. Guerrillas and collaborators have studiously ignored this tender spot as a prerequisite for permitting the collaboration wound to close naturally. The assumption has been that "time heals" and that any probing of the scar tissue might open the wound a second time with unpredictable consequences. The new blood of a new generation was thought to be a healing agent. Now, as collaboration fades into the past, the scar is barely visible to the eye.

The possibility has remained, however, that despite the superficial healing, there might be an infection below the skin of the body politic, an infection that might have carried silently the germs of the collaboration crisis elsewhere into Philippine life. As with a cancer that is secretly feared but consciously ignored in the hope that it might vanish by itself, Filipinos have gone to some lengths to avoid examining the consequences of collaboration. Psychic tension has prevented a periodic examination for the possibility of a tumor metastasizing below the skin. If a tumor were to be found, and if it were to be proven cancerous rather than benign, the original diagnosis of the society might be discredited. Moreover, at this late date, the techniques of surgery would no longer be valid. The original ailment would have spread through the social system.

The risk of unpleasant disclosure is present at every examination, but this does not negate the individual or social necessity for a check-up. The quarantine of silence around collaboration has prevented Filipinos from asking whether collaboration is at least a partial contributor to the disturbing symptoms of social malaise in contemporary Philippine life. Since the war many observers have noticed that political dishonesty, bribery, nepotism, and fraud have increased enormously. There are many causes for this. Corruption is not an abstraction isolated from social or political reality; it is part of the fabric of each society. Societies determine for themselves what constitutes a transgression of their own norms.

A part of the increase in corruption stems from the withdrawal of metropolitan supervision when the society was in shock, both physically and mentally. Independence came at a stress period, in which the fledgling government was permitted to fly from the snug nest of colonialism in a weakened state. For almost four hundred years metropolitan rule had allowed the Filipinos, at the price of their freedom, the luxury of the oversight of the Philippine ethical and moral code by the colonial country. Independence, like the transition from childhood to maturity, required that Filipinos assume this burden. Before the war independence was a gossamer of romantic notions. The disillusionment of war and reconstruction taught Filipinos that the taste of independence, like that of the apple in the garden of Eden, might be bitter as well as sweet. Reparations, foreign exchange controls, rehabilitation funds, and mutual security aid channeled billions through a government struggling for survival and a nation groping to find itself.

Another factor contributing toward the increase in corruption was the manner in which belligerent occupation upset respect for law. As Laurel wisely noted during the war, "the foundation stone of all governments is law and order. . . . And the burden of effective law enforcement falls heavily on the citizen no less than on the government."[1] Guerrilla resistance made heroes of those who violated orders from Manila. The guerrillas justified this act of disobedience on the grounds of a higher obligation, but the cleavage of the society produced as a side effect a postwar contempt for law. Roxas acknowledged this confusion when he granted amnesty "to all persons who committed acts penalized under the Revised Penal Code in the furtherance of the resistance of the enemy" in order to align the demands of law with guerrilla resistance. The proclamation specifically stated that the guerrillas "should not be regarded as criminals but rather as patriots and heroes. . . ."[2] When respect for the conventions of society embodied in law fails, this respect is difficult to reestablish.

However, might some of the increase in venality be explained by the survival of the elite in power? Laurel wrote during the war: "Public office is a public trust. The beneficiaries of an established government are the people and the people only. . . . The holding of a public office is not an occasion for personal aggrandizement but an opportunity for public service."[3] The postwar success of the elite in keeping power seemed to belie his words and to cheapen the dignity of public office. One postwar critic, Francisco Delgado, noted in 1945 that the collaborators' "feet are made of clay. . . . Leaders should be made of firmer stuff. We need men in our government who can measure up to an emergency, who are willing to suffer, even to die, for their principles, men who have a will of their own and sufficient courage to back up that will. . . ." Delgado felt that Filipinos "should not allow politics, with all its dirty underhanded maneuvers, to rob us of this chance to reshuffle our government leadership. . . ." He stated that the wartime leaders were "good demagogues, and their game is politics, and just as they maneuvered their way into power during the Japanese regime, they will try, and try hard, to do the same now." He urged that the people "not be led to believe that a premium is being paid for treachery, double-dealing, and cowardice. They [the people] should not be given grounds to feel that a man can speak and act against his nation, and, later on, again be accepted as a worthy son of that nation."[4]

The fact that no reshuffle occurred, that the same men reappeared in control of political power, and that there was no punishment for the high and mighty, probably contributed to the mood of cynicism which has been so pervasive since the war. Corruption is a "social cancer" dating back into the Spanish era, but perhaps it was nurtured to some degree by the apparently clear demonstration of the proposition that possession of the job was all that really mattered. To what extent did the success of the collaborators become a guideline for aspiring candidates? Was public office a public trust, as Laurel suggested? Since the war, venality, bribery, fraud, and corruption, usually described euphemistically as "anomalies," have made the power of office more a private preserve than a public trust.

To conduct a successful examination of collaboration requires a comparable analysis of each Philippine institution. Only a consideration of Philippine values can determine whether collaboration was benign or malignant; there exists no absolute standard of human behavior against which Filipinos can examine the Philippine specimen. In each social matrix there is a gap between what is professed and what is practiced. Every society tolerates a dynamic interaction between avowed and actual behavior. When the gulf between ideal and real becomes too great, however, the society may experience the decreasing impact of its professed norm as it becomes a distant abstraction. Members of a society with unattainable ideals of conduct become discouraged into relinquishing the attempt to achieve these ideals. In such cases the moral fiber of the society may be weakened by cynicism.

The cellular structure of Philippine loyalty holds the secret to any biopsy of collaboration. The exigencies of the occupation required each Filipino, especially the leadership, to consider whether the national response at the outbreak of the war was still worth defending at grave risk to person, kin, community, and nation. Each Filipino had to determine whether he had fulfilled his obligations by fighting honorably until he was overwhelmed by Japanese power. He had to decide why he fought initially and answer to himself whether it was *his* war or *their* war. If it was an imperial war, then he was a pawn with little obligation to the Americans. If it was *his* war, then the obligations did not end merely because the Fil-American forces were defeated. Each individual had to evolve a priority list governing his behavior. The decision to risk death or, conversely, to cooperate pragmatically could be directed only by his most cherished values.

It is of fundamental importance that both the guerrillas and collaborators listed as their prime loyalty the sacred ideal of the Philippine nation. This awareness of national identity transcended other demands of allegiance for both these groups. Modern nationalism had reached maturity in the Philippines. Each side was confident that it was preserving the nation's ideals. There has been a general tendency to argue that since both the guerrillas and the collaborators believed in and worked for the nation, that both should receive the accolade of heroes. Laurel stated that "there is 'heroism' in 'collaboration'. . . . Forced collaboration is not collaboration. Voluntary collaboration as a means of national survival and to tide over our people to better times is not punishable."[5] This argument, which has gained wide popularity since the war, raises the basic question of whether anyone who proffers his allegiance to his nation can claim that he has upheld the ideal of the nation through devotion. The heretic was devout, but was still adjudged a pariah for holding heterodox ideas. Philippine society has avoided asking whether the collaborators and the guerrillas could both have upheld the nation's ideals even though they were in some ways diametrically opposed and fiercely hostile to each other. The thorny, unposed question has been whether treason could exist even in a situation where everyone professed his allegiance to his nation? Is swearing allegiance equal to that allegiance?

The existence of very different patterns of response to the occupation by two groups of nationalists—the guerrillas and the collaborators—has been a puzzle. Part of the solution must rest in the chance of office, of residence, and of position; the national elite was caught in the capital and given less freedom of choice. But that is not the total answer. What distinguished the response of the oligarchy from that of other groups was that it held an additional loyalty, of which it alone was cognizant in 1941. One part of its value system was the deep-seated belief that it, and only it, was able to lead the nation. As the transitional force in shaping the national consciousness, the elite historically saw itself as the self-appointed guardian of cherished nationhood. As the group that determined the focus of the nation, it felt that it could not possibly transgress the sanctity of national allegiance by collaboration or any other act, because it had molded that allegiance. It was the head of the body politic. It made the decisions, generated the emotions, expressed the anxieties, and articulated goals for the people.

It saw its obligation to the nation in 1942 in the same way that it had during the Spanish and American periods. The elite had collaborated with the Spanish and with the Americans because it believed that extremism and violence were less successful than pragmatic evolution. It had cooperated with the Spanish in 1896 in negotiating a cease-fire; it had cooperated with the Americans in 1901 in establishing civilian government; why should it not do the same thing in 1941 to alleviate short-term suffering? History was full of occasions when collaboration with the superior conqueror was required to avoid useless bloodshed. Roxas, in his 1948 political amnesty proclamation, noted that "the alleged acts attributed to political collaborators . . . were performed by them in the sincere belief that it was their patriotic duty to execute them in the interest of the safety and well being of their countrymen who were then at the mercy of the enemy. . . ."[6] The elite saw its role as one of intermediary, posing itself as the living shield between the defenseless Filipino and the cruel world. For this sacrifice it demanded and received the reciprocal bonds of *utang na loob* from the masses; even more importantly, it came to view itself as a vital institution within Philippine society, replacing the ecclesiastical authority of the past with its secular strength.

Wartime governor of Leyte, Bernardo Torres, eloquently stated the collaborationist position when, during the war, he wrote that he was neither a Japanese agent nor a Japanese slave, despite the guerrilla accusations. "I am a Filipino agent," he continued, "working to the best of my ability to serve my unfortunate country at an unfortunate time in her history. I am doing what I am doing because my sincere belief is that it is for the good of our people and country under the present circumstances." Torres stated that he was a civilian official, "entrusted with the administration of government. . . ." He asked: "Who will say that I am a traitor to my country because I happen to have been called to make government—peace, order, security—function in our provinces? I was not privileged to fight in the battlefield and to make a military choice. I was fated by circumstances to be the governor of our province before and during this war."[7]

Within this broad attitude of the elite there was a spectrum of personal gradations resulting from such variables as personal ambition, degree of Japanese pressure, and internal anxieties. The remarkable thing, however, is how close the extremes of this range, represented, for example, by Benigno Aquino at one end and Jose Yulo at the other, actually were. The war leaders, including Claro Recto, Antonio de las Alas, Rafael Alunan, Quintin Paredes, Camilo Osias, and scores of others who retained power, saw their obligation to the nation and to their membership in the oligarchy as one and the same. The confusion by which they equated their own status group with the nation as a whole indicates that within their web of loyalties there was an extra factor which did not exist consciously for the masses. Membership in the oligarchy required as a condition for initiation a tacit belief in the value system of the group.

One possible exception to this elite value system was Laurel. Ironically, in order to gain postwar rehabilitation with his peers, he was forced to stand mute on why he had sought office during the war. Since most Filipinos assumed that he merely mouthed Japanese propaganda to serve as a front for the other leaders, few seriously listened to what he actually wrote and said. This put him in an exceedingly awkward situation. By accepting the role of the long-suffering servant, he could gain restoration with the rest of the elite, but only at the expense of watching his wartime ideas and reforms summarily rejected. However, if he claimed that he had really meant what he had said, he alone might have jeopardized his post-war position. He chose to appear as the self-sacrificing martyr in order to gain the opportunity to remain active in political life, but it must have galled him. During the war Laurel had wanted to alter the nature of the elite from one "whose members are good only in speeching and pork barrelling" to "the intellectual cream of the people." Laurel had to abandon his interest in "dictatorial government" and to accept his society as it was in order to remain active.[8] His portrait now hangs in the Presidential Palace with a plaque which simply reads, "President Laurel"; he was not, however, one who accepted the role of a pawn willingly. He was forced to maintain the values of the oligarchy instead of persuading it to adopt his reforms. The institution won out over the man.

Only one major figure of the prewar elite violated his loyalty to the establishment, and he did so unwittingly. Chief Justice Jose Abad Santos was the only Filipino leader who refused outright to collaborate. He made this decision early in the war, when he was isolated from his peers. Nevertheless, his refusal to cooperate became a major source of embarrassment to others who were willing to collaborate and who survived. Abad Santos, who had escaped to the Visayas with Quezon in 1942, had remained behind when Quezon left for Australia. When captured and confronted by the Japanese demand to cooperate, he consciously chose martyrdom.

The death of Abad Santos was a constant reminder to his peers of the road that they had not taken. He had died instead of compromising, and regardless of the validity of this decision, it delineated the options. Abad Santos reacted directly to his image of the ideal of the Philippines without that middle elitist allegiance of the oligarchy to itself as the only vehicle for preservation of the nation. Had Abad Santos not been caught by a regional field commander and had he been in Manila, he might have passed the war unnoticed and untested. But the reality was that when captured, he chose to die. Could Abad Santos' peers exalt his death without deprecating themselves?

Abad Santos was eulogized, but he was not glorified. In 1945, at a special memorial service in his honor at the Philippine Supreme Court, many came to extol his life, but few celebrated his death. One member of the elite, Vicente Francisco, noted that Abad Santos "could have compromised when the enemy asked him to cooperate, certain that the law of nations would have amply supported him in his stand." Francisco, defending indirectly what the others who survived had done, argued that Abad Santos could have become a "puppet" unfairly censured "like many of our political leaders who remained here believing that governments may come and go, but that there must always be men who should look after the life and welfare of the people, especially in time of distress. For his defense against such criticism, if defense he ever needed, he could have invoked what he had known, as an eminent counsel and scholar, the rule that 'military occupation creates a status of temporary allegiance. . . .'" Francisco busily argued about what Abad Santos could have done, rather than about what he did. His remarks dwelt more on the futile quality of Abad Santos' sacrifice than on his heroism. He noted that Santos chose the "way of the martyrs, for he [Abad Santos] realized the need of bolstering up the depressed spirit of the people at the time, and he wanted to give them an example. . . ."[9] Santos' heroism was explained not in terms of his own internal code of values but rather in terms of public example.

This construction of Abad Santos' death was jarred by only one speaker at that commemoration, J. Antonio Araneta. Noting that others more widely known than Abad Santos chose to live, he said that "their raucous voices, proclaiming a new brand of patriotism and a new concept of public service, are still being heard in our halls which common decency should forbid to be tainted even by their presence." Araneta spoke of those who preferred "safety and the trappings of puppetry to honor. But Jose Abad Santos, a great jurist and a greater man, shall have died in vain," Araneta continued, "if his memory does not ever remind us of our sacred duty to purge from our midst those who have failed us in the hour of need. The terrible reality of that betrayal is everywhere, creeping into every crevice of our national life." Speaking during that winter of the collaboration debate, while the Sison trial was proceeding and Hutchinson was visiting Manila, Araneta used Abad Santos' death as a whip against the collaborators. "Like hundreds of others now enjoying the comforts and rewards of high office, like hundreds of others who prostrated themselves in cringing servility before the new masters, he could have chosen the way of submission. He did not. Because unlike them," Araneta concluded, "he knew that to oppression there was only one answer—resistance. His life ended as he had lived it—with honor."[10]

The memory of Abad Santos became involved with the highly charged political and emotional accusations of treason. In his martyrdom to his country he inadvertently became a traitor to his class. Unknowingly, he broke one of the strands which made up the web of allegiance for the elite, and his rightful place as a national hero has been delayed because of the ambivalence of his peers. With candor, Claro Recto wrote that "however attractive and convenient such a theory [martyrdom] may now seem, it did not diminish one whit the brutal and irrevocable realities of the enemy rule; and not all the king's horses and not all the king's men will bring its victims back to life or ever make them whole again."[11] Recto, Laurel, Roxas, Quezon, and perhaps Osmeña saw the elite not only as the dominant social group but as the very foundation of the state, without which anarchy threatened. Consequently, it was more important for the elite to guide the nation through crisis than to sacrifice itself. Of all the vital resources of the underdeveloped country, none was more important than this core of transitional modernizing leaders. To these men the development of Philippine nationalism meant development under their guidance, and any other possibility was to be avoided at all cost.

Treason as a social crime, and its obverse, patriotism as a social virtue, are organically interwoven through other values. It is impossible to understand the dilemma of collaboration without an awareness of the elitist valuation of itself. Is the concept of national allegiance susceptible to definition according to the standards of an individual or group? Does this amount to the disintegration of the definition? The leadership of each society has always been charged with defending the explicit and implicit values of the people, but the manner of this defense is inevitably complex. As part of the social system, the elite reflects the norms of the society instinctively, and yet at the same time, the elite is usually the transitional force altering social patterns. The relationship of elite to populace should be directed toward the prevention of too great a gap between elite and popular values. The elite can neither rush too far ahead nor lag too far behind the rest of the society if dynamic relationship is to exist between leaders and led.

The collaboration dilemma revealed a schism between what the elite considered to be its obligation and the expectations of other groups. At the outbreak of the war this gap was not apparent. Both the elite and the people made a clear commitment to fight against the Japanese. Participating as equals with the United States, Filipinos fought, in Quezon's words, "for human liberty and justice, for those principles of individual freedom which we all cherish and without which life would not be worth living. Indeed, we are fighting for our own independence." Quezon, in his second inaugural address, delivered from the tunnel at Corregidor at the end of 1941, committed every Filipino resource "to maintain this independence, these liberties, and these freedoms, to banish fear and want amongst all peoples, and to establish a reign of justice for all the world. . . ." Quezon acknowledged that the war would "be long-drawn and hard-fought, . . ." but he was "absolutely convinced that final and complete victory will be ours. . . . No matter what sufferings and sacrifices this war may impose upon us," Quezon said, the nation would stand undaunted, because "upon the outcome of this war depend the happiness, liberty, and security not only of this generation but of the generations yet unborn."[12] Under the exigencies of the occupation, however, a gap appeared between the collaborators and the guerrillas.

Tomas Confesor wrote during the war that "this struggle is a total war in which . . . the question at stake with respect to the Philippines is not whether Japan or the U.S. should possess it but fundamentally, . . . what system of social organization and code for morals should govern our existence." Confesor, in rejecting an appeal to collaborate from a Filipino friend, Dr. Fermin Caram, argued that "the present war is a blessing in disguise to our people and . . . the burden it imposes and the hardship it has brought upon us are a test of our character to determine the sincerity of our convictions and the integrity of our souls." Confesor maintained that the war placed the Filipinos "in the crucible to assay the metal of our being. For as a people, we have been living during the last 40 years under a regime of justice and liberty regulated only by universally accepted principles of constitutional government. We have come to enjoy personal privileges and civil liberties without much struggle, without undergoing any pain to attain them."

Confesor disagreed with those who claimed that "there is no ignominy in surrender." He conceded that a soldier caught by a superior force was correct in surrendering, but rejected the parallel that he, as a civilian official, was in the same situation. The soldiers who surrendered to greater force "did not repudiate any principle of good government or of life which inspired them to fight heroically and valiantly. . . ." Confesor felt, however, that should he surrender, he would be giving up "something more precious than life itself: the principles of democracy and justice, the honor and destiny of our people." Confesor maintained that there are certain values which transcend short-term peace and tranquillity; he upheld ultimate national values ahead of immediate pragmatic considerations. Acknowledging that "the people may suffer now and may suffer more during the next months," Confesor affirmed his belief that such suffering was meaningful, because in the words of St. Paul "the sufferings of the present are not worthy to be compared with the glory to come that shall be revealed in us."[13]

The continuing guerrilla commitment to fight and to die, exemplified by Confesor, was based on three fundamental value judgments: the dream of independence, the belief in the ideological worth of democracy over totalitarianism, and a sense of *utang na loob* to the United States. Considerations of rationality, validity, and pragmatism in this decision were irrelevant; loyalty is rarely guided by reason. The guerrilla leadership and a large percentage of the population sensed what was expected of them even after the Fil-American defeat at Bataan. They instinctively believed that the obligations of loyalty were greater in adversity than in success. To have abandoned America when it was losing was the worst form of *walang hiya*, of shamelessness. As an emotional response, there was little room for expediency or pragmatic accommodation for most Filipinos. The abstractions of the war were personified by the towering figures of Quezon and MacArthur, to whom continuing loyalty was proffered.

To these Filipinos, enmeshed as they were in their own web of loyalties, the oligarchic response to collaborate seemed both inexplicable and treasonable. They saw the elite as having breached a vital strand of allegiance by opposing the national decision as it had been proclaimed at the outbreak of the war and articulated at that time by the elite itself. By casting their influence as a counterweight against the continuing struggle, they appeared to be *walang hiya* to Quezon, MacArthur, America, and most importantly, to the articulated values of the Philippine nationalism which the elite had been instrumental in inculcating throughout the society. Having built a national consciousness, they appeared ironically to have flouted it. Unaware of and insensitive to the subvalue system of the elite, which prompted them to do, from their point of view, what they had always done, the majority of the nation remained critical of them during the war. Neither Vargas nor Laurel received the loyalty of the people.

After the war, however, these attitudes altered, as all segments of the nation began to realize that to maintain the gap between the elite and the people would be to destroy the most potent institution within the society. Confronted with the prospect of purging the elite, as Roosevelt had wanted, the nation became conscious of the hitherto tacit role of the elite within the society. Although this was articulated less bluntly, people acknowledged that to purge the elite was to decapitate the society. Dazed by the incredible destruction and social dislocation of the country caused by the war, and frightened by the risk of further unrest caused by the Hukbalahap threat, many could not conceive of a Philippines without the establishment.[14] It became clear that within the system of Filipino values, people wanted and needed this group of secular nationalist leaders. They served as an anchor of continuity and prevented social drift. Filipinos wanted to preserve the social structure which had emerged during the colonial eras, as they searched for an independent identity. Together with ties of kinship, *compadrazgo,* ecclesiastical and regional affinities, and nationalism, Filipinos became consciously aware of this additional allegiance. Unlike Chinese society, which during these same years was repudiating its traditional social structure and its established elite, Philippine society expressed a conservative and preservative character by moving instinctively toward the elite's concept of proper wartime behavior.

The reason a thorough inquiry into a collaboration has not been held since the war is because it would require a complete examination of Philippine social organization. The society would have to ask itself if it still wanted the oligarchic structure, which, while permitting some upward mobility, has prevented many from rising to the top. It would have to ask itself whether modern nationalism, with its commitment to mass participation, and democracy, with its commitment to the individual, were well served by, in Laurel's terms, "a moral and intellectual aristocracy."[15] It would have to ask itself whether the acumen of this group was as great as the elite believed it was, and if not, whether the elite should be able to arrogate to itself the right to determine for the nation, through its control of the government, decisions affecting everyone.

An analysis of collaboration would require a reappraisal of the wartime behavior of the elite. The nation opted to retain its leaders when it recognized its dependence on them. It exercised its sovereign right to conserve the elite instead of risking further upheaval without it. However, this decision did not necessarily erase the puzzle of collaboration. The question of *hubris* remained. Was the elite arrogant in deciding in 1942 that it knew better than the people what was best for the people? Was the oligarchy insensitive to the realities of mass participation, despite its verbal pledge to this participation? Collaboration has remained a pejorative, like treason, because in Rebecca West's terms, it is "the betrayal of familiars to strangers, of those who are near to those who are far, of those to whom one is bound by real interests to those who, being foreign, will treat one as a foreigner and maybe, in the end, turn against one."[16] The difference between the oligarchic collaboration with the Spanish and American authorities and the later collaboration with Japan is that the first two occurred before a Philippine nation had emerged, while the last took place when national self-consciousness existed. Consequently, though from the elite's point of view these instances of collaboration were historically consistent, and therefore justifiable, from the nation's point of view there may have been a substantive difference between them.[17] An examination of collaboration would require that Filipinos ask whether the elite had recognized sufficiently the maturity of Philippine nationalism and the ability of the average Filipino to act within a sophisticated context. Did the elite show sufficient respect for the intelligence and integrity of its own people?

The failure to examine collaboration completely has been justified on the grounds that no human being would be capable of assessing correctly all the factors involved in such a complex social situation. The Philippines, a nation in search of its identity, has hesitated before opening what may be a Pandora's box. To resolve the moral problem, Filipinos have, characteristically, utilized another strand of their value system. Devoutly believing in redemption in the world to come, they have transferred the burden of justice from their imperfect human society to the infallible wisdom of God. That a confused and distraught society may not have dispensed total justice on earth—if the wartime leadership was indeed more culpable than Philippine society adjudged it to be after the war—did not really matter, because, in Francisco Delgado's words, "the final judgment on 'intentions'" could be left "to a Higher Power who, alone, has the power to divine men's thoughts."[18]

Notes

C H A P T E R I

[1] Henry Adams, *The Education of Henry Adams* (New York: The Modern Library, 1931), 12.

[2] *Oxford English Dictionary* (Oxford: Clarendon Press, 1933), VI, 480.

[3] *Oxford English Dictionary*, I, 231.

[4] The author is deeply in debt to Stuart Schlegel and Frazier Meade for their hours of incisive help.

[5] See Carl H. Landé, "Politics in the Philippines" (unpublished Ph.D. dissertation, Harvard University, 1958); Jaime Bulatao, "Philippine Values I: The Manileño's Mainsprings," and Frank Lynch, "Philippine Values II: Social Acceptance," *Philippine Studies*, X, 1 (January 1962), 45-99; Mary R. Hollnsteiner, *The Dynamics of Power in a Philippine Municipality* (Manila: Community Development Research Council, 1963); and Robert B. Fox, "The Filipino Concept of Self-Esteem," *Area Handbook on the Philippines*, ed. Fred Eggan, Evett Hester, and Norton Ginsburg (Chicago: Human Relations Area Files, 1956), 430-36.

[6] Mary R. Hollnsteiner, "Reciprocity in Lowland Philippines," *Philippine Studies*, IX, 3 (July 1961), 387-413; Charles Kaut, "Utang na loob: A System of Contractual Obligations among Tagalogs," *Southwest Journal of Anthropology*, XVII, 3 (1961), 256-72.

[7] The concept of *hiya* transcends simple shame since it also means embarrassment, awkwardness, and shy mortification. It is "a painful emotion arising from a relationship with an authority figure or with society, inhibiting self-assertion in a situation which is perceived as dangerous to one's ego. It is a kind of anxiety, a fear of being left exposed, unprotected, and unaccepted . . . hiya is the inner form of respect due to the group." Consequently, the accusation of

177

being *walang hiya* (shameless) is as severe a social slur as can be leveled by the group at an individual. Jaime C. Bulatao, "Hiya," *Philippine Studies*, XII, 3 (July 1964), 428 and 437.

[8] Antonio Pigafetta, *Magellan's Voyage Around the World*, ed. James A. Robertson (Cleveland: Arthur Clark, 1906), I, 153-55.

[9] Sidney W. Mintz and Eric R. Wolf, "An Analysis of Ritual Co-parenthood (Compadrazgo)," *Southwest Journal of Anthropolgy*, VI, (1950), 341-68; George Forster, "Cofradia and Compadrazgo," *Southwest Journal of Anthropology*, IX, 1 (1953), 1-28.

[10] *Area Handbook on the Philippines*, 663-64.

[11] See Horatio de la Costa, S. J., *The Jesuits in the Philippines 1581-1768* (Cambridge: Harvard University Press, 1961); John L. Phelan, *The Hispanization of the Philippines: Spanish Aims and Filipino Responses 1565-1700* (Madison: University of Wisconsin Press, 1959).

[12] Horatio de la Costa, S. J., "The Development of the Native Clergy in the Philippines," *Theological Studies*, VIII, 2 (June 1947), 219-50.

[13] W. E. Retana, *Frailes y clerigos* (Madrid: Fernando Fe, 1890), 100, cited in De la Costa, "The Development of the Native Clergy in the Philippines," 246.

[14] Carl H. Landé, *Leaders, Factions, and Parties: The Structure of Philippine Politics* (New Haven: Southeast Asia Studies Monograph No. 6, 1965), 16.

[15] Onofre D. Corpuz, *Bureaucracy in the Philippines* (Manila: Institute of Public Administration, 1957); Jean Grossholtz, *Politics in the Philippines* (Boston: Little Brown, 1964).

[16] Phelan, 121 passim.

[17] Recent scholarship has indicated that the composition of the cacique class was far more complex than was once thought. It is probable that a series of later groups including a large number of Chinese-mestizos replaced some of the original caciques. However, it is interesting that the new caciques adopted the patterns and values of the original ones, therefore perpetuating to at least some extent the traditional standards. See Edgar Wickberg, *The Chinese in Philippine Life 1850-1898* (New Haven: Yale University Press, 1965), 143.

[18] Technically, the term *Filipino* during the Spanish era meant a pure-blooded Spaniard born in the Philippines. Thus, the Filipino was a subgrouping of the generic class of creoles and was in contrast to the *peninsulares*, who were born in Spain. The natives were then called *indios*, a term which now has a strong pejorative connotation. Many Filipinos today use the term Filipino to refer only to lowland Catholics and do not include the Moros (Moslems of Mindanao) or hill peoples such as the Negritos. In time as nationalism increases the term will probably include everyone

who lives within the area. It is in this sense that it is usually now used in the West.

[19] See the seminal article by Edgar Wickberg, "The Chinese Mestizo in the Philippines," *Journal of Southeast Asian History*, V, 1 (March 1964), 62-100

[20] See William L. Schurz, *The Manila Galleon* (New York: E. P. Dutton, 1959).

[21] Wickberg, "The Chinese Mestizo in the Philippines," 68.

[22] Wickberg, *The Chinese in Philippine Life*, 31.

[23] Wickberg, "The Chinese Mestizo in the Philippines," 79-80.

[24] Wickberg, "The Chinese Mestizo in the Philippines," 84; *The Chinese in Philippine Life*, 62.

[25] Wickberg, "The Chinese Mestizo in the Philippines," 90.

[26] Wickberg, 65-66, 95.

[27] During the nineteenth century various elite organizations were created with the self-conscious intention of arrogating to themselves the most important and ceremonial activities of the society. See the discussion of the *Kapatiran ng mga Maginoo,* the "Brotherhood of the Elite," in Mary R. Hollnsteiner, *The Dynamics of Power in a Philippine Municipality,* 26 and 88.

[28] For a comparative study of elite formations throughout Southeast Asia, see the provocative article by Harry J. Benda, "Political Elites in Colonial Southeast Asia: An Historical Analysis," *Comparative Studies in Sociology and History*, VII, 3 (April 1965), 233-51.

[29] See, for example, Jose Rizal, *The Lost Eden [Noli me Tangere]* (Bloomington: Indiana University Press, 1961); *The Subversive [El Filibusterismo]* (Bloomington: Indiana University Press, 1962).

[30] Teodoro A. Agoncillo, *The Revolt of the Masses* (Quezon City: University of the Philippines Press, 1956); *Malolos: Crisis of the Republic* (Quezon City: University of the Philippines Press, 1960).

[31] Julius Pratt, *Expansionists of 1898* (Gloucester: Peter Smith, 1959); Ernest May, *Imperial Democracy* (New York: Harcourt, Brace and World, 1961); Leon Wolff, *Little Brown Brother* (London: Longmans, 1961); Dean C. Worcester, *The Philippines Past and Present* (New York: Macmillan, 1930); Garel A. Grunder and William E. Livezey, *The Philippines and the United States* (Norman: University of Oklahoma Press, 1951).

[32] For an excellent account of Quezon's power, see Theodore Friend, *Between Two Empires* (New Haven: Yale University Press, 1965); see also Manuel L. Quezon, *The Good Fight* (New York: Appleton-Century, 1946).

[33] Joseph R. Hayden, *The Philippines: A Study in National Development* (New York: Macmillan, 1947), 370-71.

[34] One of the first acts of the Philippine Congress upon gaining indepen-

dence from the United States in 1946 was its order that for per-
petuity MacArthur's name be called first at every military roll
call in the Philippines and that the senior noncommissioned
officer was always to reply, "present in spirit." Douglas Mac-
Arthur, *Reminiscences* (New York: McGraw Hill, 1964), 265-66.
[35] Pio Duran, *Philippine Independence and the Far Eastern Question*
(Manila: Community Publishers, 1935), 191, 171, 213-14.

CHAPTER II

[1] Henry F. Pringle, *Theodore Roosevelt* (New York: Harcourt, Brace
and World, 1956), 287.
[2] Tydings-McDuffie Act (Public Law No. 127, 73rd Congress) cited in
Joseph R. Hayden, *The Philippines: A Study in National Development* (New York: Macmillan, 1947), 819.
[3] Louis Morton, "War Plan Orange: Evolution of a Strategy," *World
Politics*, XI (1959), 222.
[4] Morton, 230.
[5] Occasionally, American diplomats attempted to close the gap. A continuing minority opinion within the State Department argued
along the lines originally suggested by Theodore Roosevelt. This
concept of pragmatic accommodation with Japan usually floundered against the moral commitment made by America toward
the defense of Chinese territorial integrity. For example, Secretary
of State Robert Lansing at one point considered transferring the
Philippines to Japanese influence, if not rule, as part of a general
Asian settlement with Japan. Woodrow Wilson's commitment to
China, however, aborted this idea. See Burton Beers, *Vain En-
deavor* (Durham: Duke University Press, 1962), 109.
[6] Morton, 242.
[7] Louis Morton, *The Fall of the Philippines* (Washington: Office of the
Chief of Military History, 1953), 9.
[8] Manuel Quezon, *The Good Fight* (New York: Appleton-Century,
1946), 152.
[9] Douglas MacArthur, *Reminiscences* (New York: McGraw Hill, 1964),
102; Quezon, 154-55.
[10] The Philippine Department of the American Army remained under
the Command of Major General Lucius Holbrook, who was instructed to assist MacArthur whenever possible, but to continue
his independent command. Morton, *The Fall of the Philippines*, 9.
[11] MacArthur, 103-4.
[12] Hayden, 739.
[13] Morton, *The Fall of the Philippines*, 10.
[14] Theodore Friend, *Between Two Empires* (New Haven: Yale University Press, 1965), 194.
[15] In 1939 there were about 29,000 Japanese in the Philippines with

about 5000 living in greater Manila and 18,000 concentrated in the Davao region of Mindanao. Japanese immigration had first begun in the early years of the twentieth century, when Americans brought them in to build the Baguio Road in Luzon. In 1904 a number had gone to Davao to work for an enterprising entrepreneur, Ota Kyosaburo, who saw great potential in the south. (Japanese names are given in traditional form with the family name first, but the diacritical marks have been omitted.) By 1939 Davao had become a world-wide source of abaca and copra. The Japanese had about 50,000,000 pesos invested in that one area of the Philippines alone. The Japanese, who were enormously enterprising, had a Davao Japanese Association of about 7000 members, ran twelve schools, paid about one half of the taxes of Davao, and supported nearly all the social services of the area. Japanese capital, legitimately looking for areas to invest in, also moved into the new copper and chromite mining industries as well as fishing, lumber milling, and retailing. This overseas community was a decided asset for the Philippines, and there is no evidence that it was subversive in the prewar era. It was subjected to hounding persecution, as was the Chinese community, because it was both alien and successful. For a treatment of the Japanese-Philippine relationship in the nineteenth century see Josefa M. Saniel, *Japan and the Philippines 1868-1898* (Quezon City: University of the Philippines Press, 1963). See also Hayden, 712-29, for Commonwealth tensions.

[16] Claro M. Recto as quoted in the *Manila Tribune*, September 14, 1934, cited in Hayden, 723.

[17] Uchiyama to Foreign Minister Hirota, October 8, 1935, cited in Friend, 175.

[18] Quezon, 290.

[19] Pio Duran, *Philippine Independence and the Far Eastern Question* (Manila: Community Publishers, 1935), 125.

[20] Duran, 120. Duran gave his children Japanese names.

[21] Hayden, 382-92; David R. Sturtevant, "Sakdalism and Philippine Radicalism," *Journal of Asian Studies*, XXI (February 1962), 199-214.

[22] *New York Times*, June 20, 1943, 3.

[23] For a provocative analysis of this confrontation see Paul W. Schroeder, *The Axis Alliance and Japanese American Relations* (Ithaca: Cornell University Press, 1958); see also Herbert Feis, *The Road to Pearl Harbor* (Princeton: Princeton University Press, 1950); Robert J. Butow, *Tojo and the Coming of the War* (Princeton: Princeton University Press, 1961).

[24] MacArthur, 109; Morton, *The Fall of the Philippines*, 15-19.

[25] Morton, 24.

[26] Morton, 42, table 3.

[27] Morton, 49, table 4; MacArthur, 110.

[28] Manuel L. Quezon, "Address of the President of the Commonwealth, Manuel L. Quezon, before the Senate of the United States," June 4, 1942, 3-4.

[29] Francis B. Sayre, *Glad Adventure* (New York: Macmillan, 1957), 221.

[30] *Pearl Harbor Attack Hearings*, Part 14, 1405, cited in Morton, 71.

[31] Morton, 71.

[32] Roberta Wohlstetter, *Pearl Harbor: Warning and Decision* (Stanford: Stanford University Press, 1962).

[33] Sayre, 221-22.

[34] Quezon, 181-82.

[35] Quezon, 185.

[36] Morton, 86; see also 79-90. MacArthur never admitted that the Clark Field debacle could have been avoided. He defended General Brereton, the commander at Clark, against the charge of incompetence. MacArthur, *Reminiscences*, 117-21.

[37] Morton, 90.

[38] "Interrogation of Japanese officers after the war and a study of Japanese and American records fails to support the belief that a Japanese fifth column existed in the Philippines. There is not a shred of evidence to indicate that any organized effort was made by the Japanese to utilize the sympathies of the Japanese population in the Islands or of Filipino collaborators. . . . Such an organization did not exist." Morton, 118.

[39] Carlos P. Romulo, *I Saw the Fall of the Philippines* (New York: Doubleday, Doran, 1942), 59-60; a slightly different version appears in the chapter of Quezon's autobiography written by his aide, Manuel Nieto, Quezon, *The Good Fight*, 325.

[40] The Council of State at this time included: Vice-President Sergio Osmeña, Chief Justice Jose Abad Santos, Executive Secretary to the President Jorge Vargas, Speaker of the House Jose Yulo, Floor Leader Quintin Paredes, Secretary of Justice Jose Laurel, Secretary of National Defense Teofilo Sison, Chief of the Constabulary General Guillermo Francisco; Secretary of Agriculture, Commerce, and Resources Rafael Alunan, Secretary of Public Works and Communications Sotero Baluyot, former Secretary of Finance and Senator Manuel Roxas, Secretary of Finance Serafin Marabut, Secretary of Public Instruction Jorge Bocobo, Secretary of Health Jose Fabella, Secretary of Labor Leon Guinto, and Chief of Staff General Basilio Valdes.

Virtually all these men played a major role during the war years. The only major figures absent were those key congressmen and senators who were not on the Council because of the separation of powers of the executive and legislative branches. Chief among these was Claro M. Recto, who had just been elected senator in the November 1941 ballot. Recto had placed first in the election with Roxas second, but a thousand votes behind, and Yulo fourth. In the Philippines, the top eight candidates for the Senate are elected on a nationwide basis. Laurel was initially still an associate justice of the Supreme Court when the war broke out until he resigned to accept the appointment as secretary of Justice. On December 17, 1941, General MacArthur appointed Manuel Roxas a lieutenant colonel in the American army to serve as his liaison officer with Quezon.

[41] *Manila Bulletin*, December 12, 1941, 1.

[42] *Manila Bulletin*, December 12, 1941, 1; Quezon, *The Good Fight*, 201-5.

[43] Quezon, 206.

[44] Quezon, 194-95.

[45] Quezon, 196.

[46] Quezon, 198.

[47] Quezon, 199.

[48] Morton, *The Fall of the Philippines*, 125 passim.

[49] Morton, 139 passim.

[50] Morton, 57-59.

[51] Morton, 62-64, 163-66.

[52] The heavy cruiser "Pensacola" had been leading a convoy of 4600 troops and seventy planes to the Philippines on December 7 when it was ordered back to Hawaii as a result of the heavy damage.

[53] Jose P. Laurel, *War Memoirs of Dr. Jose P. Laurel* (Manila: Jose P. Laurel Memorial Foundation, 1962), 4-5.

[54] Laurel, 5; Interview with Jorge Vargas, April 13, 1960.

[55] See, for example, Quintin Paredes, "Speech Delivered During the Amnesty Proclamation Debate, February 13, 1948" (Manila: Bureau of Printing, Special Reprint of the Congressional Debate), 18.

[56] Quezon, 208-9.

[57] Quezon, 211.

[58] MacArthur, 126.

CHAPTER III

[1] *Official Journal of the Japanese Military Administration* (Manila: Bureau of Publicity, Department of General Affairs, Japanese Military Administration), I, 1-2.

[2] It took days, however, to remove all vestiges of the prewar era. On January 16, for example, the censors missed a Donald Duck strip in which Donald bought a parrot from a sailor. Upon arrival home, the bird spoke only in pseudo-oriental characters, which made Donald furious. Filipinos laughed at such a strip, but the Japanese clearly did not.

[3] Interviews by the writer with Jorge Vargas, April 13, 1960; Quintin

Paredes, March 10, 1960; Antonio de las Alas, April 8, 1960; and Dominador Tan, March 14, 1960.

[4] *Official Gazette* (Manila: Bureau of Printing, 1942), I: 1, 19.

[5] Quintin Paredes, "Speech Delivered During the Amnesty Proclamation Debate, February 13, 1948" (Manila: Bureau of Printing, Special Reprint of the Congressional Debate), 28.

[6] *Official Gazette*, I: 1, 22.

[7] *Manila Tribune*, January 23, 1942, 1. Benigno Aquino was of "an old cacique aristocrat family with considerable Spanish blood." His father was a wealthy landowner in Tarlac, and Aquino himself was a charter member of the Nacionalista oligarchy. He was active in many prewar economic and political organizations. Office of Strategic Services, Research and Analysis Branch, United States Army, Biographical Report, "Benigno S. Aquino—Confidential," November 10, 1944, 1.

[8] *Official Gazette*, I: 1, 20. The order in which the names appeared was significant because it clearly indicated the relative ranking of these thirty-four men at the beginning of the war. In order, the list included: Jorge B. Vargas, Jose Yulo, Quintin Paredes, Jose P. Laurel, Benigno S. Aquino, Teofilo Sison, Rafael Alunan, Claro M. Recto, Jorge Bocobo, Leon Guinto, Jose Fabella (unsigned), Eulogio Rodriguez, Sotero Baluyut, Serafin Marabut, Emilio Aguinaldo, Vicente Madrigal, Ramon J. Fernandez, Antonio de las Alas, Elpidio Quirino, Jose Zulueta, Dominador Tan, Francisco Lavides, Ramon Avanceña, Miguel Unson, Alejandro Roces, Pedro Sabido, Alfonso Mendoza (unsigned), Melicio Arranz, Pedro C. Hernaez, Jose Osamiz, Jose Veloso, Ricardo Navarro, Prospero Sanidad, and Eugenio Perez. Manuel L. Quezon, *The Good Fight* (New York: Appleton-Century, 1946), 290-92. Juan Sumvlong, who declined to attend these sessions, had urged his colleagues to avoid any decision, at least until the American forces might surrender. Interview with Francisco Lavides, November 21, 1966.

[9] *Official Gazette*, I: 1, 21.

[10] *Official Journal of the Japanese Military Administration*, I, 7.

[11] Vargas initially appointed Benigno Aquino as commissioner of the Interior, Antonio de las Alas as commissioner of Finance, Jose Laurel as commissioner of Justice, Rafael Alunan as commissioner of Agriculture and Commerce, Claro Recto as commissioner of Education, Health, and Welfare, and Quintin Paredes as commissioner of Public Works and Communications.

[12] *Official Journal of the Japanese Military Administration*, I, 67.

[13] Douglas MacArthur, *Reminiscences* (New York: McGraw Hill, 1964), 136-37; Manuel Quezon, *The Good Fight*, 259-60.

[14] MacArthur, 137; Quezon, 261.

[15] MacArthur, 137.

[16] The implications of such a return are discussed in an extended speculation by James K. Eyre Jr., *The Roosevelt-MacArthur Conflict*
Chambersburg: The Craft Press, 1950), 65-74.

[17] MacArthur, 134-35; Emilio Aguinaldo and Vicente Pacis, *A Second
Look at America* (New York: Robert Speller, 1957), 182-84.

[18] MacArthur, 134-35.

[19] MacArthur, 138.

[20] MacArthur, 138.

[21] Carlos P. Romulo, *I Walked With Heroes* (New York: Holt, Rinehart
and Winston, 1961), 221.

[22] Louis Morton, *The Fall of the Philippines* (Washington: Office of the
Chief of Military History, 1953), 354-55.

[23] Eyre, 41-43.

[24] Quezon, 267-68.

[25] Quezon, 262.

[26] Romulo, 221.

[27] Rad. MacArthur to Marshall No. 358, 24 February 42, 370.05
(3/17/42) Philippines cited in Morton, 357-58.

[28] MacArthur, 145.

[29] Quezon, 280-81.

[30] Minutes of the Council of State, February 18, 1942. Malacañan Palace
(Mauro Garcia Collection) cited in Theodore Friend, *Between
Two Empires* (New Haven: Yale University Press, 1965), 224-27.
Since preparation of the manuscript of this book Mauro Garcia
has published his collection of primary documents, which is
recommended highly to all interested readers: Mauro Garcia,
Documents of the Japanese Occupation of the Philippines
(Manila: Philippine Historical Association, 1965).

[31] Jose P. Laurel, *The War Memoirs of Dr. Jose P. Laurel* (Manila: Jose
P. Laurel Memorial Foundation, 1962), 10.

CHAPTER IV

[1] General Homma Masaharu had spent five years in England as military
attache and was one of the leading military figures in prewar
Showa Japan. His relationship to General Tojo Hideki had been
strained for years as a result of factional tensions within the
Japanese military—between the Imperial Staff and the War Ministry, between the pro-German and the pro-English groups. Tojo
recalled Homma in August 1942, and Homma spent the rest
of the war in semiretirement. His replacement was Tanaka Shizu-
ichi who had also served in England and spoke English well.
Tanaka had also served as attache in Washington. He was recalled
to Japan in 1943 because of his health, and ended the war as a
member of the Supreme War Council and commandant of the
Army Staff College. His Philippine replacement was Kuroda
Shigenori, who had served in England, India, and as chief of staff

to the Southern Regions Command in Singapore (Shonan) before assuming the Philippine post. He was, in turn, replaced in October 1944 by Japan's most famous combat general, the "Tiger of Malaya," Yamashita Tomoyuki.

[2] F. C. Jones, *Japan's New Order in East Asia, 1937-1945* (London: Oxford University Press, 1954), 333.

[3] "Secret Draft of the Basic Plan for the Establishment of the Greater East Asia Co-Prosperity Sphere," January 27, 1942, cited in *International Military Tribunal Far East*, Document 2402 B, Exhibit 1336.

[4] Testimony of Yamamoto Kumaichi, March 7, 1947, *International Military Tribunal Far East*, 17926.

[5] *International Military Tribunal*, Document 837 A, Exhibit 628.

[6] *International Military Tribunal*, Document 1112 A, Exhibit 1333 A.

[7] *Official Journal of the Japanese Military Administration*, VI, 107-14. The Greater East Asia Ministry was Tojo's creation, and it retained power only as long as he did. It was opposed by bureaucratic factions in the Japanese government, which viewed this new creation with alarm. The Foreign Ministry, the Gaimusho, was hostile, and the delineation of functions was never explicit or efficient. The Greater East Asia Minister Aoki Kazuo was a close friend of Tojo's from his Manchurian days. He was nicknamed *Garikame* (stubborn tortoise) because of his reputation for getting his way. Other key officials were Ando Yoshiro who, having served in Moscow and Geneva, was chief of the Research Bureau of the Foreign Ministry before becoming chief of the General Affairs Bureau of the Greater East Asia Ministry. Mizuno Haro, the top Japanese negotiator in Thailand just before World War II, became chief of the Southern Affairs Bureau. Ogura Masatsune, the managing director of the Sumitomo Holding Company, became an adviser. Yamamoto Kumaichi, who had been vice-minister of the Foreign Affairs Ministry, became Greater East Asia vice-minister and director of the Training Institute. For a more complete list see *Japanese Government Officials* (Washington: War Department, Military Intelligence Division, 1945).

[8] *Manila Tribune*, August 23, 1942, p. 7.

[9] Many of the atrocities perpetrated by the Japanese at the end of the war can be attributed at least in part to the psychological rage of the average Japanese soldier at the Filipino rejection of this proselytism.

[10] *Official Journal*, II, v-vi.

[11] Hino Ashihei, *The Flowering of Racial Spirit*, trans. Nishina Kazeo (Manila: Imperial Japanese Army, Department of Information, 1942), 58.

[12] "Philippine Expeditionary Force" (Manila: Watari Army Group, Department of Information, May 1943), caption 49.

[13] *Official Journal,* I, 9.

[14] *Official Journal,* VI, xx.

[15] *Official Journal,* VII, viii.

[16] The Asahi Shimbun Sha was assigned responsibility for the presses in Java. Domei, the Japanese news-wire service, assumed responsibility for Sumatra and Malaya. Yomiuri Shimbun Sha had authority in Burma. T. A. Bisson, *Japan's War Economy* (New York: Institute of Pacific Relations, 1945), 88.

[17] *Philippine Review,* I, 1 (March 1943), 2.

[18] Radio speech of Claro M. Recto reprinted in the *Manila Tribune,* December 2, 1942, 6.

[19] *Manila Tribune,* January 24, 1942, 4. Years later Aguinaldo recalled that "Japanese propaganda, backed by barbaric military ruthlessness, nevertheless, created confusion among the people. Seizing Filipino nationalism, just limbering up in expectation of independence, as an ally, the Japanese dazzled the Filipinos." Emilio Aguinaldo and Vicente A. Pacis, *A Second Look At America* (New York: Robert Speller, 1957), 181.

[20] *Official Journal,* X, vi.

[21] Domingo Santiago, "Philippine Education During the Japanese Occupation" (unpublished M. A. dissertation, University of the Philippines, 1951), 53 passim.

[22] *Official Gazette,* I: 7, 359.

[23] *Official Journal,* VIII, 26-32.

[24] Executive Order No. 126 issued January 23, 1943, *Official Journal,* IX, 23-41.

[25] Manuel E. Buenafe, *War-time Philippines* (Manila: Philippine Education Foundation, 1950), 172.

[26] On February 26, 1942, a schoolbook committee of seven Japanese and three Filipinos was created. Shiohara Tamotsu headed the group and Camilo Osias, the prewar assistant commissioner of Education, and Dr. B. Gonzales, the president of the University of the Philippines, were the key Filipinos involved in this texbook review.

[27] *Tagapagturo,* I: 2, 31.

[28] *Manila Tribune,* March 15, 1943, 1.

[29] *Tagapagturo,* I: 3, 1.

[30] *Tagapagturo,* I: 3, 4-5.

[31] *International Military Tribunal,* Document 1621 C, Exhibit 1335.

[32] On June 13, 1943, for example, the mayor of Manila, Leon Guinto, led a nineteen-member mission to Tokyo. Included were Pio Duran, Hilarion Silayan, director of Plant Industry, Cornelio Balmaceda, director of Commerce and Industry, and a number of provincial governors.

[33] Willard H. Elsbree, *Japan's Role in Southeast Asian Nationalist Movements 1940-1945* (Cambridge: Harvard University Press, 1953), 38.

[34] For a discussion of the program see Grant K. Goodman, "An Experiment in Wartime Intercultural Relations: Philippine Students in Japan 1943-1945" (Ithaca: Southeast Asia Program, Cornell University, Data Paper No. 46, 1962).

The political nature of the selection is evident from an examination of the two groups sent. The first group, which arrived on July 19, 1943, contained a good percentage of older professional Constabulary officers, who were sent to learn the technical aspects of police control. It also contained Domingo Sison, a nephew of Teofilo Sison, Jesus Quiambo, a relative of Benigno Aquino, and Amado David. The second group of *pensionados,* who were younger, included Benjamin Sanvictores, whose father was assistant commissioner of Agriculture; Mama Sinsuat, whose father was a key Moro leader and former senator from Mindanao; Eduardo and Ramon Vargas, who were sons of the chairman; Virgilio de los Santos, whose father was vice-president of the Japan Philippines Society and director of Oriental Culture during the war; Alberto Lavides, son of Francisco Lavides of the Executive Commission; Cesar Alzona, son of the founder of the Fascist party of the Philippines; Dionisio de Leon Jr., whose father was a judge on the Court of Appeals; Halim Abubakar of the Jolo family; Jose Mapa, Quintin Paredes' grandson; Benjamin Osias, son of Camilo Osias; and Mariano Laurel, a son of Jose Laurel. Goodman, Appendices A and B.

Further evidence of Japanese manipulation of the children of the oligarchy was the Sailboat Shipping Corporation created in July 1942, when because of the paralysis of inter-Island shipping, great profits could be made through reopening traffic. President of this corporation was Sergio Osmeña Jr., secretary was Antonio de las Alas Jr., and directors were Serviliano Aquino, Rafael Alunan Jr., Angel Vargas, and Jorge de Leon. *Manila Tribune,* July 11, 1942, 4.

[35] *Manila Tribune,* February 20, 1942, 3.

[36] *Gunsei Jishi Gaikyo Hokoku* No. 9, April 18, 1942, comp. John Young, *Selected Archives of the Japanese Army, Navy, and Other Government Agencies 1868-1945* (Washington: Library of Congress Microfilm, 1959), reel 118, frame 31362.

[37] *Manila Tribune,* May 10, 1942, 1.

[38] *Manila Tribune,* December 13, 1942, 5-6.

[39] *Manila Tribune,* December 15, 1942, 8; see also *Manila Tribune,* June 22, 1943, 4.

[40] *Manila Tribune,* June 27, 1943, 4.

[41] *Manila Tribune,* October 8, 1943, 5.

[42] *Manila Tribune,* August 3, 1944, 4.

[43] Letter to the secretary of Justice for release to all chiefs of bureaus and offices, May 9, 1942, cited in the Department of Justice Circular No. 17 issued on May 15, 1942. In the writer's possession.

[44] The literature on the guerrilla movements is extensive, ranging from personal accounts to statistical analyses. One of the most scholarly and perceptive, suggested here merely as a representative example, is Elmer Lear, *The Japanese Occupation of the Philippines—Leyte 1941-1945* (Ithaca: Southeast Asia Program, Cornell University, Data Paper No. 42, 1961).

[45] *Official Journal*, III, iv.

[46] Guillermo Francisco, "An Open Letter" (Manila: n.pub., n.d.), cited in *The People of the Philippines v. Guillermo Francisco, Criminal Case No. 3534 for Treason*, 1. In the author's possession.

[47] Mateo M. Capinpin, "Awakening to a New Life," *The Voice of the New Philippines*, II (February 1943), 3-5.

[48] Francisco's appointment along with that of Jose de los Reyes was made on April 10, 1943, the first anniversary of the fall of Bataan. It represented a direct challenge by the Japanese to the guerrilla movement for the loyalty of the newly released Filipino prisoners of war. *Manila Tribune*, April 11, 1943, 1 and 4.

[49] Quintin Paredes was responsible for Ilocos Norte & Sur, Abra, La Union, Baguio, and the Mountain Provinces; Teofilo Sison was in charge of Cagayan, Isabela, Nueva Vizcaya, and Nueva Ecija; Antonio de las Alas had Tarlac, Bataan, Pampanga, Rizal, Cavite, Mindoro, and Palawan; Claro Recto was responsible for Tabayas, Camarines Norte & Sur, Albay, Sorsogon, and Masbate; Rafael Alunan had charge of Negros, Iloilo, and Bacolod; Benigno Aquino was given Samar, Leyte, Cebu, Bohol; and Laurel himself was responsible for Mindanao and Sulu.

[50] *Official Journal* XI, xxxi-xxxii.

[51] *Official Gazette*, II: 7, 695.

[52] Quintin Paredes, "Speech Delivered During the Amnesty Proclamation Debate, February 13, 1948" (Manila: Bureau of Printing, Special Reprint of the Congressional Debate), 42.

[53] *Official Gazette*, II: 7, 654.

[54] *New York Times*, November 4, 1943, 9.

[55] The Supreme Court, for example, included Jose Yulo, Manuel V. Moran, Roman Ozaeta, Ricardo Paras, and Jorge Bocobo.

[56] *Official Gazette*, I: 8, 442.

[57] Jose Yulo, president of the Nacionalistas, Alfonso Mendoza of the Democratistas, Benigno Ramos of the Ganaps (formerly Sakdals), Emilio Javier of the Popular Front, and Arturo Tolentino of the Young Philippines were the men who issued the order. *Official Gazette*, I: 12, 849-50.

[58] *Manila Tribune*, July 8, 1942, 1.

[59] *Official Journal*, VI, xxi.

[60] *Official Gazette*, I: 12, 857-61, 940-42; quoted from 858.

[61] Aquino's appointment led to a reshuffling of the Vargas government. Laurel became Aquino's replacement as commissioner of the In-

terior and Teofilo Sison replaced Laurel in the Justice Department.
Pio Duran became Aquino's key assistant as director of General
Affairs. Alfonso Mendoza was made director-at-large for Luzon,
Oscar Ledesma, director-at-large for the Visayas, and Juan Alanao,
director-at-large for Mindanao. Dominador Tan was appointed
director of Planning and Research, Jose P. Laurel Jr. became
director of Provincial and Municipal branches, Benigno Ramos
became director of Publicity, and Arsenio Luz became secretary
and treasurer.

[62] As a result of Executive Order No. 156 Camilo Osias became first
assistant director general, and Benigno Ramos was elevated to be
one of the four new directors-at-large. On December 15, 1943,
Arsenio Luz became acting assistant director general and Dr. Jose
de Jesus, who had been on the Malacañan staff of the chairman,
became secretary and treasurer.

[63] *Shin seiki*, I, 5 (February 1943), 32.

[64] *Official Journal*, X, xxxiv.

[65] Jorge B. Vargas, "Report of the Chairman of the Philippine Executive
Commission to the Commander-in-Chief, Covering the Period
January 23, 1942 to March 31, 1943," unpublished typescript
document of August 23, 1943, 40-41. This seventy-four page
document marked "secret" was discovered by the writer and is in
his possession.

[66] *Manila Tribune*, June 18, 1943, 4.

[67] *Official Gazette*, I: 5, 296. A number of those dropped were incarcerated
by the Japanese for anti-Japanese activities. Rodriguez, Quirino,
and Osamiz in particular were suspect. Senator Osamiz was eventually shot for anti-Japanese espionage.

[68] *Official Gazette*, I: 2, 30.

[69] Vargas, "Report . . . ," 5.

[70] Vargas, "Report . . . ," 44-45.

[71] Jorge Vargas was born August 24, 1890, in Bago, Occidental Negros.
He received a B.A. from the University of the Philippines in 1911
and a law degree in 1914. He had a long career as lawyer,
businessman, and bureaucrat, beginning in 1915 as a law clerk
to the Philippine Commission. As executive secretary to the first
independence mission of 1919, director of Lands in 1922,
secretary to the independence mission of 1922, undersecretary of
Agriculture and Commerce from 1928 to 1935, executive secretary
of the Philippine Commonwealth Inauguration Committee in
1935, and secretary to the president of the Commonwealth from
1935 to 1941, Vargas was always in the lee of Manuel Quezon.
In 1937 Quezon elevated Vargas' position to one of cabinet status
and appointed him head of the Office of the President. Vargas,
long connected with the sugar industry, served as domestic sugar
administrator in 1936-37. In August 1941, Quezon appointed

Vargas secretary of Justice. He also had served as a director of the Philippine National Bank, the Manila Railroad Company, and numerous civic groups such as the Boy Scouts. During the Commonwealth era he was considered one of the most powerful men in the country because of his loyalty and access to Quezon. Office of Strategic Services, Research and Analysis Branch, United States Army, "Biographical Report on Jorge B. Vargas (Confidential)," November 25, 1944, 1-7.

[72] John Toland, *But Not in Shame* (New York: Random House, 1961), 115.

[73] In the brief prepared against Vargas after the war the prosecution argued that "the evident purpose of divesting him of any authority that might endow him with the color of a national official figure was to remove from the enemy a possible instrument for expediting the assimilation of the occupied territory. His markedly altered status in the official hierarchy when the Japanese entered Manila circumscribed his authority within the territorial limits of the city. His powers were no greater than those of any other local executive in the different political subdivisions of the Philippines within their respective jurisdictions. . . . There was an obligation to render the enemy certain services which, however, did not include doing the things that would amount to assisting the enemy in the conduct of the war . . . against his own troops or his allies. Notwithstanding the clear definition of his duties . . . the plain implications of his demotion . . . [and] the absence of any clear justification, he spurned the comparative obscurity of a city executive's office and projected himself into the national and international limelight. . . ." Lorenzo M. Tañada, *Summary Brief Against Jorge B. Vargas*, 1 passim. Source withheld.

[74] Charles Parsons, "Conditions in the Philippine Islands Since the Japanese Occupation" ("Strictly confidential" interview between Charles Parsons and C. J. Spiker conducted on board the M.S. "Gripsholm," August 23, 1942, and prepared for the secretary of State). Source withheld.

[75] Charles Parsons, "Personalities in the Philippines," A Memorandum to Colonel J. K. Evans, Intelligence Section, General Headquarters, Southwest Pacific Area, December 12, 1942. Source withheld.

[76] Interview with Jorge B. Vargas, April 13, 1960.

[77] *Official Journal*, IV, ix-x.

[78] Charge 34, *People* v. *Vargas*, Criminal Case No. 3520, "Information" filed March 12, 1946, 25. In the author's possession.

[79] *Official Journal*, IX, xiv passim.

[80] Charge 59, *People* v. *Vargas*, 50.

[81] *Manila Tribune*, January 27, 1943, 1 and 2.

[82] *Official Journal*, IX, v-ix passim.

[83] *Official Gazette*, I: 8, 480-85 passim. Vargas repeated the same point

confidentially to the Japanese. "The most noteworthy task of building a new Philippines worthy of independence and membership in the Co-Prosperity Sphere was the degree of cooperation mutually extended by the Japanese Military Administration and the Philippine Executive Commission." Vargas, "Report . . . ," 67.

[84] *Manila Tribune*, June 18, 1943, 1.

[85] Letter from Charles Parsons to Manuel Quezon, September 27, 1943. Source withheld.

[86] Interview with the writer, April 13, 1960.

CHAPTER V

[1] "Tentative Draft of the Independence Declaration," December 12, 1942, *Hito Dokuritsu To Nippi Domei Joyaku Teiketsu Kankei*, comp. Uyehara and Beal, *Checklist of the Archives of the Japanese Ministry of Foreign Affairs 1868-1945* (Washington: Library of Congress Microfilm, 1945), code: S.1.7.0.0-47, Reel 584, frames 16-24.

[2] *Checklist of Archives . . .* , frames 31-43.

[3] *Manila Tribune*, June 18, 1943, 3.

[4] See the series of reports cited in *Checklist of the Archives . . .* , frames 1-15 and 31-43.

[5] Ramon Avanceña was born on April 13, 1872, in Iloilo. He and his family had long had distinguished careers in education, public service, and business. After serving as attorney general from 1914-17 he became a justice of the Supreme Court. From 1925 to 1941 he was chief justice of the Supreme Court. Like Quezon he had a place of honored trust among his people when he resigned in 1941 to be succeeded by Jose Abad Santos. Office of Strategic Services, Research and Analysis Branch, United States Army, "Biographical Report on Ramon Avanceña (Confidential)," November 25, 1944, 1-2.

[6] Jimbo Nobuhiko, *Dawn of the Philippines* (Tokyo: Toppan Printing, 1959), 19.

[7] Letter from Charles Parsons to Manuel Quezon, September 27, 1943. Source withheld.

[8] Letter from Charles Parsons to "Chico" [Enrico Pirovano?], n.d. Source withheld. Manuel Quezon, *The Good Fight* (New York: Appleton-Century, 1946), 310-13.

[9] Jose Paciano Laurel was born March 9, 1891, at Tanauan, Batangas Province, and died November 6, 1959. Married in 1912, he was the father of nine children. He received an LL.B. in 1915 from the University of the Philippines, a D.C.L. from Yale in 1920, and an LL.D. *honoris causa* from Tokyo Imperial University in 1938. His prewar public career included holding the office of secretary of the Interior in 1923, serving as senator and floor leader from 1925 to 1931, and associate justice of the Supreme Court from

1936-41. Office of Strategic Services, Research and Analysis Branch, United States Army, "Biographical Report on Jose P. Laurel (Confidential)," November 25, 1944, 1-7.

[10] Jose P. Laurel, *War Memoirs of Dr. Jose P. Laurel* (Manila: Jose P. Laurel Memorial Foundation, 1962), 15-16, 51, 57, 63-68 passim. These *Memoirs,* published as a part of a volume of tribute to Laurel upon his death, are alleged to have come unaltered "from the pen of Dr. Laurel" as he wrote them while in prison in Japan from September to December 1945. It is claimed that they were not altered by Laurel or his estate at any subsequent time. The reader is urged to examine them but with the caveat that like other autobiographies they may contain intentional omissions. The interested reader is also directed to the postwar defense by Senator Recto. Claro M. Recto, *Three Years of Enemy Occupation: The Issue of Political Collaboration in the Philippines* (Manila: People's Publishers, 1946).

[11] Laurel, *War Memoirs*, 21.

[12] Jose P. Laurel, *Forces that Make a Nation Great* (Manila: Bureau of Information and Public Security, 1943), 8.

[13] Laurel, *Forces*, 85.

[14] Laurel, *Forces*, 91.

[15] Laurel, *Forces*, 12.

[16] Laurel, *Forces*, 16.

[17] Laurel, *Forces*, 75.

[18] David Bernstein, *The Philippine Story* (New York: Farrar, Straus, 1947), 168. Interestingly, but perhaps not surprisingly, Laurel is quoted as saying in April 1948: "At a time like this when the young Republic of the Philippines is facing a crisis, we should adopt what other countries are doing and that is to suspend temporarily all political parties. . . . I do not want it as construed that I am against political parties. That would be undemocratic and totalitarian. But at a time like this when a country is faced with a crisis, the best way to achieve unity is to stop the political bickerings and quarrels. As a temporary measure, we should do away with partisan politics." David Bernstein, "America and Dr. Laurel," *Harper's Magazine*, CXCVII (October 1948), 87.

[19] Manuel E. Buenafe, *War-time Philippines* (Manila: Philippine Educational Foundation, 1950), 203.

[20] Laurel, *Forces*, 110.

[21] *Manila Tribune*, November 10, 1943, 6.

[22] *Ang Kapit Bahay*, I: 2, 7.

[23] Laurel, *War Memoirs*, 58.

[24] *Official Journal*, XIII, lxi.

[25] Jose P. Laurel, "The Republic's Goal," *Philippine Review*, II, 9 (November 1944), 12.

[26] "Biographical Report on Jose Paciano Laurel (Confidential)," 4.

[27] "Biographical Report on Jose Paciano Laurel (Confidential)," 6.

[28] After the war, Laurel wrote, "I was not an aspirant. I did not like to be President. . . . I wished, indeed, I had been able to fold my arms . . . and later in the end, after catastrophe had ended and the danger had disappeared, to come out from amongst the silent crowd, or from my monastic seclusion, and present myself as the archetype of genuine patriotism and proven loyalty! But it was neither my lot nor my temper perhaps. And so, I carried on, and with me the other collaborators as a matter of necessity and for the love of our people." *War Memoirs,* 59-60.

[29] Laurel was listed first, followed by Ramon Avanceña and Aquino as first and second vice-presidents. In order next came Vargas, De las Alas, Sison, Alunan, Recto, Paredes, Yulo, Aguinaldo, Unson, Osias. Roxas' name appeared seventeenth.

[30] *Checklist of the Archives . . . ,* frames 54-65.

[31] The Japanese and Laurel disagreed on some of the provisions of the new constitution. For example Laurel wanted the Church to lose its tax-exempt status as well as its rights to land ownership. He also wanted to alter the Commonwealth provision on religious education to weaken the social power of the Church in a postwar Philippines. Laurel's commitment to secular nationalism ran counter to the Japanese policy of conscious accommodation of the Church, and consequently the Japanese eliminated these provisions. *Checklist of the Archives . . . ,* frames 219-34.

[32] The official version of the constitution can be found in the *Official Gazette,* II: 9 A (September 4, 1943), 1-48.

[33] *Official Gazette,* II: 10 (October 1-14, 1943), 985. Despite the evidence to the contrary, many Filipinos still believe that the Commonwealth and Laurel constitutions were identical except for minor alterations imposed by the Japanese. Jorge Vargas claimed in an interview with the writer on April 13, 1960, that the documents were the same except for the substitution of the name of Japan for that of the United States. Vargas also claimed that the 1943 draft was "practically a replica of the present constitution." Few people seem to have noticed the authoritarian centralization by which the legislature had lost power to the executive.

[34] *Manila Tribune,* August 8, 1943, 1.

[35] *Checklist of the Archives . . . ,* frames 236-39 and 258.

[36] *Official Gazette,* II: 9, 826.

[37] *Official Gazette,* II: 9, 828-30.

[38] *Manila Tribune,* September 21, 1943, 5.

[39] *Manila Tribune,* September 24, 1943, 1.

[40] *Manila Tribune,* September 26, 1943, 1.

[41] Laurel, *War Memoirs,* 16-18.

[42] *Official Gazette,* II: 10 (October 1-14, 1943), 983.

[43] Murata's staff contained many men of experience, English language ability, and knowledge of Southeast Asia. Murata's minister was

Tajiri Akiyoshi, an expert on the overseas Chinese, who later became Greater East Asia vice-minister. The embassy councilor was Ishii Tasushi, a professional diplomat with experience in New York and former head of a section of the American Affairs Bureau in Tokyo. The legal adviser and Murata's closest aide was Morishige Takeo, who had served in the Kwantung government, the Korean Affairs Bureau, the East Asia section of the Overseas Bureau, and the puppet government of Manchukuo. First secretary was Fukushima Shintaro, who had been consul in New York and Los Angeles and had served in Australia. Consul General Shionoya Suekichi had long experience in the colonial areas of Kwantung and Manchukuo. Among the holdovers from the Military Administration was Kobayashi Ichizo, a former minister of Commerce and Industry under Konoe who had been president of the Tokyo Electric Company and had headed one of the oil missions to Batavia in 1940.

⁴⁴ Laurel swiftly constructed his new government. By Executive Order No. 1, he created a Council of State embracing primarily the elder statesmen like Avanceña, Aunario, Unson, and Fernandez. At the same time he appointed the younger members of the elite to a National Planning Board chaired by Rafael Alunan and including Yulo and Roxas. His cabinet appointments included Recto as foreign secretary, De las Alas as finance secretary, Sison as secretary of Justice, Alunan as Agriculture and Commerce secretary, Paredes as secretary of Public Works and Communications, and Osias as secretary of Education.

⁴⁵ Jose P. Laurel, "Plea for Recognition of and Respect for Philippine Independence," *Ministry of Foreign Affairs Bulletin*, I, 1 (Manila: Bureau of Printing), 15.

⁴⁶ Theodore Friend, *Between Two Empires* (New Haven: Yale University Press, 1965), 237.

⁴⁷ *New York Times*, September 25, 1943, 3; October 17, 1943, IV, 8; November 4, 1943, 8; November 10, 1943, 15; July 1, 1944, 6. Joint Resolution 93, 78th Congress, 2nd Session (Approved June 29, 1944) cited in the *Official Gazette*, XLI; 1, 81-83.

⁴⁸ *Department of State Bulletin*, IX, 226, October 23, 1943, cited in Hernando J. Abaya, *Betrayal in the Philippines* (New York: A. A. Wyn, 1946), 47-48.

⁴⁹ *Checklist of the Archives . . .* , frame 83 passim.

⁵⁰ *Official Gazette*, I: 1, 13. (With the establishment of the Laurel government, the *Official Gazette* was issued in a new serial from that of the Vargas Philippine Executive Commission.)

⁵¹ Shirley Jenkins, *American Economic Policy Toward the Philippines* (Palo Alto: Stanford University Press, 1954), 37-41; J. E. Spencer, *Land and People in the Philippines* (Berkeley: University of California Press, 1952), passim.

⁵² *Official Journal*, VI, 29-36; *Manila Tribune*, October 8, 1942, 4.

[53] Murata Shozo was president and the three vice-presidents were Kodera Gengo, chairman of the Board of the Nippon Cotton Growing Association; Yamagoshi Michizo, director of the Military Administration's Department of Commerce and Industry; and Rafael Alunan who served as Vargas' commissioner of Agriculture and Commerce. *Manila Tribune*, February 12, 1943, 3.

A comparable five-year plan was drawn to increase ramie production based primarily on the Davao Japanese community. The Mitsubishi Commercial Company (Mitsubishi Shoji Kaisha) and the Mitsui Agriculture and Forestry Company (Mitsui Norin Kaisha) were given the prime responsibility to increase jute production. *Official Journal*, VII, 15-19.

[54] In a propaganda pamphlet in 1943, the Filipinos were informed that "the duty of the Filipino people, therefore, is clear: they must work harder to produce more and better quality Cotton—now." "Let us Produce More Cotton," (Manila: Department of Information, May 1943), 10.

[55] See, for example, the "Outline of Economic Policies for the Southern Areas (Nampo keizai taisaku yoko)" adopted at the Liaison Conference December 12, 1941, cited in Benda, Irikura, and Kishi, *Japanese Military Administration in Indonesia: Selected Documents* (New Haven: Yale University Southeast Asia Translation Series No. 6, 1965), 17-25.

[56] For a general analysis of Japan's wartime economic problems, see David H. James, *The Rise and Fall of the Japanese Empire* (London: Allen and Unwin, 1951).

[57] *Official Journal*, VI, 111.

[58] "The circulation of yen paper money (paper money issued by the Imperial Japanese Government, yen notes issued by the Bank of Japan, yen notes issued by the Bank of Chosen [and] . . . Taiwan, and military notes other than peso military notes), . . . and all other currencies of foreign countries shall be prohibited." *Official Journal*, I, 39.

[59] *Manila Tribune*, July 18, 1943, 1.

[60] A. V. H. Hartendorp, *History of Industry and Trade of the Philippines* (Manila: American Chamber of Commerce of the Philippines, 1958), 74.

[61] In 1941 the Bank earned 2,484,023 pesos, but in the first fifteen months of the occupation, the earnings, despite the inflation, fell to 413,765 pesos. Jorge B. Vargas, "Report of the Chairman of the Philippines Executive Commission to the Commander in Chief, covering the period January 23, 1942 to March 31, 1943," unpublished typescript document, 34.

[62] *Manila Tribune*, February 19, 1944, 4.

[63] *Official Journal*, VI, 25-29, passim.

[64] Revenues in 1940-41 were 158,668,000 pesos, but in the first six months of the occupation revenues fell to 3,152,340 pesos, or,

on a yearly basis, one twenty-fifth of the prewar levels. Spencer, 232; Vargas, "Report . . . , " 8.

[65] *Official Gazette*, I: 2, 50.

[66] *Manila Tribune*, January 10, 1943, 1; January 27, 1943, 1; February 17, 1943, 3.

[67] Government attempts to curb the black market never succeeded. Executive Order No. 157 establishing an Economic Police Force to limit the black market had almost no effect. Department of the Interior, Philippine Constabulary Circular No. 45, n.d. In the author's possession.

[68] "Get the Most out of Controlled Economy" (Manila: Bureau of Information and Public Security, n.d.), 4; Act No. 65 signed by Laurel March 3, 1944. *Official Gazette*, I: 6, 642-46.

[69] *Official Gazette*, I: 6, 619-20.

[70] An effort was made to shift the blame to the Chinese community, frequently a scapegoat in Philippine history. The *Tribune* editorialized that "selling our land to alien speculators is like selling our country away." (*Manila Tribune*, April 4, 1943, 4.) Similarly, the government attempted to link the inflation to the Chinese traditional power in retail trade (*Manila Tribune*, November 21, 1943, 2). Republic Act 43 and 45 (cited in the *Official Gazette*, I: 5, 497-98 and 500) threatened to intern the Chinese for any "act inimical to the peace, security, or interest of the Republic." However, while the Chinese were certainly involved in what the Japanese and Laurel felt to be inimical acts, these same crimes were as widely practiced by Filipinos.

[71] *Official Journal*, IV, 31.

[72] Hartendorp, *History of Industry and Trade* . . . , 81ff; *Manila Tribune*, October 5, 1942, 1.

[73] *Official Journal*, XI, 7.

[74] *Official Gazette*, I: 2, 111-16; *Manila Tribune*, December 3, 1943, 1; *Manila Tribune*, December 4, 1943, 1.

[75] *Manila Tribune*, January 6, 7, 8, 1944, 1.

[76] *Official Gazette*, I: 1, 53.

[77] *Official Gazette*, I: 1, 53-54.

[78] *Ang Kapit Bahay*, I, 2 (May 1943), 8.

[79] Laurel, "The Republic's Goal," 4.

[80] John Young, comp. *Selected Archives of the Japanese Army, Navy, and other Government Agencies 1868-1945* (Washington: Library of Congress Microfilm, 1959), reel 118, frame 31553 ff; reel 119, frame 31891 ff. See also, for example, the long nonmilitary report by Counsellor Morishige Tateo to Foreign Minister Shigemitsu indicating the frustration felt by the Japanese at their inability to control the guerrilla movement, in this case, in Cebu. *Checklist of the Archives of the Japanese Ministry of Foreign Affairs 1868-1945*, frames 357-79.

[81] *Manila Tribune*, November 4, 1943, 1.

[82] *Official Gazette*, I: 3, 199.

[83] *Manila Tribune*, January 7, 1944, 2.

[84] *Manila Tribune*, February 5, 1944, 1 and 2.

[85] *Official Gazette*, I: 10, 5.

[86] *Manila Tribune*, January 4, 1944, 1.

[87] *Official Gazette*, I: 8, 857-61.

[88] *Manila Tribune*, May 20, 1944, 2.

[89] *Official Gazette*, I: 5, 492-94. In mid-June Laurel issued Executive Order No. 61, which transferred the administration of the city of Manila directly to him because of the "exigencies of the situation." (*Manila Tribune*, June 16, 1944, 1.) A Civilian Protection Service, the CPS, was created to prepare the city for air raids, especially after the fall of Saipan placed Manila within American bombing range. (*Official Gazette*, I: 5, 457.)

[90] "Our Independence Is at Hand" (Manila: Bureau of Information and Public Security, 1943), 6.

[91] Jose P. Laurel, "One Nation, One Heart, One Republic," September 7, 1943, cited in the *Official Journal*, XIII, lvii; *Manila Tribune*, September 14, 1944, 2.

[92] *Manila Tribune*, September 23, 1944, 1.

[93] *Checklist of the Archives . . .* , frame 44, 275.

[94] *Manila Tribune*, September 24, 1944, 1-2. During the Council of State discussion of the Proclamation, it was modified slightly. Recto suggested that the clause which stated that the United States was "intent upon a reconquest of the Philippines and an invasion of our soil made sacred and hallowed by the blood of our fore-fathers" be eliminated. Arsenio Luz also persuaded Laurel to drop a passage in which the people were to "be ready and willing to pledge our fortunes, our lives, and our sacred honor." Cited in Friend, *Between Two Empires*, 243. Recto, 49-55. Laurel, 23-24.

[95] *Manila Tribune*, November 10, 1944, 1.

[96] *Manila Tribune*, November 15, 1944, 4.

[97] Executive Order No. 37 issued on February 23, 1944, cited in the *Official Gazette*, I: 5, 458-59.

[98] *Manila Tribune*, July 12, 1944, 4; April 11, 1944, 2.

[99] Laurel, *War Memoirs*, 60.

[100] Laurel, *Forces That Make a Nation Great*, 109.

CHAPTER VI

[1] Douglas MacArthur, *Reminiscences* (New York: McGraw Hill, 1964), 198.

[2] James A. Field, *The Japanese at Leyte Gulf: The Sho Operation* (Princeton: Princeton University Press, 1947).

[3] The lure of this confrontation had led many people to write accounts of the invasion. Among the numerous army and navy accounts see M. Hamlin Cannon, *Leyte: The Return to the Philippines*

(Washington: Office of the Chief of Military History, Department of the 'Army, 1954).

4 Cannon, *Leyte*, 26.

5 Manuel L. Quezon, "Report to the Filipino People" (Washington: Office of Special Services, February 20, 1943), 10.

6 Letter from Harold Ickes to Franklin Roosevelt, September 1, 1943, *Foreign Relations of the United States, Diplomatic Papers,* 1943 (Washington: Government Printing Office, 1963), III, 1099.

7 James K. Eyre Jr., *The Roosevelt-MacArthur Conflict.* (Chambersburg: The Craft Press, 1950), 131.

8 Joint Resolution No. 95, 78th Congress, 1st Session cited in the *Official Gazette,* XLI: 3 (June 1945), 241.

9 *New York Times,* November 10, 1943, 15; Garel A. Grunder and William E. Livezey, *The Philippines and the United States* (Norman: University of Oklahoma Press, 1951), 244.

10 Carlos P. Romulo, *I See the Philippines Rise* (New York: Doubleday & Co., 1946), 51-52.

11 MacArthur, *Reminiscences,* 265.

12 *Official Gazette,* XLI: 2 (May 1945), 145-46.

13 MacArthur, *Reminiscences,* 234-35.

14 *Manila Tribune,* April 12, 1944, 1; Marcial Lichauco, *Dear Mother Putnam: A Diary of the War in the Philippines* (Manila: Private Printing, 1949), 177.

15 *Official Gazette,* I: 7, 751; *Official Gazette,* I: 8, 899.

16 *Official Gazette,* I: 8, 856; *Manila Tribune,* June 6, 1944, 1.

17 *Manila Tribune,* September 12, 1944, 1; January 7, 1945, 1; January 12, 1945, 1.

18 The directors included L. R. Aguinaldo, Dr. Melquiades G. Virata, Dr. Jose Lara, and Benigno Ramos. General Ricarte was President, while Jose S. Laurel III, the president's son, was secretary general. The organization was the technical sponsor for an Institute of Oriental Culture. *Manila Tribune,* July 18, 1944, 3; November 4, 1944, 1; January 16, 1945, 2.

19 John Young, comp. *Selected Archives of the Japanese Army, Navy, and Other Government Agencies 1868-1945* (Washington: Library of Congress Microfilm, 1959), reel 119, frame 31912.

20 The Makapili was established on November 10, 1944, in Quezon City The key figures included Pio Duran, Benigno Ramos, Marcos P. Ramos, Generals Artemio Ricarte, Leon Villafuerte, and Andres Villanueva (all of the 1898 Insurrection), Pablo Capa, Jose Baluyot, and Aurelio Alvero. The organization was formally launched by Yamashita on December 8, 1944, the third anniversary of the war. See A. V. H. Hartendorp, *History of Industry and Trade of the Philippines* (Manila: American Chamber of Commerce of the Philippines, 1958), 74; and the *Manila Tribune* throughout this period.

[21] Interview with General Wachi Takagi cited in Theodore Friend, *Between Two Empires* (New Haven: Yale University Press, 1965), 244.

[22] Jose P. Laurel, *The War Memoirs of Dr. Jose P. Laurel* (Manila: Jose P. Laurel Memorial Foundation, 1962), 25.

[23] Of the six thousand Filipinos investigated by the American Counter-Intelligence Corps after the fighting ceased, over half were members of the Makapili. In a subsequent Philippine Court trial, it was ruled that "being a Makapili is in itself constitutive of an overt act [of treason.] It is not necessary except for the purpose of increasing the punishment that the defendant actually went to battle or committed nefarious acts against his country or his countrymen. . . . It furnished the enemy aid in that his cause was advanced, his forces augmented, and his courage was enhanced by the knowledge that he could count on such men as the accused. . . . The practical effect of it was no different from that of enlisting in the invader's army." *People* v. *Adriano, Official Gazette*, XLI: 11, 4300-4304.

[24] *New York Times*, July 1, 1944, 6.

[25] Eyre, *The Roosevelt-MacArthur Conflict*, 141-42.

[26] *Official Gazette*, XLI: 2, 148-49.

[27] Friend, *Between Two Empires*, 249.

[28] In 1942 Quezon had written Secretary of the Navy Frank Knox, urging that derogatory information about the collaborators not be released because he felt it would be "harmful to our cause." Expressing his oligarchic view, he noted that "while if they [the elite in Manila] had to be killed in the interests of the cause, I am sure they would willingly die, their replacement by the few who are really pro-Japanese and who are trying to get their jobs would definitely jeopardize the effectiveness of the help that the Filipino people would want to render us when the proper time arrives for lack of intelligent leadership." Letter from Manuel Quezon to Frank Knox, August 27, 1942. Source withheld.

[29] *Official Gazette*, XLI: 1 (April 1945), 101-2. *New York Times*, November 24, 1945, 3.

[30] *Official Gazette*, XLI: 1, 43-45; *New York Times* November 7, 1944, 5.

[31] *New York Times*, November 19, 1944, 34.

[32] *Manila Tribune*, January 7, 1945, 1.

[33] Printed handsheet in the Worcester Collection, University of Michigan, Ann Arbor.

[34] See Frank A. Reel, *The Case of General Yamashita* (Chicago: University of Chicago Press, 1949); Aubrey S. Kenworthy, *The Tiger of Malaya* (New York: Exposition Press, 1953); *Report on the Destruction of Manila and Japanese Atrocities* (Washington: Office of the Philippine Resident Commissioner, 1945); Robert Ross Smith, *Triumph in the Philippines* (Washington: Depart-

ment of the Army, 1963); Douglas MacArthur, *Reminiscences* (New York: McGraw Hill, 1964), 237-66.

[35] Smith, *Triumph in the Philippines*, 249.

[36] *Official Gazette*, XLI: 1, 86-87; MacArthur, *Reminiscences*, 251-52.

[37] Laurel, *War Memoirs*, 27-28, 34-48.

[38] *Victory News*, April 18, 1945, 1; *Guerrilla*, April 18, 1945, 1.

[39] MacArthur, *Reminiscences*, 236-37.

[40] Emilio Aguinaldo and Vicente Pacis, *A Second Look at America* (New York: Robert Speller, 1957), 189.

[41] *New York Times*, February 11, 1945, 28.

[42] Eyre, *The Roosevelt-MacArthur Conflict*, 29; Friend, *Between Two Empires*, 248, 251.

[43] Eyre, *The Roosevelt-MacArthur Conflict*, 155, 244.

[44] *Official Gazette*, XLI: 1, 89-90.

[45] *Victory News*, March 18, 1945, 1. Letter from Secretary of Instruction and Information Maximo M. Kalaw to Dr. Arturo Tolentino, April 15, 1945 (Lopex Museum, 3630).

[46] *Official Gazette*, XLI: 1, 89.

[47] "An Open Letter from Antonio Barredo y Padagas to President Osmeña," June 7, 1945 (Manila: Bureau of Printing, 1945), 1-26.

[48] "An Open Letter . . . ," 12-13; *New York Times*, June 10, 1945, 4.

[49] *Official Gazette*, XLI: 2, 161-75.

[50] Roxas answered from the Senate floor, asking, "What is collaboration? There are no puppets and collaborationists in this house. I am against every collaborator. I would be the first to bring them to justice. But the mere fact of service under the Japanese is not conclusive evidence of collaboration! *Not a single senator can justly be accused of collaboration.*" Cited in Hernando J. Abaya, *Betrayal in the Philippines* (New York: A. A. Wyn, 1946), 91-92.

[51] Abaya, 153-54.

[52] Abaya, 152.

[53] David Bernstein, *The Philippine Story* (New York: Farrar Straus, 1947), 207.

[54] MacArthur, *Reminiscences*, 253.

[55] *Official Gazette*, XLI: 4, 289-90.

[56] Hartendorp, *History of Industry and Trade in the Philippines*, 152.

[57] *Official Gazette*, XLI: 6, 494-95.

[58] *New York Times*, August 24, 1945, 6.

CHAPTER VII

[1] J. E. Spencer, *Land and People in the Philippines* (Berkeley: University of California Press, 1952), 222-23.

[2] *Official Gazette*, XLI: 3, 202-4.

[3] *Official Gazette*, XLI: 7, 565-67.

[4] *New York Times*, August 24, 1945, 6.

[5] *Manila Daily News*, August 24, 1945, 3.

[6] *Official Gazette*, XLI: 6, 416-17.

[7] *Official Gazette*, XLI: 7, 583-84.

[8] *Official Gazette*, XLI:6, 491-92.

[9] Claro M. Recto, *Three Years of Enemy Occupation* (Manila: People's Publishers, 1946), 127.

[10] Recto, 128.

[11] *New York Times*, September 11, 1945, 2.

[12] *New York Times*, September 17, 1945, 3.

[13] *Official Gazette*, XLI: 7, 690-91; *New York Times*, September 26, 1945, 14.

[14] *Manila Post*, September 6, 1945, 1; Interviews with Lorenzo Tañada, March 9, March 17, March 19, and March 24, 1960.

[15] In a letter to General Charles Willoughby, Tañada wrote that "the Filipino officials who accompanied Laurel . . . are, to say the least, reluctant to testify, and we find it imperative that we utilize Japanese witnesses to prove the charges. . . ." Tañada continued by requesting the use of a military plane to fly the witnesses to Manila, because his budget was so tight that he could not afford to pay for the witnesses. Letter from Lorenzo Tañada to Charles Willoughby, December 11, 1946. In the author's possession.

[16] McNutt, Fortas, "Memorandum for the President Relative to Enemy Collaboration in the Philippine Government," September 29, 1945, cited in Theodore Friend, *Between Two Empires* (New Haven: Yale University Press, 1965), 254.

[17] Walter R. Hutchinson, "Preliminary Report on the Progress of the Investigation and the Trial of Collaborationists . . . and Recommendations for Immediate Action by the United States," submitted to Attorney General Tom Clark and High Commissioner Paul McNutt, January 28, 1946, 1. Source withheld. Recto, *Three Years of Enemy Occupation*, 128-29.

[18] *New York Times*, November 25, 1945, 5.

[19] *New York Times*, December 10, 1945, 4.

[20] *New York Times*, December 3, 1945, 3.

[21] *Manila Daily News*, July 27, 1945, 1.

[22] Hernando J. Abaya, *Betrayal in the Philippines* (New York: A. A. Wyn, 1946), 124.

[23] Manuel Roxas, *Papers, Addresses, and Other Writings of Manuel Roxas* (Manila: Bureau of Printing, 1945), I, 10-11.

[24] Abaya, *Betrayal in the Philippines*, 241.

[25] Hutchinson, "Preliminary Report . . . ," 20.

[26] Hutchinson, 4-5.

[27] Hutchinson, 14.

[28] Hutchinson, 19.

[29] Hutchinson, 2-4.

[30] Office of Strategic Services, Research and Analysis Branch, United States Army, "Biographical Report on Teofilo Sison (Confidential)," November 10, 1944, 1-2.

[31] "Biographical Report . . . ," 3.

[32] *Official Gazette,* XLII: 4, 748-98; "Memorandum" of the Prosecution submitted to the People's Court, February 9, 1946, 67. In the author's possession.

[33] "Memorandum," 76.

[34] "Memorandum," 91.

[35] "Memorandum," 104.

[36] Hutchinson, "Preliminary Report . . . ," 16-17.

[37] "Memorandum," 122.

[38] *de Jager* v. *Attorney General of Natal* (1907) A.C. 326, 328 cited in "Memorandum," 124.

[39] "Memorandum," 128-29. A similar argument was made by the judges at the Quisling trial in Norway. The Court stated that "if, therefore, accused [Quisling] is aware that he willfully cooperated to surrender his country to the hands of its enemies, he acted in bad faith, even if he argues that it was for the good of the country. It may, indeed, be further remarked that even in the event that later happenings justify accused's assertion and prove his acts to have, in fact, been for the good of the country, he would not be free of the guilt for having committed treason. The person who surrenders a place or a fighting unit in time of war to the enemy is guilty of treason, even if he saves human lives through doing so. If the ideas and wishes of the individual are to be placed above the law, then every law concerning treachery becomes illusory." Cited in Margret Boveri, *Treason in the Twentieth Century* (London: MacDonald, 1961), 95.

[40] "Memorandum," 132.

[41] Filemon Poblador, *Philippine Chronology, January 1, 1946 to July 3, 1946* (Manila: Philippine Liberal Publishing Co., 1946), 43.

[42] See the three articles on the American treason law written by William Hurst, "Treason in the United States," *Harvard Law Review,* LVIII, 2 (December 1944), 226-72; 3 (February 1945), 395-444; 6 (July 1945), 806-46. See also Bradley Chaplin, *The American Law on Treason* (Seattle: University of Washington Press, 1964).

[43] *Official Gazette,* XLII: 4, 748-98; *New York Times,* March 8, 1946, 12.

[44] *Lawyer's Journal,* XI, 6 (June 1946), 275.

[45] Interview with Antonio Quirino, March 24, 1960.

[46] *Lawyer's Journal,* XI, 7 (July 1946), 329-31.

[47] *New York Times,* March 13, 1946, 9; March 15, 1946, 6.

[48] *New York Times,* March 17, 1946, 28.

[49] Recto, *Three Years of Enemy Occupation,* 87.

[50] Quintin Paredes, "Speech Delivered During the Amnesty Proclamation Debate, February 13, 1948" (Manila: Bureau of Printing, Special Reprint of the Congressional Debate), 50.

[51] Jose P. Laurel, *The War Memoirs of Dr. Jose P. Laurel* (Manila: Jose P. Laurel Memorial Foundation, 1962), 57.

[52] Jose Ma. Veloso, "Collaboration as a National Problem," *Lawyer's Journal*, X, 3 (November 1945), 114.

[53] *Official Gazette*, XLII: 4, 845.

[54] *New York Times*, May 16, 1946, 17.

[55] *New York Times*, May 26, 1946, 16; May 27, 1946, 5; Luis Taruc, *Born of the People* (New York: International Publishers, 1953), 221-27.

[56] The twelve Roxas supporters unanimously altered the Senate rules while Confesor and the Nacionalistas boycotted the sessions. Confesor threatened to take the issue to the Philippine Supreme Court, but Osmeña refused to support him and the issue faded.

[57] *New York Times*, May 27, 1946, 22.

CHAPTER VIII

[1] *New York Times*, August 6, 1946, 14.

[2] Letter from Attorney General Tom Clark to Solicitor General Lorenzo Tañada, December 6, 1946. In author's possession.

[3] Letter from Solicitor General Lorenzo M. Tañada to President Manuel Roxas, October 21, 1946. In author's possession.

[4] *Official Gazette*, XLII: 6, 1278. On September 3, 1946, Manuel Escudero was confirmed in his appointment. *Official Gazette*, XLII: 9, 2222. The judges were: Leopoldo Rovira (Presiding), Salvador Abad Santos, Jose Bautista, Jose Bernabe, Manuel Calleja, Pompeyo Diaz, Arsenio Dizon, Manuel Escudero, Angel Gamboa, Eusebio Lopez, Ricardo Nepomucena, Antonio Quirino, Emilio Rilloraza, Florintino Saguin, Tiburcio Tancinco, Fortunato Borromeo Veloso, and Jose Veluz.

[5] "Minutes of the Executive Session of the People's Court in Banc to consider the Resolution of Judge Eusebio Lopez to dismiss the treason case against Dr. Camilo Osias. Held in the office of Presiding Judge Fortunato Borromeo Veloso, January 13, 1946," 2. In author's possession.

[6] "Resolution of Eusebio Lopez," November 6, 1946, *People* v. *Aquino*, 21-23. In author's possession.

[7] "Resolution," 7, 12, 26, 27, 29.

[8] Hernando Abaya, *Betrayal in the Philippines* (New York: A. A. Wyn, 1946), 82.

[9] In 1950, when the political explosiveness of this issue was long past, the Supreme Court, freed from the inhibitions of the Roxas era, ruled more impartially. In *People* v. *Antonio* (47 *Official Gazette* 3514) the Court upheld a lower court conviction which had established that the defendant had actively attempted to convince his fellow Filipinos that they should not aid the guerrillas unless they were willing to be mistreated by the Japanese. The Court then felt that such propaganda in itself gave the Japanese aid and comfort by weakening the will to resist. In *People* v.

Pañganiban (47 *Official Gazette* 3454) the Court supported another conviction in which it was proven that the defendant had, among other things, made speeches for the Japanese warning the guerrillas that the Japanese would win. He was convicted for other crimes committed, but Justice Torres, in the majority decision, held him guilty of treason for his language and implied that he would have been convicted on that charge alone. Whether either of these decisions would have had importance in the political trials is subject to dispute.

[10] The justification of the seizure was most directly stated by Justice M. L. de la Rosa in his concurring opinion (G.R. No. L-342). He wrote "La ley basica del Commonwealth contiene una declaración de derechos individuales e incluye el privilegio contra registros y secuestros irrazonables, que se invoca en este recurso. Pero esta es una garantía constitucional condiciona pro la lealtad. . . . La deslealtad por lo tanto, inherente a la traición, supone renuncia a los beneficios de la garantía, que ha sido repudiada. . . . La estabilidad y preservacion, necesarias en todo gobierno, requieren medidas drasticas, el uso de la fuerza armada, inclusive, de mayor transcendencia que la retirada de una garantía constitucional, para reprimir, frustrar la traición." (The basic law of the Commonwealth contains a declaration of the rights of the individual and includes a provision against unreasonable search and seizure, which has been invoked in this appeal. However, this is a constitutional guarantee, conditional on loyalty. . . . The disloyalty inherent in treason assumes a renunciation of the guaranteed benefits which have been repudiated. . . . The establishment and preservation of the state necessary for every government may require drastic measures, including the use of armed force and most importantly the suspension of constitutional guarantees in order to curb and defeat treason.)

[11] *Manila Tribune,* January 20, 1943, 1, 6.

[12] Jose P. Laurel, *War Memoirs of Dr. Jose P. Laurel* (Manila: Jose P. Laurel Memorial Foundation, 1962), 52-53.

[13] Interview with Chief Justice Ricardo Paras, March 5, 1960; Dissenting opinion, 1, 4, 5, 7. *Official Gazette,* XLIV: 4, 1199-1215.

[14] *Official Gazette,* XLIV: 4, 1176-78.

[15] Teofilo and Jose del Castillo, *The Saga of Jose P. Laurel* (Manila: Associated Authors', 1949), 47.

[16] *People* v. *Bagalawis* (78 Phil 174), *People* v. *Fernando* (79 Phil 719), and *People* v. *Munoz* (79 Phil 702).

[17] By contrast the postwar Dutch courts ruled that the only effective defense to the charge of collaboration was *force majeure.* The Dutch courts argued that the individual was under no compulsion to serve the enemy conqueror even though The Hague convention of 1907 permitted the requisitioning of local aid to maintain peace

and order. (*In re Contractor Worp* (1946) Na-oorlogse Recht-spraak, Tribunalen in Nederlland, 1946, No. 519; *In re van Huis*, No. 605; *In re Heinemann*, 1947, No. 763, cited in Richard R. Baxter, "The Duty of Obedience to the Belligerent Occupant," *The British Yearbook of International Law*, XXVII (1950), 257.

Professor Baxter commented that "there is a strong tendency in modern law . . . to deny that there is any duty of obedience founded on any legal or moral obligation with which international law concerns itself. The occupying power's ability to enforce respect for its legitimate interests is not a creation of the law. It springs from superior military power and from factual capacity to compel obedience. International law suffers the occupant to legislate but it will not lend its authority or its assistance to the enforcement of such legislation (243)." Another expert noted that "just as . . . officials have the right to agree to stay in office, so they have the right to resign. If such should happen, the occupant does not normally possess the right to regard such resignation as a punishable offense and the persons concerned should not be molested because of their actions." Gerhard von Glahn, *The Occupation of Enemy Territory—A Commentary on the Law and Practice of Belligerent Occupation* (St. Paul: University of Minnesota Press, 1957), 132.

[18] See *People* v. *Prieto, People* v. *Gonzales, People* v. *Escleto, People* v. *Alacion, People* v. *Abad, People* v. *Agpangan, People* v. *Mateo, People* v. *Cantos, People* v. *Flores,* and *People* v. *Concepcion.*

[19] *Official Gazette,* XLII: 4, 748-98.

[20] *Lawyer's Journal,* XI, 5 (May 1946), 225.

[21] Office of Strategic Services, Research and Analysis Branch, United States Army, "Biographical Report on Guillermo Francisco (Confidential)," November 25, 1944, 1-3.

[22] *The Philippine Herald,* December 22, 1941, 1.

[23] The decision in *The People of the Philippines, Plaintiff,* v. *Guillermo B. Francisco, Accused, Criminal Case No. 3534, for Treason* appears in the *Official Gazette,* XLII: 10 (October 1946), 2452-2500. The author has in his possession additional documentation of this case including the "Information" (17 pages), the motion, the order, the subpoenas, the list of exhibits (27 pages), the majority decision of Salvador Abad Santos delivered August 15, 1946, (42 pages), and the concurring opinion of Eusebio Lopez (37 pages). *People* v. *Francisco,* majority decision, 13.

[24] Majority decision, 41.

[25] Concurring opinion of Eusebio Lopez, 2, 4.

[26] Lopez, 36, 37.

[27] *New York Times,* August 25, 1946, 29.

[28] *New York Times,* September 4, 1946, 8; September 5, 1946, 5.

[29] *New York Times,* September 15, 1946, 6.

[30] *New York Times*, December 29, 1946, 15.

[31] *New York Times*, June 1, 1947, 6; October 15, 1947, 18.

[32] *New York Times*, October 21, 1947, 9.

[33] *New York Times*, June 28, 1947, 4.

[34] *New York Times*, July 8, 1947, 9; July 12, 1947, 4.

[35] Lorenzo M. Tañada, "Summary Brief against Jorge Vargas," 1. Source withheld.

[36] "Summary Brief," 102 passim.

[37] Roxas was *compadre* to Laurel's son, Arsenio.

[38] *Official Gazette*, XLIV: 2 (February 1948), 408-11.

[39] Manuel Roxas, *Papers, Addresses, and Other Writings of Manuel Roxas* (Manila: Bureau of Printing, 1954), II, 606 passim.

[40] *New York Times*, February 14, 1948, 6.

[41] *Official Gazette*, XLI: 7, 690-91.

[42] In 1960 the author found the last extant record of the People's Court at the Department of Justice in Manila. The cited figures are based on the author's tabulations, which apparently were the first ever made on the Court records.

After the amnesty, others were convicted in regular courts, where People's Court cases not governed by the amnesty were transferred. In October 1946 there were 1172 political prisoners in prison, but by June 1948, the number, excluding Hukbalahap, had dropped to 229. One prisoner, Teodoro Barrameda, was executed and thirty-five had death sentences commuted. Approximately two-thirds of all those convicted by the People's Court appealed their conviction to the Supreme Court. Based on Prison Records, Department of Justice, New Bilibid Prison, Muntinlupa, Rizal Province.

[43] The Office of Strategic Services and the F.C.C. prepared a series of large volumes in which every monitored radio broadcast was cross-filed by subject matter. They contain many inaccuracies but are a valuable source of supplementary information. Widener Library, Harvard University.

CHAPTER IX

[1] Jose P. Laurel, *Forces That Make a Nation Great* (Manila: Bureau of Printing, 1943), 31.

[2] *Official Gazette*, XLII: 9 (September 1946), 2072-73.

[3] Laurel, *Forces* . . . , 32.

[4] Francisco A. Delgado, "Memorandum on the Policies of the Commonwealth Government Regarding the Collaborators of the Japanese," Submitted to Acting Secretary Tomas Confesor (Manila: Bureau of Printing, 1945), 23-24.

[5] Jose P. Laurel, *The War Memoirs of Dr. Jose P. Laurel* (Manila: Jose P. Laurel Memorial Foundation, 1962), 57.

[6] *Official Gazette*, XLIV: 2, 408-11.

⁷ Bernardo Torres, "Proclamation on Philippine Independence [1943]," 4-5, cited in Elmer Lear, *The Japanese Occupation of the Philippines, Leyte, 1941-1945* (Ithaca: Southeast Asia Program, Cornell University, Data Paper, No. 42, 1961), 228-29.

⁸ Jose P. Laurel, fragmentary essays entitled "Political" and "Moral" [December 1944?], cited in Theodore Friend, *Between Two Empires* (New Haven: Yale University Press, 1965), 245.

⁹ "Jose Abad Santos—Patriot and Martyr," a reprint of addresses delivered in the Supreme Court Chambers, December 2, 1945 (Manila: Bureau of Printing, 1945), 13-14.

¹⁰ "Jose Abad Santos—Patriot and Martyr," 10-11.

¹¹ Claro M. Recto, *Three Years of Enemy Occupation* (Manila: People's Publishers, 1946), 68.

¹² Manuel L. Quezon, *The Good Fight* (New York: Appleton, Century, 1946), 231-34.

¹³ Letter from Tomas Confesor to Dr. Fermin Caram, February 20, 1943, cited in Courtney Whitney, *MacArthur: His Rendezvous with History* (New York: Alfred Knopf, 1956), 136-38.

¹⁴ In a recent work by Professor Teodoro A. Agoncillo, which was published while this work was in its final stages, he wrote that during the war he had "looked upon all those who worked in the government as traitors or collaborators." However, he writes that with time many of his impressions were proved inaccurate. He states that "if there is any value attached to those impressions [of the war], it is that they represent, in the historical sense, the contemporary thoughts and feelings of the great majority of the people during that most difficult period." Agoncillo eschews "extended character portrayal of the most important men during the occupation." Except for a few brief concluding comments, he avoids dealing with the postwar political rehabilitation of the elite, though he does state his belief that "the Filipino people should sympathize with them [the collaborators] and recognize that they, too, like the guerrillas in the mountains and the Escolta, performed their duty to the country in a different way but without any thought of personal aggrandizement. They were the victims of circumstances and as such they should be treated more with understanding than with contempt or hatred. Forgiveness is not for them, for it implies guilt. . . ." Teodoro A. Agoncillo, *The Fateful Years: Japan's Adventure in the Philippines, 1941-1945* (Quezon City: R. P. Garcia, 1965), I, viii-ix; II, 911.

¹⁵ Laurel, *Forces* . . . , 109.

¹⁶ Rebecca West, *The Meaning of Treason* (New York: Viking Press, 1947), 276.

¹⁷ Recto, 99-101.

¹⁸ Delgado, "Memorandum . . . ," 21.

Bibliography

Japanese Documents

Benda, Harry J., Irikura, James K. and Kishi Koichi (comp.). *Japanese Military Administration in Indonesia: Selected Documents.* New Haven: Southeast Asia Studies Translation Series No. 6, 1965.

Communiqués Issued by the Imperial General Headquarters, December 8, 1941-June 30, 1943. University of the Philippines Library, Quezon City.

Enosawa Hisashi. "The Significance of the Greater East Asia Co-Prosperity Sphere" [pamphlet]. Propaganda Corps, n.d.

——. "America: A Revelation of Her True Character" [pamphlet]. Propaganda Corps, n.d.

Hino Ashihei. "The Flowering of Racial Spirit." Nishina Kazeo trans. Propaganda Corps, 1942.

Ideals of the New Philippines (A collection of speeches). Propaganda Corps.

    1—Homma Masaharu. "Day of Deep Significance," April 29, 1942.

    2—Hayashi Yoshide. "The Future of the New Philippines," May 18, 1942.

    3— ——. "Route to a New Glorified Philippines," May 19, 1942.

    4—Vargas, Jorge. "Philippines Grateful to Japan," May 18, 1942.

New Order Short Essays. Propaganda Corps, n.d.

The Official Journal of the Japanese Military Administration (13 volumes). Japanese Military Administration, January 2, 1942-September 30, 1943.

"Prelude to Philippine Independence" [A record of Premier Tojo's visit]. Propaganda Corps, May 1943.

Saito Jiro. *Ang Dinmaan ng Lalong Malaking Silangang Asia (Greater East Asia War: A Historical Analysis of Its Background, Causes, Strategy, and Significance)*. Department of Information, April 1943.

Uyehara and Beal (comp.). *Checklist of the Archives of the Japanese Ministry of Foreign Affairs, 1868-1945*. Washington: Library of Congress Microfilm, 1954.

    Code S.1.6.0.0-5. *Sho gaikoku naisei kankei zassan (Hirippin no bu)*, October, 1943-August, 1944. I.P.S. Document No. 973, Reel 707.

    Code S.1.7.0.0-47. *Hito Dokuritsu To Nippi Domei Joyaku Teiketsu Kankei*, May-October, 1943 [284 pages], Reel 584. [Greater East Asia and Foreign Ministry files combined.]

Young, John (comp.). *Selected Archives of the Japanese Army, Navy, and Other Government Agencies, 1868-1945*. Washington: Library of Congress Microfilm (Georgetown University Press), 1959.

    T. 1106 (Reel 118). *Gunsei Jisshi Gaikyo Ho koku*. 14th Army, January 18, 1942. *Riku A Mitsu Dai Nikki*, Vol. 6, No. 35.

    T. 1112 (Reel 118). *Ibid.*, March 14, 1942, Vol. 12, No. 117.

    T. 1116 (Reel 118). *Ibid.*, April 18, 1942, Vol. 21, No. 124.

    T. 1122 (Reel 118). *Ibid.*, September 1-10, 1942, Vol. [?], No. 98.

    T. 1123 (Reel 118). *Ibid.*, August 21-31, 1942, Vol. [?], No. 99.

    T. 1124 (Reel 118). *Ibid.*, August 1-10, 1942, Vol. 25, No. 32.

    T. 1125 (Reel 118). *Dai Ni Kai Gunseikanbu Shibucho Kaido Jisshi. Riku A Mitsu Nikki*, Vol. 39, No. 32.

    T. 1128 (Reel 119). *Dai Toa Sho Ni Kansuru Ken*, September 7, 1942. *Riku A Mitsu Dai Nikki*, Vol. 41, No. 122.

    T. 1131. (Reel 119). *Gunsei Jishi Gaikyo Ho koko*, June 30, 1942. *Riku A Mitsu Dai Nikki*, Vol. 43, No. 49.

Documents of the Philippine Executive Commission and the [Laurel] Republic of the Philippines

Constitution Adopted by the Preparatory Commission for Philippine Independence. Philippine Executive Commission. September 4, 1943.

Correspondence of the Republic of the Philippines. [Uncatalogued and unpublished correspondence held by the University of the Philippines Library.]

Foreign Affairs Bulletin. Ministry of Foreign Affairs. Vol. 1, No. 1, October 14, 1943-February 15, 1944; Vol. 1, No. 2, February 16, 1944-March 31, 1944; Vol. 1, No. 3, April 1944.

Francisco, Guillermo and Quimbo, J. G. "An Open Letter to Our Countrymen." Manila: Philippine Executive Commission, December 25, 1942.

The Kalibapi:

    Ano Ang Kalibapi: (What Is Kalibapi). Manila: Department of Information, 1943.

    "The Kalibapi and the Filipino." Manila: Bureau of Printing, 1943.

    "Know Your Constitution." Manila: Bureau of Printing, September 1944.

"The Kalibapi: The People's Party." Manila: Bureau of Printing, 1944.

"The Kalibapi Worker's Handbook." Manila: Bureau of Printing, 1943.

Laurel, Jose. *Forces That Make a Nation Great.* Manila: Bureau of Information, Republic of the Philippines, 1943.

Leon, Jacinto de. "The Rise of Jose P. Laurel" [pamphlet]. Manila: E. Floro (publisher), 1944.

Official Gazette. Philippine Executive Commission: Vol. 1, No. 1-12, January 1942-December 1942; Vol. 2, No. 1-9, January 1943-September 1943; Vol. 2, No. 9a, September 4, 1943; Vol. 2, No. 10, October 1-14, 1943.

Official Gazette. Republic of the Philippines: Vol. 1, No. 1-10, October 15, 1943-July 1944.

"Our Independence is at Hand" [pamphlet]. Philippine Executive Commission, October 6, 1943.

National Assembly Yearbook. Republic of the Philippines, 1943.

Philippine Executive Commission, Department of the Interior, Bureau of the Constabulary, Circular No. 45, Manila, June 3, 1943.

———. Department of Justice, File of Circulars, Manila, March 23, 1942-May 9, 1944.

"Proposed Opening of German School by the German Community," Memorandum from Foreign Minister Claro Recto to President Laurel, June 13, 1944.

"Questions Between Japan and the Philippines Arising from the Philippine Independence" [confidential marking], Memorandum from Foreign Minister Claro Recto to President Laurel, October 1943. University of the Philippines Library.

Voice of the New Philippines (A collection of speeches). Department of Information. Vol. 1, October 31, 1942.

    1—Hayashi Yoshide. "Address to the War Prisoners." September 18, 1942.

    2—Tokugawa, Marquis. "Cultural Movement." September 11, 1942.

    3—Katsuya T. "Address at the Opening of the School for Training Prisoners of War." July 20, 1942.

    4— ———. "Address at School for Training . . ." July 27, 1942.

    5— ———. "Commencement Address." August 9, 1942.

    6—Vargas, Jorge. "Address before the Second Convention of City Mayors and Provincial Governors." August 12, 1942.

    7—Aquino, Benigno. "Speech at Naga, Camarines Sur." July 1942.

    8—Guinto, Leon. "Speech at the Prisoner's Training School." September 15, 1942.

    9—Duran, Pio. "Speech at the Prisoner's Training School." n.d.

    10—Mochizuki S. "The Burning Faith at Calvary—An Address to the Christian Leaders in the Philippines." October 18, 1942.

Voice of the New Philippines. Vol. 2, February 1943.

1—Capinpin, Mateo. "Awakening to a New Life."

2—Enosawa Hisashi. "Why This War Is Self-Defense."

3—Guerrero (Bishop), Cesar. "Working for Our Salvation."

4—Guinto, Leon. "The Japanese Occupation Is Compatible with Filipino Aspiration."

5—Pilar, Filemon del. "Nippon's Unshakeable Position in Greater East Asia."

6—Alunan, Rafael. "Economic Adjustment to the Present Situation."

7—Ponce, Ernesto. "What Did American Democracy Give to the Philippines."

8—Benitez, Conrado. "Present Progress of the Coconut Industries."

9—Samson, Bayani. "The American People's Declining Confidence in President Roosevelt and Their Navy."

10—Guerrero, Leon Ma. "Rizal and the New Order."

Voice of the New Philippines. Vol. 3, n.d.

1—Vargas, Jorge. "Independence for the Filipinos." February 8, 1943.

2—Aquino, Benigno. "The Task of National Reconstruction." February 25, 1943.

3—Guinto, Leon. "March onto Destiny."

4—Recto, Claro. "Fundamental Aim of the New Philippines." January 19, 1943.

5—Paredes, Quintin. "Perspective for Our Country's Future."

6—Vargas, Jorge. "Rizal and the Kalibapi." December 30, 1942.

7—Alas, Antonio de las. "The Public Servant." February 5, 1943.

8—Recto, Claro. "Onward to Liberation." January 23, 1943.

9—Osias, Camilo. "The Rizal Way for Youth." December 29, 1942.

10— ———. "The Rizal Way for Adults." December 30, 1942.

11—Alas, Antonio de las. "Financing the New Philippines." February 24, 1943.

[Many of these speeches along with hundreds of others appeared in the *Official Journal* published by the Military Administration, in the *Official Gazette* published by the Vargas and Laurel regimes, in the *Manila Tribune,* and in the *Philippine Review.* The above speeches are a representative listing.]

Newspapers and Periodicals

Ang Kapit Bahay (Official Publication of the District and Neighborhood Associations of the Philippines). No. 1-5, May 1943-February 1944.

Davao Times, March 1943.

Domei Releases (A collection of news releases, February 1, 1945-April 3, 1945), United States Embassy Library collection.

Filipina, No. 1-5, July 1944-December 1944.

Guerrilla, April 11, 1945-August 31, 1945.

Leyte Shimbun, August 26, 1942-November 14, 1942.

Liwanag (Light) (Official publication of the Federation of Evangelical Churches in the Philippines).

Manila Bulletin, December 8, 1941-January 2, 1942.

Manila Daily Mail, April 21, 1945-July 10, 1945.

Manila Free Philippines, February 9, 1945-March 19, 1945.

Manila Tribune, January 5, 1942-February 3, 1945.

New York Times, July 1941-February 1948.

Philippine Review, Vol. 1, No. 1-12, March 1943-February 1944; Vol. 2, No. 1-10, March 1944-December 1944.

Pillars (Official publication of the New Philippines Cultural Institute at Tagaytay), No. 1-5, December 1943-May 1944.

Shin Seiki (New Era), Vol. 1, No. 4-12, January 1943-September 1943; Vol. 2, No. 1-12, October 1943-September 1944.

Tagapagturo (Official publication of the diocesan church—imprimatur of Bishop Cesar Ma. Guerrero), No. 2, February 2, 1943; No. 3, March 25, 1943; No. 5, December 8, 1943.

Victory News, February 25, 1945-May 24, 1945.

Postwar Material Relating to the Collaboration Issue

Barredo y Padagas, Antonio. An Open Letter to President Sergio Osmeña of June 7, 1945. Manila: Bureau of Printing, 1945.

Clark, Tom. Letter from the Attorney General to Lorenzo Tañada, December 6, 1946.

Confesor, Tomas. Speech delivered at the Lotus Theater, Manila, on April 1, 1945, under the Auspices of the Manila Civilian Anti-Japanese Association. Manila: Department of Information, 1945.

Delgado, Francisco A. "Memorandum on the Policies of the Commonwealth Government Regarding the Collaborators of the Japanese" to Tomas Confesor. Manila: Bureau of Printing, 1945.

Hutchinson, Walter A. "Preliminary Report on the Progress of the Investigation and Trial of the Collaborationists by the Commonwealth Government of the Philippine Government and Recommendations for Immediate Action by the United States Government." Memorandum to Attorney General Tom Clark and High Commissioner Paul McNutt, January 28, 1946.

Lim, Manuel. "Memorandum Concerning the Amnesty Proclamation" from Solicitor General Lim to Judge Juan R. Liway, February 3, 1948.

MacArthur, Douglas. Communication to the author. April 14, 1961.

Official Gazette. Commonwealth of the Philippines. Vol. 41, No. 1-12, April 1945-March 1946; Vol. 42, No. 1-3, April 1946-June 1946.

Official Gazette. Republic of the Philippines. Vol. 42, No. 4-12, July 1946-March 1947; Vol. 43, No. 1-12, April 1947-March 1948; Vol. 44, No. 1-12, April 1948-March 1949; Vol. 45, No. 1-12, April 1949-March 1950.

Osmeña, Sergio. "Speech on the Occasion of the Induction into Office of the Members of the New Cabinet," March 8, 1945. Manila: Bureau of Printing, 1945.

Paredes, Quintin. "Speech on the Amnesty Proclamation delivered to the House of Representatives, February 13, 1948." Manila: Congressional Reprint, 1948.

Parsons, Charles. "Conditions in the Philippine Islands Since the Japanese Occupation." Interview between Charles Parsons and C. J. Spiker conducted on board the M.S. "Gripsholm," August 23, 1942, and prepared for the Secretary of State.

———. "Personalities in the Philippines" to Colonel J. K. Evans, Intelligence Section, General Headquarters, Southwest Pacific Area Command, December 12, 1942.

———. Letter to Manuel Quezon, September 27, 1943.

———. "Report on Conditions in the Philippines Gathered March 5, 1943-July 8, 1943," to General Headquarters, Southwest Pacific Area Command, August 20, 1943.

People's Court Records. (Material in the author's possession.)

Alphabetical listing of all persons indicted before the People's Court, including a partial indication of the outcome of individual cases. This record was discovered in a damaged state at the Department of Justice, Manila, and was microfilmed by the author. A second microfilm is on deposit in the archive collection of the Ateneo de Manila library.

Certification of the List of Appeals to the Philippine Supreme Court from the People's Court, September 24, 1947. Microfilm of the original.

Executive Session of the People's Court in Banc to Consider the Resolution of Associate Judge Eusebio Lopez to Dismiss the Treason Case Against Dr. Camilo Osias. Held in the office of the Presiding Judge, Fortunato V. Borromeo [Veloso] on January 13, 1948. Carbon of the original.

People v. Aquino (Criminal Case No. 3527). Resolution of Eusebio Lopez, November 6, 1946. Original copy.

People v. Arcache (Criminal Case No. 729). "Information," April 8, 1946. Original copy.

People v. Francisco (Criminal Case No. 3534). "Information," motion, order, subpoenas, list of exhibits, majority decision, concurring opinion. Microfilm of the original.

People v. Laurel (Criminal Case No. 3519). Order, February 16, 1948. Carbon copy.

People v. Manayao, Flores, and Flores (Criminal Case No. 15). Decision, January 24, 1946. Carbon copy.

People v. Moncado (Criminal Case No. 3522). Order, July 9, 1946. Carbon copy.

People v. Osmeña [Sergio Osmeña Jr.] (Criminal Case No. 3462). "Information," March 13, 1946. Carbon copy.

People v. *Paredes* (Criminal Case No. 3530). Order, February [?], 1948.

People v. *Racaza* (Criminal Case No. 207). Decision, February 15, 1946. Original copy.

People v. *Recto* (Criminal Case No. 3533). "Information" [Written by Ramon Nolasco and Emmanuel Pelaez], March 14, 1946. Carbon copy.

People v. *Sison* (Criminal Case No. 1). Memorandum for the Prosecution [144 pages], February 9, 1946. Carbon copy.

People v. *Vargas* (Criminal Case No. 3520). "Information" March 12, 1946. Carbon copy.

Quezon, Manuel. Letter to secretary of the Navy, Frank Knox, August 27, 1942.

Republic of the Philippines. *An Act Abolishing the People's Court and the Office of Special Prosecutors, Providing for the Trial and Disposition of Treason Cases not Embraced by Proclamation No. 51 Granting Amnesty to Political and Economic Collaborators.* First Congress, Third Session, H. No. 1621, May 20, 1948.

Roosevelt, Franklin D. "America's Pledge to the Philippines," Radio Broadcast on August 13, 1943. Special Folder, New York Public Library.

Roxas, Manuel. *Papers, Addresses, and Other Writings of Manuel Roxas.* Manila: Bureau of Printing, 1954.

Santos, Jose Abad. "Jose Abad Santos, Patriot and Martyr." A collection of speeches delivered at the Philippine Supreme Court Chambers, December 2, 1945. Manila: Bureau of Printing, 1945.

Supreme Court Records. (Material in the author's possession)

Aurelio S. Alvero v. *Arsenio P. Dizon* (G.R. No. L-231). Decision (DeJoya), Concurring opinion (Perfecto), Concurring (De la Rosa). Carbon copy.

Pio Duran v. *Salvador Abad Santos* (G.R. No. L-99). Decision (Jaranilla), Concurring (De la Rosa), Dissenting opinion (Perfecto), November 16, 1945. Carbon copy.

Anastacio Laurel v. *Eriberto Misa* (G.R. No. L-409). Decision, January 30, 1947. Carbon copy.

Hilario Camino Moncado v. *People's Court* (G.R. No. L-824). Petition for Certiorari and Injunction. n.d. Carbon copy.

People v. *Beato* (G.R. No. L-524). Decision (Perfecto), July 2, 1947. Original copy.

People v. *Logo* (G.R. No. L-1317). Decision (Moran), February 27, 1948. Carbon copy.

Tañada v. *Quirino* (G.R. No. L-237). Order, January 15, 1946. Original copy.

[Except for those folders which have been lost intentionally or unintentionally, the original files of each People's Court case are held at the Department of Justice, Manila. To the best of the author's knowledge, most of the decisions and rulings of the People's Court are held by Fiscal Agapito Conchu in his private collection. If the Department of Justice has copies of these records, the author was not able to find them.

Tañada, Lorenzo. Letter from the solicitor general to Major General Charles Willoughby, G-2 Section, Supreme Command Allied Powers, in Tokyo, December 11, 1946.

———. Letter to President Manuel Roxas, October 21, 1946.

———. Letter to Attorney General Tom Clark, December 21, 1946.

Miscellaneous Material

Epic of Bataan. Background material for feature articles and editorials prepared by the Philippine Government in Exile, Washington.

The Hague Conventions and Declarations of 1899 and 1907. London, Oxford University Press, 1915.

International Military Tribunal, Far East. Tokyo: General Headquarters, Supreme Commander for the Allied Powers, International Prosecution Section, 1948.

Japanese Government Officials, 1937-1945. Washington: Military Intelligence Division, Department of War, 1945.

Philippine War-time Officials. 441 reports on "Persons on Whom Adverse Information Has Been Submitted to the Government of the Commonwealth of the Philippine Islands." Washington: Counter-Intelligence Corps, United States Army, 1944. Mimeographed.

Programs of Japan in the Philippines. Extracts from Monitored Shortwave Radio Broadcasts, Vol. 1, Vol. 2, Supplement 1-3. Honolulu: Office of Strategic Services, 1943-45.

Report on the Destruction of Manila and Japanese Atrocities. Prepared by the Office of the Resident Commissioner of the Philippines to the United States. Washington: February 1945.

Report of the Special Mission [Wood-Forbes] on Investigation to the Philippine Islands to the Secretary of War. Washington: Government Printing Office, 1921.

United States Congressional Record. Vol. 90, No. 163 (A 4855), November 27, 1944.

United States Senate. "Laws Against Treason, Sedition, Etc. Communication from the Law Officer of the Division of Insular Affairs, Making a Comparison Between the Existing Laws of the United States Against Treason, Sedition, and Misprision and the Provisions of Act No. 292 of the Philippine Commission." 57th Congress, 1st Session, Document No. 173. 1902.

Interviews with the Author

Alas, Antonio de las. 484 Rosario Street, Manila. April 8, 1960.

Bautista, Felix Angelo. Supreme Court Building, Manila. March 15, 1960.

Conchu, Agapito R. Department of Justice Building, Manila. March 17, 1960.

Dizon, Arsenio. Court of Appeals Building (Florida Street), Manila. March 7, 1960.

Lagman, Eligio G. Samarinillo Building, Escolta, Manila. March 17, 1960.

Langcauon, Prudencio. University of the East, Manila. March 16, 1960.

Lavides, Francisco. Great Eastern Hotel, Manila, March 8, 1960.

Ledesma, Oscar. Senate Office Building, Manila. March 10, 1960.

Leon, Dionisio de. Court of Appeals Building, Manila. March 15, 1960.

Lim, Manuel C. Commerce Department (Boston Street), Manila. April 4, 1960.

Martinez, Jesus I. United States Embassy, Manila. March 11, 1960.

Ocampo, Antonio R. New Bilibid Prison, Muntinlupa, Rizal. February 15, 1960.

Osias, Camilo. Shaw Boulevard, Mandaluyong. March 9, 1960.

Paez, Jose. 1360 Pennsylvania Avenue, Manila. March 4, 1960.

Paras, Ricardo. Supreme Court Building, Manila. March 5, 1960.

Paredes, Quintin. Senate Office Building, Manila. March 10, 1960.

Poblador, Honario. "Welfareville," Mandaluyong. March 16, 1960.

Perez, Jesus. City Hall Building, Manila. March 12, 1960.

Quirino, Antonio. 404 Guerra, San Juan, Manila. March 24, 1960.

Recto, Claro. Adriana Street (Intramuros), Manila. March 17, 1960.

Tan, Dominador. Congressional Office Building, Manila. March 14, 1960.

Tañada, Lorenzo. Senate Office Building, Manila. March 9, 1960; March 17, 1960; March 24, 1960.

Tolentino, Arturo. Senate Office Building, Manila. March 12, 1960.

Vargas, Jorge B. 11 Vargas Street, Mandaluyong. April 13, 1960.

SECONDARY SOURCES

Articles

Agpalo, Remigio E. "Pro-Deo Et Pro Patria: The Political Philosophy of Jose P. Laurel," *Asian Studies,* III, 2 (August 1965), 163-92.

Baxter, Richard R. "The Duty of Obedience to the Belligerent Occupant," *The British Yearbook of International Law, 1950,* XXVII, 235.

Benda, Harry J. "Political Elites in Colonial Southeast Asia: An Historical Analysis," *Comparative Studies in Society and History,* VII, 3 (April 1965), 233-51.

——. The Structure of Southeast Asian History: Some Preliminary Observations," *Journal of Southeast Asian History,* III, 1 (March 1962), 106-38.

Bradley, Harold W. "Observations on American Policy in the Philippines," *Pacific Historical Review,* XI (1942), 43-53.

Bulatao, Jaime C. "Hiya," *Philippine Studies,* XII, 3 (July 1964), 424-38.

——. "Philippine Values I: The Manileño's Mainsprings," *Philippine Studies,* X, 1 (January 1962), 45-81.

Collection of newspaper clippings and articles, United States Embassy Library, Manila, Republic of the Philippines.

Corpuz, Onofre D. "Western Colonisation and the Filipino Response," *Journal of Southeast Asian History*, III, 1 (March 1962), 1-23.

Costa, Horatio de la. "The Development of the Native Clergy in the Philippines," *Theological Studies*, VIII, 2 (June 1947), 219-50.

Crowley, James B. "Japanese Army Factionalism in the Early 1930's," *Journal of Asian Studies*, XXI, 3 (May 1962), 309-26.

——. "A Reconsideration of the Marco Polo Bridge Incident," *Journal of Asian Studies*, XXII, 3 (May 1963), 277-91.

Delgado, Francisco A. "Collaborators of the Japanese," *Lawyer's Journal*, X, 2 (October 1945), 50-60.

Feliciano, Florentino P. "Criminal Liability of Specific Crimes," *Philippine Law Journal*, XXVII (1952), 292.

Forster, George. "Cofradia and Compadrazgo," *Southwest Journal of Anthropology*, IX, 1 (1953), 1-28.

Friend, Theodore. "The Philippine Sugar Industry and the Politics of Independence, 1929-1935," *Journal of Asian Studies*, XXII, 2 (February 1963), 179-92.

Goodman, Grant K. "An Experiment in War-time Intercultural Relations: Philippine Students in Japan, 1943-1945," Ithaca, New York: Data Paper No. 46, Southeast Asia Program, Cornell University, 1962.

——. "The Japanese Occupation in the Philippines Was a Success," paper delivered at the Fifteenth Annual Meeting of the Association for Asian Studies, Philadelphia, Pennsylvania, March 26, 1963.

Gunther, John. "Manuel Quezon," *Atlantic Monthly*, CLXIII, (January 1939), 59-70.

Hart, Donn V. "Filipino Resistance on Negroes, 1942-1945," *Journal of Southeast Asian History*, V, 1 (March 1964), 101-25.

Hollnsteiner, Mary R. "Reciprocity in Lowland Philippines," *Philippine Studies*, IX, 3 (July 1961), 387-413.

Hurst, Willard. "Treason in the United States," *Harvard Law Review*, LVIII, 2 (December 1944), 226-72; 3 (February 1945), 395-444; 6 (July 1945), 806-46.

Iriye, Akira. "Japanese Imperialism and Aggression: Reconsiderations," *Journal of Asian Studies*, XXIII, 1 (November 1963), 103-13.

Kaut, Charles. "Contingency in a Tagalog Society," *Asian Studies*, III, 1 (1965), 1-15.

——. "Utang na loob: A System of Contractual Obligations Among Tagalogs," *Southwest Journal of Anthropology*, XVII, 3 (1961), 256-72.

Kirk, Grayson. "The Filipinos," *Annals of the American Academy of Political and Social Science*, CCXXIII (September 1942), 45-48.

Lattimore, Eleanor. "Decline of Empire in the Pacific," New York: Institute of Pacific Relations, 1947. Pamphlet No. 25.

Lilienthal, Philip and Oakie, John H. "Asia's Captive Colonies," New York: Institute of Pacific Relations, 1944. Pamphlet No. 6.

Lynch, Frank. "Philippine Values II: Social Acceptance," *Philippine Studies*, X, 1 (January 1962), 82-99.

Macapagal, Diosdado. "Lack of Solidarity in the Supreme Court," *Lawyer's Journal*, XI, 6 (June 1946), 246.

——. "Who are Collaborators?" *Lawyer's Journal*, XI, 1 (January 1946), 6.

Marcq, Rene. "Collaboration Under Enemy Occupation," *Lawyer's Journal*, XI, 11 (November 1946), 514.

McHale, Thomas R. "American Colonial Policy Towards the Philippines," *Journal of Southeast Asian History*, III 1 (March 1962), 24-43.

——. "The Philippines in Transition," *Journal of Asian Studies*, XX, 3 (May 1961), 331-41.

Mill, Edward W. "One Year of the Philippine Republic," Department of State Publication 2877—Far Eastern Series No. 23, Department of State Bulletin (Washington), June 29, 1947.

Mintz, Sidney W. and Wolf, Eric R. "An Analysis of Ritual Co-parenthood (Compadrazgo)," *Southwest Journal of Anthropology*, VI (1950), 341-68.

Morton, Louis. "War Plan ORANGE: Evolution of a Strategy," *World Politics*, XI (1959), 221-50.

Pastrana, Vicente L. "The Road to Unity," *Lawyer's Journal*, X, 2 (October 1945), 50-60.

Rosinger, Lawrence K. "The Philippines—Problems of Independence," *Foreign Policy Reports*, XXIV, 8 (September 1, 1948).

Sayre, Francis B. "Freedom Comes to the Philippines," *Atlantic Monthly*, CLXXV, 3 (March 1945), 83.

Seeman, Bernard and Salisbury, Lawrence. "Cross Currents in the Philippines," New York: Institute of Pacific Relations, 1946. Pamphlet No. 23.

Sturtevant, David R. "Sakdalism and Philippine Radicalism," *Journal of Asian Studies*, XXI, 2 (February 1962), 199-214.

United States Army, Philippine Information Training Program, "We Return to the Philippines," Education packet prepared by the Information and Education Section, United States Armed Forces Far East.

Veloso, Jose Ma. "Collaboration as a National Problem," *Lawyer's Journal*, X, 3 (November 1945), 114.

Vinacke, Harold M. "Implications of the Japanese Foreign Policy for the Philippines and Southeastern Asia," *Annals of the American Academy of Political and Social Science*, CCXXVI (March 1943), 50.

Wickberg, Edgar. "The Chinese Mestizo in the Philippines," *Journal of Southeast Asian History*, V, 1 (March 1964), 62-100.

Yarnell, H. D. "The War in the Western Pacific," *Annals of the American Academy of Political and Social Science*, CCXXVI (March 1943), 62.

Books

Abaya, Hernando J. *Betrayal in the Philippines.* New York: A. A. Wyn, 1946.

Achutegui, Pedro S. and Bernad, Miguel A. *Religious Revolution in the Philippines.* Manila: Ateneo de Manila, 1960.

Agoncillo, Teodoro A. *The Fateful Years: Japan's Adventure in the Philippines, 1941-1945.* Quezon City: R. P. Garcia, 1965. 2 vols.

——. *Malolos: The Crisis of the Republic.* Quezon City: University of the Philippines, 1960.

——. *The Revolt of the Masses: The Story of Bonifacio and the Katipunan.* Quezon City: University of the Philippines, 1956.

Aguinaldo, Emilio and Pacis, Vicente Albano. *A Second Look at America.* New York: Robert Speller & Sons, 1957.

Anderson, Benedict R. O'G. *Some Aspects of Indonesian Politics Under the Japanese Occupation: 1944-1945.* Ithaca: Interim Report Series, Southeast Asia Program, Cornell University, 1961.

Area Handbook on the Philippines. ed. Fred Eggan, Evett Hester, and Norton Ginsburg. Chicago: Human Relations Area Files, 1956.

Atlas of Philippine Statistics. Manila: Bureau of Printing, 1939.

Baclagon, Uldarico S. *Philippine Campaigns.* Manila: Graphic House, 1952.

——. *They Chose to Fight.* Manila: n.p., 1962.

Benda, Harry J. *The Crescent and the Rising Sun—Indonesian Islam Under Japanese Occupation.* The Hague: W. van Hoeve Ltd., 1958.

Benedict, Ruth. *The Chrysanthemum and the Sword.* Cambridge: Houghton Mifflin, 1946.

Bernstein, David. *The Philippine Story.* New York: Farrar Straus & Co., 1947.

Bisson, T. A. *Japan's War Economy.* New York: Institute of Pacific Relations, 1945.

Blount, James H. *The American Occupation of the Philippines.* New York: Putnam's, 1912.

Borg, Dorothy. *The United States and the Far Eastern Crisis of 1933-1938.* Cambridge: Harvard University Press, 1964.

Borton, Hugh. *Japan's Modern Century.* New York: Ronald Press, 1955.

Boveri, Margret. *Treason in the Twentieth Century.* London: MacDonald & Co., 1956.

Brown, Charles. *Bars from Bilibid Prison.* San Antonio (Texas): The Naylor Co., 1947.

Brown, Delmer. *Nationalism in Japan: An Introductory Historical Analysis.* Berkeley: University of California Press, 1955.

Buenafe, Manuel E. *War-time Philippines.* Manila: Philippine Education Foundation, 1950.

Butow, Robert J. C. *Tojo and the Coming of the War.* Princeton: University Press, 1961.

Byas, Hugh. *The Japanese Enemy.* New York: Knopf, 1942.

Cannon, M. Hamlin. *Leyte: The Return to the Philippines.* Washington: Office of the Chief of Military History, 1954.

Castillo, Teofilo, and Jose del. *The Saga of Jose P. Laurel.* Manila: Associated Authors, 1949.

Chapman, James and Ethel. *Escape to the Hills.* Lancaster (Pennsylvania): Jaques Cattell Press, 1947.

Corpuz, Onofre D. *Bureaucracy in the Philippines.* Manila: Institute of Public Administration, 1957.

——. *The Philippines.* Englewood Cliffs: Prentice-Hall, 1965.

Costa, Horatio de la. *The Background of Nationalism and Other Essays.* Manila: Solidaridad, 1965.

——. *The Jesuits in the Philippines, 1581-1768.* Cambridge: Harvard University Press, 1961.

Duran, Pio. *Philippine Independence and the Far Eastern Question.* Manila: Community Publishers, 1935.

Eichelberger, Robert L. *Our Jungle Road to Tokyo.* New York: Viking Press, 1950.

Elsbree, Willard H. *Japan's Role in Southeast Asian Nationalist Movements, 1940-1945.* Cambridge: Harvard University Press, 1953.

Espiritu, Socorro C. and Hunt, Chester L. *Social Foundations of Community Development—Readings on the Philippines.* Manila: R. M. Garcia, 1964.

Eyre, James K. Jr. *The Roosevelt-MacArthur Conflict.* Chambersburg: The Craft Press, 1950.

Feis, Herbert. *The Road to Pearl Harbor.* Princeton: Princeton University Press, 1950.

——. *Japan Subdued. The Atomic Bomb and the End of the Pacific.* Princeton: Princeton University Press, 1961.

Ferrell, Robert H. *American Diplomacy in the Great Depression.* New Haven: Yale University Press, 1957.

Field, James A. *The Japanese at Leyte Gulf: The Sho Operation.* Princeton: Princeton University Press, 1947.

Forbes, William Cameron. *The Philippine Islands.* Cambridge: Harvard University Press, 1945.

Francisco, Vicente J. *The Law on Treason.* Manila: Privately Printed, 1945.

Friend, Theodore. *Between Two Empires: The Ordeal of the Philippines, 1929-1946.* New Haven: Yale University Press, 1965.

Glahn, Gerhard von. *The Occupation of Enemy Territory—A Commentary on the Law and Practice of Belligerent Occupation.* Minneapolis: University of Minnesota Press, 1957.

Greenspan, Morris. *The Modern Law of Land Warfare.* Berkeley: University of California Press, 1959.

Grew, Joseph C. *Ten Years in Japan.* New York: Simon & Schuster, 1944.

Griswald, A. Whitney. *The Far Eastern Policy of the United States.* New York: Harcourt Brace, 1938.

Grossholtz, Jean. *Politics in the Philippines.* Boston: Little Brown, 1964.

Grunder, Garel A. and Livezey, William E. *The Philippines and the United States.* Norman: University of Oklahoma Press, 1951.

Gunther, John. *The Riddle of MacArthur.* New York: Harper & Brothers, 1950.

Hartendorp, A. V. H. *A History of Industry and Trade of the Philippines.* Manila: American Chamber of Commerce of the Philippines, 1958.

Hayashi Saburo and Coox, Alvin D. *Kogun, The Japanese Army in the Pacific War.* Quantico (Virginia): Marine Corps Association, 1959.

Hayden, Joseph Ralston. *The Philippines—A Study in National Development.* New York: Macmillan & Co., 1942.

Henderson, James A. *Republic of the Philippines Digest.* Manila: Lawyer's Cooperative Publishing Co., 1961. Vol. 7.

Hollnsteiner, Mary R. *The Dynamics of Power in a Philippine Municipality.* Quezon City: University of the Philippines, 1963.

Ind, Allison. *Allied Intelligence Bureau.* New York: David McKay & Co., 1958.

——. *Bataan: The Judgment Seat.* New York: Macmillan & Co., 1944.

Ingham, Travis. *Rendezvous by Submarine—The Story of Charles Parsons.* New York: Doubleday Duran & Co., 1945.

Iriye, Akira. *After Imperialism: The Search for a New Order in the Far East 1921-1931.* Cambridge: Harvard University Press, 1965.

James, David H. *The Rise and Fall of the Japanese Empire.* London: Allen & Unwin, 1951.

Javellana, Steven. *Without Seeing the Dawn.* Boston: Little Brown, 1947.

Jenkins, Shirley. *American Economic Policy Toward the Philippines.* Stanford: Stanford University Press, 1954.

Jimbo Nobuhiko. *Dawn of the Philippines.* Tokyo: Toppan Printing Co., 1959.

Jones, F. C. *Japan's New Order in East Asia, 1937-1945.* London: Oxford University Press, 1954.

Kalaw, Pura Villanueva (Mrs. Teodoro). *Osmeña—From Newspaperman to President.* Manila: Privately Printed, 1946.

Kase, Toshikazu. *Journey to the Missouri.* New Haven: Yale University Press, 1950.

Kenworthy, Aubrey Saint. *The Tiger of Malaya.* New York: Exposition Press, 1963.

Kirk, Grayson V. *Philippine Independence.* New York: Farrar & Rinehart, 1936.

Landé, Carl H. "Politics in the Philippines" (Unpublished Ph.D. dissertation, Harvard University, 1958).

——. *Leaders, Factions, and Parties: The Structure of Philippine Politics.* New Haven: Southeast Asia Studies Monograph Series No. 6, 1965.

Lasker, Bruno. *Filipino Immigration to Continental United States and to Hawaii.* Chicago: Chicago University Press, 1931.

Laurel, Jose P. *War Memoirs.* Manila: Lyceum Press, 1962.

Lear, Elmer. *The Japanese Occupation of the Philippines—Leyte 1941-1945.* Ithaca: Data Paper No. 42. Southeast Asia Program. Cornell University, 1961.

Lee, Clark. *One Last Look Around.* New York: Duell, Sloan & Pearce, 1947.

——. *They Call It Pacific.* New York: Viking Press, 1943.

Lichauco, Marcial. *Dear Mother Putnam: A Diary of the War in the Philippines.* Manila: Private Printing, 1949.

Lu, David J. *From the Marco Polo Bridge to Pearl Harbor.* Washington: Public Affairs Press, 1961.

MacArthur, Douglas. *Reminiscences.* New York: McGraw Hill, 1964.

——. *Revitalizing a Nation—Public Pronouncements of Douglas MacArthur.* Chicago: Heritage Foundation, 1952.

Maki, John. *Japanese Militarism: Its Cause and Cure.* New York: Knopf, 1945.

Malcolm, George A. *American Colonial Careerist.* Boston: Christopher Publishing House, 1957.

——. *The Commonwealth of the Philippines.* New York: Appleton-Century, 1936.

——. *First Malayan Republic.* Boston: Christopher Publishing House, 1951.

Marquardt, Frederic S. *Before Bataan and After.* Indianapolis: Bobbs Merrill, 1943.

Maxon, Y. C. *Control of Japanese Foreign Policy: A Study of Civil-Military Rivalry, 1930-1945.* Berkeley: University of California Press, 1957.

May, Ernest. *Imperial Democracy.* New York: Harcourt Brace & World, 1961.

Mendelssohn, Peter de. *Japan's Political Warfare.* London: Allen & Unwin, 1944.

Meyer, Milton Walter. *A Diplomatic History of the Philippines.* Honolulu: University of Hawaii Press, 1965.

Monaghan, J. Forbes. *Under the Red Sun—A Letter from Manila.* New York: Declan X. McMullen Co., 1946.

Morison, Elting E. *Turmoil and Tradition: A Study of the Life and Times of Henry L. Stimson.* Boston: Houghton Mifflin, 1960.

Morison, Samuel Eliot. *Leyte: June 1944-January 1945.* Boston: Little Brown & Co., 1958.

——. *The Liberation of the Philippines: Luzon, Mindanao, the Vizayas, 1944-1945.* Boston: Little Brown & Co., 1959.

——. *The Rising Sun in the Pacific, 1931-April, 1942.* Boston: Little Brown & Co., 1948.

Morton, Louis. *The United States Army in World War Two—The Fall of the Philippines.* Washington: Office of the Chief of Military History, 1953.

Neumann, William L. *America Encounters Japan from Perry to MacArthur.* Baltimore: Johns Hopkins Press, 1963.

Padilla, Ambrosio. *Criminal Law—Revised Penal Code, Book Two: Crimes and Penalties.* Manila: F. C. P. Publications, 1951.

Panilio, Yay. *The Crucible: An Autobiography.* New York: Macmillan & Co., 1950.

Phelan, James L. *The Hispanization of the Philippines: Spanish Aims and Filipino Responses 1565-1700.* Madison: University of Wisconsin Press, 1959.

Poblador, Filemon. *Philippine Chronology January 1 to July 3, 1946.* Manila: Philippine Liberal Publishing Co., 1946.

Porter, Catherine. *Crisis in the Philippines.* New York: Alfred Knopf, 1942.

Pratt, J. W. *America's Colonial Experiment.* New York: Prentice-Hall & Co., 1950.

——. *The Expansionists of 1898.* Baltimore: Johns Hopkins Press, 1936.

Quezon, Manuel. *The Good Fight.* New York: Appleton-Century & Co., 1946.

Quirino, Eliseo. *A Day to Remember.* Manila: Benipayo, 1958.

Recto, Claro M. *Three Years of Enemy Occupation: The Issue of Political Collaboration in the Philippines.* Manila: People's Publishers, 1946.

Reel, Frank A. *The Case of General Yamashita.* Chicago: University of Chicago Press, 1949.

Reischauer, Edwin O. *Japan, Past and Present.* New York, Knopf, 1964.

——. *The United States and Japan.* Cambridge: Harvard University Press, 1957.

Romulo, Carlos P. *I Saw the Fall of the Philippines.* New York: Doubleday Duran & Co., 1942.

——. *I See the Philippines Rise.* New York: Doubleday Duran & Co., 1946.

——. *I Walked with Heroes.* New York: Holt, Rinehart & Winston, 1961.

Romulo, Carlos P. and Gray, Marvin M. *The Magsaysay Story.* New York: Pocket Books, Inc., 1957.

Rubens, Doris. *Bread and Rice.* New York: Thurston Macauley Associates, 1947.

Saniel, Josefa M. *Japan and the Philippines, 1868-1898.* Quezon City: University of the Philippines, 1963.

Santiago, Domingo B. "Philippine Education During the Japanese Occupation" (Unpublished master's thesis, University of the Philippines, 1951).

Savary, Gladys. *Outside the Walls.* New York: Vantage Press, 1954.

Sayre, Francis. *Glad Adventure.* New York: Macmillan, 1957.

Scaff, Alvin H. *The Philippine Answer to Communism*. Stanford: Stanford University Press, 1955.

Schroeder, Paul W. *The Axis Alliance and Japanese American Relations*. Ithaca: Cornell University Press, 1958.

Shigemitsu Mamoru. *Japan and Her Destiny*. London: Hutchinson & Co., 1958.

Smith, Robert Aura. *Philippine Freedom, 1946-1958*. New York: Columbia University Press, 1958.

Smith, Robert R. *Triumph in the Philippines*. Washington: Office of the Chief of Military History, 1963.

Soriano, Rafaelita Hilario. "The Japanese Occupation of the Philippines with Special Reference to Japanese Propaganda, 1941-1945" (Unpublished Ph.D. thesis, University of Michigan—Microfilm No. 1078—1948).

Spencer, J. E. *Land and People in the Philippines*. Berkeley: University of California Press, 1952.

Stimson, Henry L. and Bundy, McGeorge. *On Active Service in Peace and War*. New York: Harper & Co., 1947.

Stone, Julius. *Legal Controls of International Conflict*. London: Stevenson & Co., 1959.

Storry, Richard. *The Double Patriots: A Study of Japanese Nationalism*. Boston: Houghton Mifflin, 1957.

Taruc, Luis. *Born of the People*. New York: International Publishers, 1953.

Taylor, George E. *The Philippines and the United States: Problems of Partnership*. New York: Frederick A. Praeger, 1964.

Togo Shigenori. *The Cause of Japan*. New York: Simon & Schuster, 1956.

Toland, John: *But Not in Shame: The Six Months After Pearl Harbor*. New York: Random House, 1961.

U Hla Pe's Narrative of the Japanese Occupation of Burma. Recorded by U Khin. Ithaca: Data Paper No. 41, Southeast Asia Program, Cornell University, 1961.

Vaughan, Elizabeth Head. *Community Under Stress*. Princeton: Princeton University Press, 1949.

Verosa, Paul Rodriguez. *Re-examining Japan*. Manila: Reverend Yamanouchi Hideo (Publisher), 1940.

Villanueva, Ines S. "The Development of Philippine Nationalism and Its Implication to Education" (Unpublished master's thesis, University of the Philippines, 1954).

Vinacke, Harold M. *Far Eastern Politics in the Post-War Period*. New York: Appleton-Century-Crofts, 1956.

Volckmann, R. W. *We Remained*. New York: Norton & Co., 1954.

Wainwright, Jonathan. *General Wainwright's Story*. New York: Doubleday & Co., 1946.

Ward, Robert S. *Asia for the Asiatics? The Techniques of Japanese Occupation*. Chicago: University of Chicago Press, 1945.

Weinstein, Alfred A. *Barbed Wire Surgeon*. New York: Macmillan & Co., 1956.

West, Rebecca. *The Meaning of Treason*. New York: Viking Press, 1947.

Whitney, Courtney. *MacArthur: His Rendezvous with History*. New York: Alfred Knopf, 1956.

Wickberg, Edgar. *The Chinese in Philippine Life, 1850-1898*. New Haven: Yale University Press, 1965.

Willoughby, Charles A. and Chamberlain, John. *MacArthur, 1941-1951*. New York: McGraw Hill, 1954.

Wohlstetter, Roberta. *Pearl Harbor: Warning and Decision*. Stanford: Stanford University Press, 1962.

Wolfert, Ira. *American Guerrilla in the Philippines*. New York: Simon & Schuster, 1945.

Wolff, Leon. *Little Brown Brother*. London: Longmans, Green & Co., 1960.

Woodward, C. Vann. *The Battle for Leyte Gulf*. New York: Ballantine Books, 1947.

Worcester, Dean C. *The Philippines Past and Present*. New York: Macmillan, 1930.

Yanaga, Chitoshi, *Japan Since Perry*. New York: McGraw Hill, 1949.

Zaide, Gregorio F. *Philippine Political and Cultural History*. Manila: Philippine Education Co., 1953. Vol. 2.

Index

227